Lake Beykal

U N I O N

TER
GOLIA

○Ulan Bator

MANCHURIA

Vladivostok ○

Peking
○

Dairen ○

Seoul ○

KOREA

VLADIVOSTOK

JAPAN

Tokyo ○

H I N A

HONG KONG ○

0 Miles   500

0 Km.   800

BODIA

VIETNAM

D1446744

MANCHURIAN ADVENTURE

THE STORY OF
LOBSANG THONDUP

SYLVAIN MANGEOT

WILLIAM MORROW & COMPANY, INC.,
NEW YORK, 1975

Published in Great Britain under the title *The Adventures
of a Manchurian: The Story of Lobsang Thondup*.

Printed in the United States of America.

1 2 3 4 5 79 78 77 76 75

Library of Congress Catalog Card Number 74-12173

ISBN 0-688-00224-2

CONTENTS

ILLUSTRATIONS

FOREWORD BY LOBSANG THONDUP

This biography is an account of events as I
experienced them and as they affected me. It
necessarily reflects my own view. Others may
have seen the same events in quite a different
light. If my interpretation offends anyone, I
would like to apologise to them in advance as
that has never been my intention.

LOBSANG THONDUP

INTRODUCTION TO LOBSANG

Getting to know Lobsang was a minor adventure in itself. In 1963, in the Himalayan kingdom of Bhutan, someone pointed out a tall, jaunty figure swinging down a gangplank over a moat during the demolition and rebuilding of the great fortress-monastery-cathedral of Thimpu Dzong, and told me that he was a Chinese engineer who had escaped from Tibet after the Chinese Communist takeover and the Dalai Lama's flight from Lhasa.

A couple of years later, in the upheaval in Bhutan which followed the assassination of the Prime Minister, Jigme Dorji, travellers recently in the country spoke of a mysterious Chinese who had been arrested by the King and confined in the dungeon of the same dzong at Thimpu. Their accounts did not make his offence clear, but there was vague talk of conspiracy and suspected espionage.

Then, in 1966 in London, I was introduced to Lobsang. He was, it transpired, both the engineer and the prisoner in the dzong. He looked as jaunty as when I had first seen him, apparently none the worse for his experiences.

Lobsang's English at that time was execrable – fluent to a fault but almost totally incomprehensible. My knowledge of Mandarin, Tibetan or any of his other working languages was non-existent. But I was able to piece together enough of his story to realise that it must be told. By the time he left London, we had agreed in principle to collaborate in a biography.

Our language barrier had one advantage. The less a person knows of a language, the more direct he has to be. If we had had a common language, I doubt if I would have had such a quick insight into Lobsang's character or have established with him the same relationship of mutual confidence. Like strangers marooned on a desert island, we had to go straight to the heart of things. I asked the bluntest of questions and he gave the straightest of answers, because any frills would have made our conversation unintelligible.

Lobsang returned to London briefly in 1968. His English had improved a little and I acquired fuller notes and an overwhelming curiosity to know the whole story. In 1972, on Easter Day, Lobsang arrived in London overland from Nepal. He stayed for the rest of the year while we finished this book.

On his last visit Shui Chien-Tung, of the Chinese Service of the BBC, tape-recorded many conversations with Lobsang in their native Mandarin, and transcribed them for me.

As we pieced together Lobsang's story, two distinct strands emerged. There was the element of pure adventure, extraordinary by any standards; then, as the story unfolded, it shed a great light of human understanding on the upheavals which have transformed China and her neighbours during the last twenty-five years.

These convulsions shook Lobsang's world and sent him, in an effort to live his life in his own way, on an Odyssey which took him from his native Manchuria across China, Korea, Siberia, Sinkiang and Tibet and finally landed him up in India, Bhutan and Nepal. He learnt, the hard way, a great deal about the passions and divided loyalties of ordinary people in China and Central Asia during and after the Chinese Civil War – people who have never had an opportunity to tell their story and which we in the West have only been able to guess at obscurely through what has been written by ideological apologists or political historians. He shared their problems with compassion and often at their own level, even though he emerges as a slightly over-life-size figure by the ebullience of his personality, his vitality and his sheer capacity for physical survival.

His adventures, which took him not only to some of the least known corners of Asia but also on journeys through time, back into societies whose manners and ways of life were purely medieval, may tax the credulity by their sustained improbability. As we discussed them in detail, such inconsistencies as did crop up were of the kind one would expect from someone, without notes or diaries, trying to recall complicated events over a long period of years. Where it was possible to check his accounts of places, people and events from other sources, they have turned out to be remarkably accurate.

There are times when Lobsang himself finds it difficult to believe that so many bewildering things really happened to him; or, if they did, that he is really the same person as the little rich boy in pre-war Manchuria, or the lieutenant in the Japanese air force who spent two years as a prisoner of the Russians in Siberia, or the colonel in Mao's first tank corps, or the lover of a girl whom Tibetans revered as an incarnate Living Buddha, or Lhasa's first mechanical tycoon who in the space of a year became a penniless fugitive through guerrilla territory, or, finally, the King's favourite in Bhutan who ended up in irons in a rat-infested dungeon.

Lobsang searches vainly for a connecting link to explain the pattern of his life. He does not see himself as a heroic figure who set out in search of adventure; more as a headstrong young man whose urge to live an independent life gradually turned him into a whole-time escapist from the advance of the Chinese Communist Revolution.

For years, not even his determination and ingenuity could keep him more than half a step ahead of Chairman Mao's stealthy expansion into Central Asia. Twice he was obliged to coexist with it, precariously and occasionally hilariously, before he finally succeeded in putting himself beyond its reach. Even then it continued to dog his footsteps, landing him in prison in India on suspicion of being its undercover agent.

When at last he thought he had found sanctuary in the little house he had built for himself, his Bhutanese wife and their family in the pleasant foothills of the Himalayas, fate was waiting again to shatter his dream of contented domesticity.

'Your life', Lobsang says, 'is not determined by you or your background. In times of trouble, circumstances decide what happens to you and where you go.'

The only part of his life that was not lived 'in times of trouble' was his secure and apparently stable childhood in pre-war Manchuria. It provided him with roots which he has tried to replant in at least two of his countries of adoption. Tame as these early days may be compared with what followed, it is essential to go back to the beginning to understand the rest of his story, with all its twists and ironies.

The chapters of this book dealing with the early part of his life before he left China contain deliberate omissions and gloss over certain facts and events which might still bring trouble to surviving members of his large family. Lobsang himself, in order to protect himself during the period of the Chinese Civil War and the years which immediately followed it, had to dissemble his Japanese connections so thoroughly and for so long that he still prefers not to dwell in detail on this chapter of his life.

All this, and a deep-rooted reluctance to bare his emotions in situations which he still finds it unbearable to think about – for example the moments of separation from his mother and his second and third wives – may leave readers feeling that Lobsang is holding back things that are needed for a full and sympathetic understanding of his character.

Lobsang admits that these early chapters are sketches rather than rounded pictures. But, once outside China, released from inhibitions of family and security, his reticences disappear. Having escaped from the systems which had obliged him to be a wary conformist, he starts to live his own sort of life and the shadowy monochrome is replaced by an adventure serial in full colour.

Finally, LOBSANG THONDUP is, of course, not his Chinese name. It is a Bhutanese name of fortune and convenience and it appears on the only passport he has ever held. I have used it throughout for simplicity and for reasons of security. To list all the successive aliases he used would confuse the reader as surely as it would tax Lobsang's own memory.

SYLVAIN MANGEOT

PART I

China

I

BEFORE THE STORM

Lobsang was born in 1925, in Dairen, the great sea-port of Manchuria, in the peninsula known as Kwan Tung Chou which Japan annexed from Russia in 1905, after the Russo-Japanese war. It was a mercantile city, the centre for Japan's imports of raw materials from Manchuria and her exports of manufactured goods to the mainland. His father was a prosperous Chinese business-man, whose family had been settled in Manchuria for several generations. His mother belonged to one of the big land-owning families, which used to be known as Banner Manchurians, with estates in the rich rice-growing district of Antung, up against the border of Korea.

Lobsang was the youngest of her eleven children – eight boys and three girls. At times, and particularly during his middle twenties, at a moment when he was bordering on despair, he was very close to her, and yet, try as he may, he says that he is never able to recall his mother's face in any detail. This puzzles and troubles him. The only explanation he can think of is that he has led so many different lives that his childhood has become overlaid by subsequent events and has receded to a point where he feels that it was lived by an entirely different person. It is the same with the boys in his class in his first primary school. 'I cannot see a single distinct face.'

Lobsang thinks that the easy circumstances of his childhood may have something to do with the vagueness of these boyhood memories. 'When you come home from school and your mother is wondering where the next bowl of rice is coming from, you remember every detail. We never had to worry about things like that.'

Home for Lobsang was a great family mansion in the affluent

Chinese business quarter of Dairen. The houses on its broad avenues had been built during the days of the Russian occupation, but were architecturally in the Chinese style. Lobsang's father's house ran the depth of a whole block between Fu Tor-Jai Street and Yun Nor-Jao Street. Behind the main frontage, there were several courtyards and gardens, with storehouses and go-downs where the numerous household servants had their quarters. His parents occupied the front part of the house, with guest rooms and grand reception rooms where his father's business friends were entertained. The children occupied the middle section, which also included the main kitchens. Apart from his father's own family, one of his younger brothers lived in the same mansion, with his own household and guest rooms backing on to the street at the rear. The servants lived in first-floor rooms above the go-downs.

Lobsang's father, as the eldest brother and head of the family, was treated with the respect due to his seniority and wealth. When he entered the room, everyone rose and Lobsang's memory of him is that he was always too busy, when he was not away on business trips, to play with the children or devote much time to them. He was a shipowner, trading almost entirely between China and Japan, and owned engineering workshops and many other business enterprises. He left the management of the household entirely to his wife. She it was who held the pursestrings for the whole family as far as domestic expenditure was concerned. In the huge central dining-room, the grown ups would eat at one table, and the children at another, with the smaller ones up to the age of five or six having their meals first, attended by their ayahs. Most of these nursemaids came from his mother's family estates in Amdung under the old system where the landlord paid his tenants a down sum for a daughter who then passed into his service and became his charge. If Lobsang's uncle and his wife wished to eat or entertain privately, they had to buy their own food more or less secretly and serve it in their own apartments.

Each of the children had their own bedroom and living-room with one ayah in attendance for two or three children. Lobsang describes the style of the decoration and furniture as 'heavy and old-fashioned'. Clearly it was both solid and prosperous. Lobsang remembers paintings by the famous artist Tang Po-Hu, done on silk and depicting a tiger or three goats or a composition of flowers. His own concern with Chinese art or culture during his boyhood was compulsory rather than voluntary. From the age of five onwards, his formal schooling was in Japanese schools. Under the Japanese occupation, this was the only way for a Manchurian to get a modern education which qualified him for a good job. Lobsang's father's import-export business was almost entirely with Japan and as a resident of Kwan Tung Chou he was technically a Japanese national.

At the same time, he and his wife attached the greatest importance to their children being aware of their national identity and cultural heritage. Besides his Japanese schooling, Lobsang was taught the traditional Confucian disciplines by an elderly Mandarin tutor. He regarded this venerable gentleman as an anachronism and a nuisance. He interfered with Lobsang's leisure, and had exasperatingly old-fashioned ideas about homework and discipline. When Lobsang failed to come up to scratch with his set tasks, he had no hesitation in beating him – 'the only time any of my masters hit me during my schooldays.' Lobsang admits, a trifle grudgingly, that the old tyrant's method produced results. It gave him a solid grounding in the history, art and philosophy of China, and of the subtle intricacies of Mandarin, not only as a means of expression, but as a yardstick of the degree of education, measured by the rigid hierarchical standards of pre-revolutionary China. Lobsang still applies these standards to other Chinese, sometimes in unexpected contexts.

Chairman Mao's speeches, in their deliberate use of simple conversational idiom, still sound rather plebeian to Lobsang and *The Little Red Book* or Mao's poems, which avoid the subtlety of classical Mandarin, have a workaday ring. He himself can still write formal Mandarin poetry – very respectable in form and content – without apparent effort, and his exquisite running calligraphy, even when scribbled with a ballpoint instead of the traditional brush and ink, is a legacy of his early instruction of which his old tutor would no doubt have been slyly proud.

Above all, his private education gave him an insight into and understanding of his father's vanished world. He was an old-fashioned Chinese gentleman. 'Long before I was born, in 1906 or 1907, when he was away from home on business, Sun Yat-Sen's revolutionaries cut off his pigtail in the street of a provincial town. My mother told me that he wept. For someone of his standing and upbringing, it was worse than losing his life. It was the loss of the symbol of a whole way of life – the end of a civilisation.' This understanding of traditional upper-class Chinese values remains, sometimes rather incongruously, an important ingredient in Lobsang's complex make-up. He is broadminded and often surprisingly detached in his judgment of the conflicting systems of the contemporary world, but when it comes to fundamentals, he remains not only impenitently Chinese, but Chinese with deep roots in the Confucian tradition. When he is speaking Mandarin, particularly with another educated person, his manner and even his appearance change. He speaks with heightened animation and eloquence and, above all, with an evident sense of relief at being able to converse in a civilised medium.

His lack of enthusiasm for his Chinese tutorials does not seem to have prevented him being a dutiful scholar. His father, apart from presiding over family meals, at which thirty or forty people commonly sat down to table, always found time to check on his progress with his Chinese studies. From the age of five, Lobsang spent eight hours a day at a Japanese school. He travelled on a monthly season ticket by train, taking his lunch of rice and vegetables, packed in layers in a special container and putting it on top of the central heating to warm. At the age of six he became a weekly boarder in a hostel at the same school. This was in the residential outer ring of Dairen where the Japanese occupiers had built their own quarter when they first took over the area. Compared with home, school life was fairly spartan, with cold showers in the dormitory and P.T. every morning. Lobsang seems to have accepted it in the spirit that, since it was unavoidable, it was easier to conform. He cannot recall ever feeling victimised or under-privileged as one of a small minority of Manchurian pupils among a Japanese majority. It is difficult in any case to imagine Lobsang allowing himself to be victimised or dominated in any society or circumstances. Asked what sort of school-boy he was, he replies unhesitatingly 'Always fighting.' He admits to an almost Irish delight in fighting for fighting's sake, and he often returned home at weekends battered and bruised.

This brought him into disgrace with his mother, whose strict Buddhist principles made her deplore anything involving violence or bloodshed. She used to order him to the family chapel, where he spent many hours of penance for his bloody encounters. Whether his antipathy to organised religion and ceremonial demonstrations of piety dates from these enforced prayer sessions is difficult to establish. His own philosophy is that an 'open heart' in all one's dealings and civilised behaviour towards people in all walks of life is more admirable than any ritual devotions. He thinks most of his seven brothers, some of whom had already left home before he was born, were as lukewarm in their religious observance as himself, but his three sisters inherited their mother's piety and were all practising Buddhists.

At school, his teachers were all Japanese. He wore the stock uniform of khaki cap, jacket and shorts, being promoted to long trousers when he had reached the sixth grade. Whenever a new item of clothing was issued, everyone immediately took the starch out of it by crumpling it, stamping on it, rolling it in the dust and otherwise reducing it to the fashionable state of well-worn scruffiness that custom demanded. For Lobsang, this was quite out of character. Throughout his adventures, he has remained a fastidious dresser, very conscious of his appearance, and with an unerring eye for good quality materials and fashionable cut.

He describes himself as a very average scholar. In the large classes of over sixty, he regularly came out between twentieth and thirtieth. He cannot remember ever having felt any sense of vocation or having any clear idea in which direction his studies would lead him. The fact that his father, besides his shipping and banking interests, owned saw-mills and workshops, which he often visited, got him early into the habit of handling tools and simple machinery. In Middle School, a master advised him to concentrate on engineering. This was agreed, without Lobsang being either enthusiastic or reluctant. He remained an average pupil, who always got by without ever being brilliant. 'I've noticed that in engineering schools and colleges, the top boys in the class are seldom among the best when it comes to practical work in the field.' It was the practical field that appealed to Lobsang. From an early age he always wanted to make things and handle everything himself. 'I used to do my own repairs to bicycles and toys, and when I was about twelve I remember being scolded by my father for interfering with what people were doing in one of his workshops.'

His happiest and most vivid recollections are of the long holiday days on the beaches round Dairen, swimming and picnicking and pottering about in small boats. Besides being a thriving mercantile and naval port, Dairen was a great holiday resort. From Russian days, it had a tradition of cosmopolitan good living and easygoing enjoyment. It had an unusually good climate and even in term time Lobsang used often to dash down to the sea in a tram for a quick swim or picnic at all seasons. After the Second World War and the Communist takeover in 1949, Lobsang returned to Dairen in melancholy circumstances, to find the beaches deserted. The bathing tents and the holiday-makers had vanished, and with them the old atmosphere of leisure and gaiety. It was the forsaken beaches of Dairen that brought home to Lobsang, more poignantly than anything, that the way of life he was born into had gone for ever.

Other happy occasions were the visits to his mother's family in the country near Amtung. Sometimes he stayed with his grandparents in their big country house near the Korean border. His grandfather was the chairman of the local branch of the Tao Teh-Hui, a Buddhist religious and charitable organisation which seems to have combined the functions of a form of freemasonry with the good works of the Salvation Army. It distributed warm winter clothing to the poor, with a distinctive emblem, in the form of a swastika, embroidered on the jacket. Even well-to-do people prized these quilted jackets for their children, because of a superstition that they brought happiness and long life to their wearers.

By his own admission, Lobsang as a small boy was considered a bit of a handful for his grandparents' orderly household. His mother used to dispatch him on these visits with admonitions against noisy and rumbustious behaviour. More often than not, he spent most of his country holidays in a smaller house belonging to an elder married sister, where his energies were less disturbing. There were outings in exciting local buggies drawn by a troika of horses, with one between the shafts, and two leaders on a free rein, whose movements were controlled by the expert cracking of a long whip. At this time, there was an open border between Manchuria and Korea, both being under Japanese control, and Lobsang remembers driving through the mulberry forests and small rolling hills just over the Korean border.

Altogether, his childhood, apart from school, seems to have been lived in a comfortable patrician world which kept him insulated from Chinese politics under Japanese occupation. He was never required or encouraged to worry his head with political problems or ideologies. 'My father was a business man who had accepted the Japanese rule in Manchuria as a fact of life. We preserved our Chinese identity, of course, but I don't think he ever felt that trading within this system was either unpatriotic or against the interests of China. Some of my elder brothers who had studied in China, had joined the Kuomintang Nationalist movement in the early 1920's and were already caught up in the tide of Chinese nationalism. But they were not in Dairen when I was a schoolboy, so that I never really questioned my father's way of life. Looking back, I suppose he would have been well advised to sell out his interests in Manchuria and to transfer to some part of China under direct Chinese administration while the going was good. As it was, when Japan entered the Second World War, all his ships were requisitioned for the Japanese war effort. I think that worry over their loss was, as much as anything, responsible for his death, while only in his sixties, in 1942.'

This rather sheltered and privileged upbringing, combined with the discipline of hard study in two languages, seems to have given Lobsang a basic sense of security and self-confidence which was to stand him in good stead in the upheavals and buffetings which were to come. While he was at school, his only serious clash with students of his own age was, curiously enough, not with Japanese, but with fellow Manchurians. A school outing had been arranged to the great industrialist city of Mukden, to the north of Dairen. Lobsang, arriving late at the railway station, missed his own train and had to travel with a party of schoolgirls who were on the same excursion. At Mukden, in the great railway terminal, they found no trace of the rest of their party. While they were wondering what to do, some older local boys began teasing the girls and jostling Lobsang. He allowed himself to be provoked into a fight with two of them and, when they began to be worsted, was set upon by a dozen others who knocked him senseless. The girls managed to revive him, and the outing ended sadly, with them all returning to Dairen on the next available train with their tails between their legs. 'I never really made out whether it was because they were jealous of me being alone with so many girls, or whether there was some rivalry between Mukden and Dairen which I had never run into before.'

At the age of three, as was the traditional custom among Manchus of substance, he was betrothed to the daughter of a wealthy and influential government official. Her name was Fu Pi-Dze, and her family lived in Dairen. Sometimes in the street people would point her out to him and say 'Look, that's your bride.' Even as a small boy, this always embarrassed him, so that he immediately turned away and looked in the opposite direction. During all the years of their betrothal, he never made any attempt to visit her or get to know her. He felt a growing resentment that such an important decision should be taken for him. As the years went by, it was no longer a question of shyness. With eight elder brothers and three sisters, he had plenty of opportunity of meeting girls, and was an experienced ladies' man long before he left school. Being tall and well set-up, he looked older than his years, and was not slow to take his opportunities when his brothers' girl friends began to make a fuss of him. Without being exactly permissive, life in the family mansion made the conduct of amorous escapades comparatively easy. The convention seems to have been that there was respectability in numbers and, from

the age of twelve or thirteen, Lobsang used to invite a gaggle of
girls home to listen to records after school in his room – demure
little parties which were not necessarily quite as childish or
innocent as everyone assumed. Adolescence was in fact such a
natural process that Lobsang has some difficulty in recalling the
exact age at which he had his first love-affair, dismissing the
question airily as a half-forgotten triviality by saying 'When I was
twelve or thirteen, I think.'

By the time he was fifteen, Lobsang's schooling was complete.
He had finished the ten-year curriculum, and his schoolmaster's
advice had proved sound. He had won a place in the faculty of
mechanical engineering at Tokyo University – a rare distinction
in those days for a non-Japanese. From 1940 to 1943, he lived in a
students' hostel in the Japanese capital, and shared the life of his
Japanese fellow-students. Even before Pearl Harbor and Japan's
entry into the Second World War, in 1941, Japanese universities
were being organised on a semi-war footing. Japan had been
fighting with Chiang Kai-Shek's nationalist China since 1937, and
on the Chinese mainland the Communist challenge had also to
be met. By the time Lobsang arrived in Tokyo, university life in
Japan, like everything else, was gradually being integrated into
the war effort. Ordinarily, his courses in theoretical and practical
engineering would have taken up eight hours of his working day,
but already in his first year students were farmed out to work in
war factories and, after 1941, this war-work was gradually
increased until Lobsang eventually found himself doing six hours
a day in factories on top of his university course.

From the beginning, university life was mostly hard work and
austerity, with an increasingly military flavour. First and second
year students had to salute their seniors. Each day began with an
assembly and a silent prayer to the Emperor. The students, in
their severe black uniforms, and square-topped caps, had little
time for recreation or the kind of social life which undergraduates
in western universities enjoy. Lobsang does not remember the
university as a place where he made intimate or life-long friends.
This may have been partly because the hostel in which he lived
was mainly for non-Japanese students, most of them Koreans.

For some reason, there was never much love lost between this Korean majority and the small minority of Manchurians, who thought the Koreans tried to put on airs by aping the Japanese and were altogether too big for their boots. The nearest thing that Lobsang can remember to organised sport is the periodic battles arranged between the Manchurians and the Koreans. Any sort of brawling or unruliness in the precincts of the university was strictly forbidden, so the word had to be secretly passed around: 'Meet at the Japanese bridge at seven o'clock.' There, when both sides had assembled, a pitched battle would be fought with fists and bicycle chains. There seems to have been no ideological reason for this rivalry, but Lobsang confesses that he used to look forward to these fights and enjoyed letting off steam after the monotony of a hard day's work in the lecture rooms and factories.

During his university years, the Japanese were already beginning to tighten their belts. Even when he first arrived, the food in his hostel was unpleasantly austere compared with the easy living at home in Dairen. Lobsang is no admirer of Japanese cooking at the best of times, and he recalls with disgust that by the time he graduated in 1943, 'everything was fifty per cent soya.'

As always, when confronted with some disciplined course of study, Lobsang seems to have accepted that the only sensible thing to do was to conform. The teaching staff in his Faculty of Engineering was excellent, and the workshops modern and well equipped. He found plenty of outlet for his natural interest in practical work and his quick brain, allied to a strong sense of self-respect and a fair streak of competitiveness, made it easy for him to satisfy his lecturers and instructors.

During his vacations he returned home and, on his last visit to Dairen before he graduated, he was married off to his child-hood fiancée with the full ceremonial of a traditional Manchu wedding. At the reception, guests remarked on what a handsome couple he and Fu Pi-Dze made, both tall and elegant, and apparently so ideally matched. In fact, for both of them, it was a constrained and dutiful occasion. Lobsang was simply obeying his parents' wishes. At the same time, he sympathised with his bride's predicament. By this time, it was already decided that he would go into the Japanese air force. If he had gone to the wars and been killed, without them marrying, she would have been prevented by the fact of their betrothal from marrying anyone else. Tradition would have demanded that she move to his mother's house and live there to all intents and purposes as a widow.

On their wedding night, they shared the same room but slept in separate beds. Lobsang was frankly exasperated by the whole situation. Poor Fu Pi-Dze made it worse by trying to make the best of it, attending to his smallest needs and making dutiful and conventional conversation. To add to the irony, Lobsang's father-in-law, as a wedding present, had ordered him a collection of expensive suits which, under any other circumstances, would have delighted him but now seemed to stare at him reproachfully from the nuptial wardrobe. His bride, decked out entirely in scarlet, in Manchu tradition, was pathetic in her oppressive finery. After two or three days of this distressing pantomime, Lobsang woke one night to find her asleep. She looked so forlorn and lonely that he was suddenly overcome with compassion and took her in his arms to comfort her.

'She burst into tears and told me that she too felt an absolute fool. She was a nice, intelligent, well-educated girl, and good-looking besides. I did my best to be kind to her, and after that we did sleep together a few times. Perhaps, if we had remained together, we might even eventually have made a go of it. But I couldn't get over the feeling that she had been foisted on me without my having any say in the matter. The whole situation was so artificial that I found it impossible to behave naturally with her. When I left to go back to Tokyo, she went through the motions of being sad to see me go, but I can't help feeling that it came as a relief to both of us. I never saw her again. When I next returned to Dairen, the Communists were in control of the city, and Fu Pi-Dze had long since left my mother's house to return to her father or to stay with married brothers or sisters.'

2

PRISONER IN SIBERIA

In the normal course of events Lobsang, after completing his three-year degree course in Mechanical Engineering, would have done two more years of higher studies in Tokyo. By 1943, however, things were far from normal. The requisitioning of his father's ships had been a bad financial blow and after his father's death family fortunes were drastically depleted and seemed threatened with further setbacks.

Instead of going back to Tokyo at the beginning of the new academic year in 1944, it was decided that Lobsang should go straight into the armed forces. He accordingly enrolled at an engineering training centre at Pu Lan Den near Mukden.

From Pu Lan Den, where he specialised in aircraft engineering, he joined the air force proper with the rank of Pilot Officer in the engineering branch. He was posted to 688 squadron of the Japanese Kwantung Chou army in the summer of 1944. This army was a special force created when the Japanese took over the province in 1903 after the Russo-Japanese war. It had its own naval arm, and later its own air arm, and enjoyed almost complete autonomy in its task of enforcing order in the annexed territory. If Lobsang had not joined the Kwantung army, the chances are that he would in due course have been drafted into some branch of the armed forces of Manchukuo, the puppet state which the Japanese set up in 1932 in the rest of Manchuria under the last of the Manchu Emperors, Pu Yi. To belong to the Kwantung army at least preserved for Lobsang an official link with his native province.

In August, 1944, his squadron, the 688 squadron, was sent to Korea to a station near Seoul. By this time most of the heroics had gone out of the Japanese air force. American air supremacy was virtually unchallenged and the old-fashioned fighter-bombers of 688 squadron, meant for low-level attacks on shipping and ground targets, had neither the speed nor the altitude to engage the American B29 bombers which made high-level raids in their area. 'When the B29s came over, there wasn't much we could do but stay in the shelters.' In any case Lobsang's flying was limited to what was necessary for his duties as a technician and maintenance engineer. 'We did routine training flights to keep the squadron efficient and airborne, but at this time Korea was something of a backwater for the air force.'

Lobsang recalls that even Seoul, which was still called Keijo, its Japanese name, was little more than an overgrown village and that Korea was still essentially an underpopulated rural area, of relatively little interest to American air strategy in the autumn or winter of 1944.

Still, morale in 688 squadron was as high as ever. Among his fellow officers there was no hint of defeatism, or even any sense of impending defeat. It was assumed that in due course they would get the necessary new planes in time to launch a great counter offensive and that, although the war might go on for many years, it would end in a final Japanese victory.

In this connection Lobsang remembers talk in his squadron of the whole of the army of Kwan Tung Chou and Manchuria being held in reserve for a great second front which Japan would launch against the Soviet Union in due course. At the time Lobsang was inclined to regard it as mere propaganda, designed to boost morale and explain away the squadron's almost total inactivity against the Americans. But later, after the end of the war, he met an old fellow student from Tokyo, also a Manchurian, who had served as a medical officer in the Kwan Tung Chou army. He told Lobsang that he had been attached to a special force which had been used to construct a strategic highway from the Dairen region up to the Manchurian-Siberian frontier. They had worked in very trying conditions and been harassed by Chinese Communists who hid in the forests along the route of the projected highway. According to this friend the plan included the building of a tunnel under the Yalu River through which it was planned to launch the spearhead of a great offensive into Siberia. He told Lobsang that preparatory work for this tunnel was actually in progress and that huge quantities of steel were brought up to the frontier for use to reinforce the tunnel. This was the same area where Soviet and Communist Chinese troops were later to clash in border skirmishes, emphasising how sensitive the Russians felt it to be strategically for the defence of the Soviet Union against any incursion from the East.

In these circumstances Lobsang's short spell of service in the Japanese air force, which might have been a formative experience, turned out to be a period of tedium and frustration. By this time his own feelings towards Japan in general and his fellow Japanese officers in particular were distinctly mixed. In the mess, attention to rank and seniority was so meticulous that almost no informal relationship existed between junior and more senior officers. As a non-Japanese, he was always aware that he was held at a distance and never quite accepted as a full member of this exclusive caste. The Japanese air force was intensely status-conscious. Although in the past the navy had been regarded as the senior service, the army and navy were now required to salute air force officers on all occasions. Lobsang, who to this day resents any hint of being patronised or treated with condescension, never felt quite at home in this atmosphere of artificial etiquette. He does not recall making one intimate or memorable friendship in his squadron. 'It was just not that kind of life. Private feelings or relationships were not things that were allowed to matter.'

Lobsang's fellow officers also looked down with contempt on the local Koreans, whom they referred to as *Kori Panzi*, meaning 'wooden sticks'. They were despised for their habit of eating dog meat, which the Japanese found repulsive, and for their alleged obstinacy and stupidity. Lobsang himself, as a Manchurian, felt a mixture of pity and irritation for the Koreans because they seemed half ashamed of being Korean, and made the fatal mistake of trying to be half Japanese, only to be rebuffed and ridiculed. 'They were very tough fellows all the same and, if provoked, had the disconcerting habit of suddenly lowering their heads, with their hands still in their pockets, and butting you with incredible force. They were also very hot-tempered, and it was just as well not to tease them too far.'

In this outpost of the Japanese empire, nothing had prepared 688 Squadron for the drama of Hiroshima and the Emperor's call to the nation to surrender. The first reaction was blank incredulity. It had become so much part of the accepted credo that every Japanese was prepared to die or fight to a finish that no one could understand the logic of the Emperor's appeal. Why should two atomic bombs, whatever the casualties, be accepted as decisive?

Lobsang's squadron was not given much opportunity to reflect on the cause or responsibility of defeat. As part of the Kwantung army, it was ordered to return immediately to its headquarters near Dairen. Its planes were grounded and it was sent home ignominiously by rail. Already the railways were in chaos, and by the time Lobsang's train crossed the Korean border, law and order had broken down in Manchuria. There were endless unscheduled halts. No one on the train had any clear idea of what was happening in the world outside. At first, they received scraps of news at stations where the stationmaster's communications had not broken down. Then, all communications were cut and the stations themselves were wrecked, looted and deserted, with broken windows in the offices adding to the general air of desolation. As the train crawled on, it became clear that the people of Manchuria had risen spontaneously against their Japanese overlords and taken the law into their own hands. Lobsang later heard stories of wholesale massacre of Japanese residents and officials, and the Japanese officers on the train were afraid to leave it during halts. 688 Squadron tightened its belts and did its best to keep a stiff Japanese upper lip. 'The old arrogance had vanished. The officers were dazed, dispirited and completely disorientated. There was no one to issue orders or a directive from above.' Without a mainspring, the clockwork precision of the Japanese military machine had come to a standstill. Along the line, Lobsang had noticed that the Japanese railway workers were preparing to defend themselves with crude swords that they had forged out of old rails. Whether they expected to be attacked by the local population or were simply arming themselves to carry on the war against foreign invaders, he was not certain.

After seven days, the train limped into Mukden, the great industrial city which the Japanese had made the capital of Manchukuo. The Japanese engine-driver had to grope his way unassisted into the terminal because the stationmaster and his staff had either run away or been dealt with by the mob. The great hall of the station, where Lobsang had been assaulted on his school outing, was full of people, milling around in total confusion. The squadron's orders had been to proceed to Dairen, but at Mukden the train came to a final stop. The officers stayed in the train, afraid to alight and waiting for movement orders that never came. By this time, everyone was starving, and finally Lobsang decided to get out and explore. The Manchurian mob had looted the military stores, and many of them were wearing Japanese field boots or bits of uniforms. Lobsang decided that, even in his uniform, they might mistake him for one of themselves, and he at least had the advantage of being able to speak to them in their native Mandarin.

His foray into the crowd, unexpectedly, turned into a moment of truth. 'Suddenly, everyone was talking my own language. I had stepped out of an atmosphere of shame and humiliation into a world of hope and joy – joy that Japan was defeated and that the war was over. I felt a surge of sympathy for my own people. I was also desperately hungry. The clothing warehouses were not the only ones that had been looted. Everyone seemed to be carrying tins of canned food. Tinned meat, tinned sausages, even tins of bread. Tins were strewn all over the ground. I just grabbed one big one and went back to the train to share it with the other officers in my carriage. When I got there, I was back in Japan, and what a Japanese reception I got from my brother officers. They were as hungry as I was, but discipline was discipline and looting was looting. They all refused to touch the food, and I heard a voice say with a sneer: "You Chinese are all the same. Once a Chinese, always a Chinese." '

For a moment, Lobsang's Japanese training held. 'I felt a pang of shame and threw the tin out of the window.' Then a wave of dull fury welled up inside him. What slavish dolts these Japanese were. 'I could understand their stubbornness, and their rigid observance of rules and regulations as long as there was a war on to be fought and won. But now the war was over, and people had to eat and drink and live. I had offered these arrogant bastards food, and risked my life to fetch it for them, and all they did was look down their noses at me.'

For the first time in his story, as he tells it, the real Lobsang was beginning to break out of the strait-jacket of his Japanese uniform and all that it stood for. He was being swept along on a tide of pent-up nationalism, and the spell of passive acceptance of authority was broken.

Lobsang was so overwhelmed by conflicting emotions that his capacity for clear thinking and quick decisions seems temporarily to have deserted him. 'Looking back, I might have been able to run away and fade into the landscape. If I had had a home or even friends in Mukden, I think that is probably what I would have done. But I wasn't sure whether the Chinese might not try to kill me. I had no civilian clothes and no money. I now longed to be finished with war and to get back to my family and a peaceful life. It has often happened to me to find myself caught between conflicting anxieties which paralyse decisive action, but this was the first time and I had not yet learned how fatal it can be to delay.'

During the week that Lobsang's train struggled on from Korea to Mukden, the Soviet army had swept into Manchuria. Hitler's defeat the year before had left it free to make its plans against the day of Japan's defeat. Its first objective was to lay its hands on Japan's great industrial hinterland in Manchuria before its ally, the Nationalist Chinese Army of Chiang Kai-Shek, was able to forestall it. Mukden and the area surrounding it was the industrial as well as the administrative heart of Manchuria. So, while the luckless remnants of 688 squadron were sitting tight in their train, waiting for orders, the Soviet military authorities arrived to claim their surrender. To be confronted once again with precise military orders came almost as a relief. The Japanese were disarmed, but officers were allowed to keep their swords. A

Japanese major was appointed to maintain official liaison with the Russians, and the squadron was taken to the west of Mukden, where it spent a few weeks in a tented camp near the railway. At least they were able to eat again without dishonour. 'I remember' says Lobsang prosaically, 'we were given lots of pork and potatoes. There didn't seem to be any other kind of vegetables available.'

If the Japanese prisoners were still dazed and unprepared for the situation they now found themselves in, the Russians seemed to have a very clear plan of action. There were engineering teams from every branch of the armed forces – with specialists from the army, air force and tank corps who knew exactly where all the industrial resources of Manchuria were located, and had already detailed plans for the removal of plant and machinery in carefully listed categories. Lobsang, having missed his opportunity to escape, still half expected that the Russians would not treat Manchurians like himself, who had been drafted into Japanese service, as enemies. The Russians, however, made no such fine distinctions. To carry out their programme of lightning looting, they needed all the skilled labour and technical expertise they could lay their hands on. The pilots and ground staff of the Japanese air force were ready to hand as an invaluable addition to their own labour force. It is true that they progressively weeded out non-Japanese personnel to form special detachments, pre-sumably on the assumption that they would be more co-operative than hard-core Japanese élite, but this did not happen for several months.

After a few weeks, Lobsang and the detachment he had been assigned to were packed into military trucks and driven to Anshan, the centre of China's iron and steel industry. There had been wholesale destruction and sabotage of the blast furnaces and rolling mills by the Japanese army before it withdrew, but in this huge industrial complex there was still a mass of machinery and plant that the Russians coveted, and Lobsang's detachment was put straight to work. They slept where they could, in trucks or improvised shelters, but always on the job so as to lose no time. 'It was hard and rough work, but under the circumstances we were not treated inhumanely. Nearly all the officers were European Russians but the bulk of the Soviet occupation troops were from the Soviet Asian republics, or Outer Mongolia. They were not bad fellows. Rough and ready, hard drinkers, and pretty terrible with the girls, but when they worked alongside us they treated us more as fellow-workers than prisoners of war. When it got cold, they would pull out a bottle of vodka and call to us to come and have a swig. We were given the same rations and living quarters as the Russians who were directing operations, and there were no rigid barriers of rank or nationality. The kind of work we were doing and the hurry would in any case have made them impossible. So I soon began to pick up a smattering of Russian.'

The dismantling at Anshan lasted several months. Machinery was packed, numbered and crated, and Lobsang was sent twice by rail to Siberia in a working party to check the safe arrival of certain plant.

Before the Chinese nationalist army arrived to take over Manchuria towards the end of 1946, the Soviet specialists had completed a gigantic looting operation. In his assessment of relations between China and the Soviet Union, Lobsang always attaches great importance to what he sees as the ruthless selfishness of the Russians in taking everything they could from China – even after the Communists took over in 1949 – and driving a very hard bargain over such aid as they eventually provided in return.

In the summer of 1946, his detachment was sent to a prisoner-of-war camp in Vladivostok, where the first systematic interrogation and sorting out since surrender took place. Once again, he was given no opportunity to claim any sort of privileged treatment as a non-Japanese, but he was assigned to an engineering unit which contained no Japanese prisoners. It was mainly made up of Koreans. There was one other Chinese whom he had known in the air force.

For the rest of his captivity, the itinerary of his new unit was a cartographer's nightmare. The sites chosen on Soviet territory for reassembling the dismantled Japanese plant were often located in desolate places whose names and military significance Lobsang has forgotten, if indeed he was actually ever aware of them at the time. All his work was connected with military projects, and generally took him to army camps or emplacements which appeared to be situated in the middle of nowhere. He remembers, for instance, doing a big job 'somewhere near Lake Beykal', but never got a chance to see the huge inland sea itself. 'All we really knew was that we were somewhere along the interminable length of the Trans-Siberian railway. The distances seemed at times so enormous that in the end, if I had been told that I was near Stalingrad or in the Ukraine, it would not have surprised me very much.'

Time passed quickly, and the constant heavy work and fatigue left the prisoners no time for introspection. 'The curious thing is, I never got ill. The Siberian winter is supposed to be very hard, but is not so different from a Manchurian winter. We were given Soviet army sheepskin coats and felt boots. I soon learnt the trick of putting dried maize leaves inside the boots instead of wearing socks – it is a wonderful way of keeping your feet and legs dry and warm. In Manchuria, they do the same thing. In fact, there is an old saying that the three most precious things that Manchuria produces are *tiao pi* (mink fur), *yin shen* (a root that is used all over China and is believed to have almost magic properties as a cure for practically everything) and *uru tz'ao* (the maize grass). The food, though it was often strange, and occasionally nauseating to anyone brought up on good Chinese food, was copious enough to keep us strong and healthy. With that sort of work and that sort of climate, one is ready to eat anything, even if the cabbage soup had a foetid taste like the smell of stale urine.'

As it pushed westward across the emptiness of Siberia, Lobsang's unit shook down into a seasoned task-force of nomadic mechanical tinkers. No matter how carefully the looted plant had been crated and dispatched, there was never any guarantee that all the component parts would arrive at their destination, but the orders were to reassemble it, and reassembled it had to be. Improvisation came to be a second nature, and to this day Lobsang has a barely concealed contempt for engineers who are lost if the right spare parts are not available on the spot or who cannot roll up their sleeves to make or mend virtually anything with the most primitive equipment.

In an outlandish way, he found some things about Siberia almost congenial, 'What I found sympathetic was that so many of the local people or their families had originally been sent to Siberia because they were at loggerheads with the regime or in disgrace with authority; so that it wasn't even necessary for them to pretend to be Communists. And that, in its own curious way, made the atmosphere much less stiff and constrained than in other places I've been in under Communist rule.' Not that the members of Lobsang's party were allowed any contact with the civilian population. Their only casual acquaintances were with local temporary workers, known as *lobode*, who were recruited and paid by the army.

Lobsang's Russian was by now getting fluent, fluent enough, at any rate, to join in the banter and chaff between the Russian soldiers and the local labour force. 'When there were any women among them, we all used to joke with them, and I generally found them cheerful and amusing and not at all put out by the outrageous compliments we tried to pay them. Some of the Siberian girls were beautiful and very sexy looking.'

Lobsang is still not sure whether the various representations he tried to make had anything to do with the timing of his release. More likely, he thinks, it was simply the result of some arbitrary decision which happened to come into operation while he was in Siberia. There were long and complicated negotiations between Moscow and the Chinese nationalists over the withdrawal of Soviet occupation forces from Manchuria, with the Russians procrastinating and using every pretext to stay and keep control of the resources and communications through Manchuria to the seaboard south of Vladivostok.

'I think there must have been a political deal between Stalin and Chiang Kai-Shek in which the repatriation of prisoners was used as a bargaining counter. In any event, half a dozen of us, all Chinese, were sent back by rail by stages to Mukden, where we were handed over to the Kuomintang military authorities.'

The KMT general commanding the Mukden military region at

this time was General Ma Chan-San. 'He was,' says Lobsang, 'one of the more eccentric of the old-time war-lords. He was a confirmed opium-smoker, and very stout. But what I remember best about him was his ludicrously short legs. When he was sitting on his horse, he managed to look almost a life-size general. But when he dismounted, he turned out to be a pigmy.'

It was now 1947. Lobsang was back among his own people, but in his absence the Chinese Civil War between Chiang Kai-Shek's nationalists and Mao Tse Tung's Communists had moved towards its climax. Manchuria was the strategic cockpit of China, where the decisive battles of the war were already being fought out.

3

KMT COLONEL

During his captivity in Siberia, Lobsang had often wondered what sort of life he would return to. If there had been no Civil War in China, he thinks he would probably have gone into some part of his father's business, probably on the engineering side. He felt that his abbreviated wartime course at Tokyo University had left gaps, particularly on the theoretical side, which he wanted to fill. He had heard that at Mukden there was a new nationalist university, and his original idea was to explore the possibilities of either doing some post-graduate work or combining it with teaching.

But before he could make any plans, his first task was to regularise his position with the Kuomintang military authorities and, if possible, make contact with his family. Here he was in luck. His eldest brother was in Mukden itself. He had joined the KMT back in 1931 as a Chinese-trained civil engineer. By virtue of his wartime work, which was semi-military, semi-civilian, he carried the military rank of General. Thanks to this, Lobsang had little difficulty in satisfying the military authorities that he was not a Communist sympathiser.

His brother's advice was simple and categoric. 'Forget all this nonsense about becoming a student again. Civilian life in Manchuria has become too chaotic, too dangerous. The only thing for you to do is to get into the army, because only the army guarantees you a living and some kind of security.' Quite apart from the respect due to an elder brother in Chinese families, Lobsang had to admit the force of his argument.

Mukden, which he had last seen in the turmoil and euphoria of liberation from Japanese rule, had become the headquarters of the KMT army as well as the administrative capital of Manchuria. It had also become the graveyard of the hopes of the younger generation of Manchurians. Nowhere was this more evident than at the university. Most of the students, who received no grants or assistance from the KMT authorities, were penniless. The teaching staff was almost as insecure and impecunious as the students, and as a result the standard of tuition in most of the faculties was either second-rate or frankly deplorable.

Worst hit of all were the sons and daughters of upper- and middle-class families from areas which had been overrun by the Communists, and whose parents had already been dispossessed. Often they were in desperate straits to maintain themselves and help their surviving relations. Daughters of good families, enrolled as university students, were driven to casual prostitution in order to support a mother, a younger brother or sister, or simply to find the price of their next meal.

Lobsang's brother had not exaggerated. The plight of much of the civilian population was as desperate as that of the students. Largely as a result of the Soviet army's dismantling policy, and Japanese sabotage at the moment of surrender, industry was almost at a standstill. At Anshan alone, the iron and steel area which Lobsang remembered so well, he was told that there were between three and four million unemployed workers. Where jobs were available, the KMT military authorities had no scruples about giving redundant officers priority over civilians. Lobsang has no doubt that this monumental indifference to the welfare of the workers and the civilian population was one of the important causes of the KMT's downfall.

Admittedly, when the nationalist army took over Manchuria from its Soviet allies, it had inherited almost insoluble problems. At the moment of the Japanese collapse, Manchurians all over the country had looted shops and business premises. There had been indiscriminate killings and settling of scores with real or supposed collaborators. There had been several months without an effective government of any kind. Nameless groups, prompted by conflicting ideologies or simply a lust for power, had tried to set up local revolutionary organisations. Ill-gotten gains were frittered away by people who often hardly knew where their wealth had come from. It was common to see people gambling in the streets, or spending with grotesque lavishness in restaurants and night-clubs.

When the KMT did arrive, the political and economic rot was already so deep that only the most coherent, disciplined adminis-tration could have kept it in check. As it was, by this time the Kuomintang was neither coherent nor disciplined. It had become a corrupt, selfish, privileged caste. Ordinary people found them-selves caught between the arbitrary exactions of the KMT and the creeping advance of the Communists in all those parts of the country where there was no effective KMT military control.

Militarily, the nationalists still looked secure enough. The Americans were pouring arms and money into China, and the army was, if anything, overpaid and over-equipped. 'How,' says Lobsang, 'did they manage to lose the war? They had something like eight million troops – more than half of them in Manchuria. At that time, I doubt if the Communists had more than a million soldiers – unpaid, ragged and pathetically armed and equipped. I myself have seen them go into action with only four hand-grenades. And yet, in less than a couple of years after I got home, it was all over. How?'

Lobsang's considered explanation comes from a man with first-hand experience of service in both the nationalist and com-munist armies. 'From what I saw, practically everyone in the KMT army, from top to bottom, was on the make. Drivers used to hire out their trucks to deliver goods in the markets. Officers flagrantly fiddled their accounts, drawing pay for twice the num-ber of men they actually commanded, and pocketing the differ-ence. Army stores of every description were sold on the black market. The only things the KMT seemed to think of were money, food, drink and girls. When I returned to Mukden from Siberia, there were so many army brothels there that they had to be divided into four authorised categories. Class I: Guaranteed really lovely girls. Class II: Medically inspected by the army, guaranteed no V.D. – what a joke! Class III: Be careful, use contraceptives. Class IV: Only fit for civilians. On the parade ground, before morning drill, I've often heard soldiers greeting each other, "How was the fucking last night?" And, in earshot of their officers, the boastful answer, "Thanks, four or five. How about you?" ' Morality apart, Lobsang draws his own simple military conclusion. 'When soldiers are living like that, they don't want to fight and they don't want to die. In any case, there was no sense of a cause which men were ready to sacrifice or die for. None of the men in the KMT had any respect for their officers, or the officers for their generals, or the generals for their leader, Chiang Kai-Shek. I saw respect and readiness to die for a cause in the Japanese air force and later in the Chinese communist army, but never in the KMT in my day.'

But this was the army that Lobsang was persuaded to join. Two months after his return to Manchuria, he entered it, at the age of twenty-three, as a lieutenant-colonel. No doubt his engineering qualifications and his technical skills counted for something, but Lobsang has no illusions that he would have received such astonishing preferment if he had not had the right sort of family connections and, he adds with disarming candour, the right sort of family money. 'What to do?' he asks simply. 'I felt more than anything that it was important to get myself organised.' Even with the KMT he was careful not to disclose that he had been in the Japanese air force.

What he had seen and heard about the general situation in Manchuria since his return was not reassuring. Everywhere outside the main towns the Communists were very strong. In Dairen, where Lobsang's mother was still living, they had quietly taken control under the umbrella of the Soviet occupation force. Moscow, notwithstanding the Communist revolution, continued to regard the Kwan Tung Chou peninsula as stolen Russian territory and, after the Japanese surrender, in 1943, continued to maintain a Soviet military presence there throughout the entire Chinese Civil War.

At the time of Lobsang's return, travel in the Manchurian countryside was always hazardous and often restricted. From Mukden he had only been able to communicate with his mother in Dairen and with other members of his family in the country by smuggling messages to them through refugees returning to those areas or through dubious characters who, for one reason or another, were able to move freely from KMT-controlled territory to Communist strongholds. 'This was a time when spies, informers and obscure agents were two-a-penny, most of them willing to act as couriers or as double agents if anyone cared to pay them.'

The stories Lobsang heard were often as discreditable to the Communists as to the KMT. Many of his family's friends and acquaintances had been dispossessed, imprisoned or killed. The Communists' techniques of public denunciations and trials of landlords were already sickeningly familiar. It was part of their campaign of distributing land to the peasants and recruiting peasants' sons for the People's Army. For Lobsang, in these early months, it was one more depressing piece of evidence of the plight of his country and the bitterness of the hatreds which divided its people.

When a landlord or wealthy businessman was put up for public investigation, the Communists had invariably studied his record and discovered someone with a personal grudge against him. This person would tax him with the responsibility for past hardships or injustices inflicted on his family until someone in the crowd would raise the cry of 'Beat him, beat him.' Then first one peasant, then another fell on him with sticks. The victim's land was then parcelled out among the local peasants. For this, the Communist army presented its own bill. 'Now that the land is yours,' its officers told the peasants, 'it is your duty to defend it against the enemies of the people. If you have three sons, one of them must stay to work for the land. Send the other two to fight with the People's Liberation Army.' So two more willing or reluctant recruits went to swell the ranks of the threadbare army of unpaid volunteers, and the Communists' stealthy but relentless grip on the Manchurian countryside tightened.

'They took such pains to convince ordinary simple people that the Communist army belonged to them. You have to give them credit for brilliant organisation and for the skill with which they always managed to identify their actions with the interests of the people. The KMT army oppressed and robbed the people, taxed them to the limit and lived off their local resources. The Communists, when they arrived in a rural area, did none of these things. When they were not training, fighting or studying, they worked in the fields, sharing the produce with the whole community. They paid for anything they commandeered for the army. On pain of the severest punishments, they were forbidden to molest women. In areas which had seen the KMT army, their puritan discipline increased the hatred for the excesses and arrogance of the licentious and rapacious KMT soldiers. It is also my experience that the more sacrifice you demand from fighting troops, the more they respond – provided, of course, that their leaders always set the example and that the troops themselves have a clear idea of what it is they are supposed to be fighting for.

'The Communist plan of recruitment, indoctrination and military strategy was all of a piece. It was a masterly blend of reasoned persuasion, appeal to self-interest, exploitation of grievances, and straight-forward, old-fashioned nationalism. People knew that, even in the days before the defeat of Japan, the Communists had always been eager to fight the foreign army of occupation first, and their Chinese opponents afterwards. It had been exactly the opposite with the KMT. Whatever their ideological differences, the ordinary people had always felt that the Communists were at least fellow Chinese.'

Lobsang delivers this judgment objectively and with hindsight. When he joined the KMT, however, he saw things differently. By background and up-bringing, he was disinclined to make common cause with the Communists. His spell in the Soviet Union had opened his eyes to the seamier side of life under a Communist regime. His sister in Amdung, who had married a poor but handsome husband and been given a modest farm by her grandfather, had been publicly tried by a People's Court, and savagely flogged. 'She was given three hundred blows simply for belonging to a family of landowners. When we met, long afterwards, the scars on her bottom were still atrocious.'

Apart from these personal prejudices, the temptation for a young man of twenty-three, after more than two years of isolation and hard labour, to taste some of the creature comforts of life must have been very strong. Lobsang never pretends to have been either a Puritan or an ideological crusader. His concern for ordinary people stems from personal compassion and understanding of how the under-privileged live and suffer, and has nothing to do with systems or nationalities. Over-privileged people offend him collectively because he has often found them oppressive and greedy. As individuals, he accepts or rejects them on their merits. He has never spurned the fleshpots, probably because his opportunities to indulge himself have been so limited and intermittent. Not that his own brief career as a KMT officer seems to have been particularly debauched. One of his first steps, in fact, after being commissioned, was to marry one of the Mukden students in distress. Her family, including younger brothers and sisters, was destitute, and she was at her wits' end to help provide for them.

Li Chin-Fung was a gifted pianist. Lobsang met her in a café and married her almost immediately. Luckily for both of them KMT officers at general headquarters in Mukden, to which Lobsang was then attached, did not have to live in camp. On his lieutenant-colonel's pay, he was able to install his wife in decent lodgings and, within the limits of his military duties, lead quite a satisfactory domestic life.

Already he had seen and heard enough of the Civil War in Manchuria to determine him to get as far away from it as possible, as fast as he could.

'This was, I am sure, the cruellest and most murderous part of the war. Both sides realised that whoever controlled Manchuria would control China. The Communists' hold on the countryside was increasing all the time. Whenever they dared, they would try to encircle a KMT garrison in a town. Then everything depended on whether the KMT could call up reinforcements in time to trap the Communists in the middle. It did not happen very often but, when it did, the slaughter was merciless.'

Eventually, after a few months of string-pulling, Lobsang managed to get himself transferred from the Manchurian command to the Chinese centre-north army, with its headquarters at Tung-Hsien. Its commander, General Fu Tso-Yi, had been appointed in the belief that he, if anyone, would defend Peking with the resolution and efficiency which the situation demanded. Once again, Lobsang was attached to army headquarters, roughly a hundred miles from Peking, on the road to Tientsin. He worked in the adjutant-general's office, as a special adviser on training and supply for mechanised units. If Fu Tso-Yi had lived up to expectations, and fought to a finish, it could have been a stirring command for Lobsang. In the event, it turned out not to be particularly testing or arduous. Lobsang was responsible for the supply and maintenance of armoured vehicles. It involved a good deal of travelling to local commands, and this in turn gave him an insight into the whole KMT military machine.

In the technical services, corruption was less flagrant than, for example, in the quarter-master-general's branch. Even so, the hiring of military transport to commercial enterprises and traffic in spare parts were everyday practices which Lobsang's superiors and subordinates made no serious effort to control.

'Chiang Kai-Shek had at one stage tried to stamp out corruption in the KMT army. He had even appointed his son, Chiang Ching-Kuk, to lead a special unit – the so-called "Tiger Squadron" – to eliminate abuses. He was given special powers to ferret out and punish the worst offenders, but most of them were so well entrenched that he failed to make any impression on them, and ended by becoming almost as venal as the rest of them.' The whole exercise demonstrated how limited Chiang Kai-Shek's authority was over his own generals, many of whom in reality remained old-fashioned war-lords in their own right.

Throughout 1948 the KMT's situation deteriorated with frightening speed. In Manchuria, the situation grew catastrophic. By the summer, the Communists were everywhere threatening to gain control. The fall of Chinchow, the gateway to China proper, at the south-western tip of Manchuria, marked the turning-point of the war. No fewer than thirty-seven KMT generals were trapped and taken prisoner, and the Communists began openly threatening the remaining commanders who continued to resist them. According to Lobsang, they informed Fu Tso-Yi that he was number one on their list of major war-criminals, and that, if captured, he would be publicly exhibited in a cage and allowed to starve to death. What is certain is that, about this time, he secretly began negotiations for the surrender of Peking and bargaining terms for himself and his whole army.

More than any single person, General Fu Tso-Yi held the key to the duration, if not the final outcome, of the war. His army held the whole of China north of Shanghai and up to the border of Manchuria. Apart from his reputation as a fighting general, he enjoyed widespread popularity and esteem unique among the KMT commanders. He was something of an intellectual – a graduate of the famous Nankai University, and, in Lobsang's opinion, the one truly educated KMT general in the whole of northern China. In earlier days, he had marked himself out as a patriot who had never been afraid of denouncing inefficiency, selfishness and corruption inside the Kuomintang. He had made a famous speech in 1942 to the KMT Consultative Council, which included all the top brass, in which he had told his audience, 'At the front, I see soldiers fighting desperate battles. At the rear, I see only people eating themselves to death.' The students and intellectuals, as well as the fighting troops, respected him. Lobsang says that Generalissimo Chiang Kai-Shek became jealous of his popularity and that, in the period leading up to his surrender, Chiang had deliberately denied Fu Tso-Yi's army the reinforcements and equipment it had urgently requested. Another cause of the Generalissimo's jealousy may have been that the American Aid mission had voted Fu Tso-Yi special funds on the ground that he was one of the only generals in the field they could trust to use them honestly and effectively.

Like Lobsang himself, Fu Tso-Yi is by training an engineer, which may have something to do with the obvious admiration, bordering on affection, in which Lobsang holds him. To this day, he holds high office in Peking as a top military adviser and a member of the Communist Central Committee. Under Mao Tse-Tung, he has carried out many great engineering projects, including the world's longest bridge which spans the Yangtse River from Pukow to Nanking. As a builder of political bridges, his achievement is no less remarkable. Of those who made the perilous leap from the Kuomintang on to the Communist bandwagon, he proved himself the most successful survivor. And, while he still held Peking, he contrived a bridge for his entire army to cross into the ranks of the victorious People's Army, without a single shot being fired.

In taking his decision to surrender, Fu Tso-Yi was influenced by two main considerations. He had been watching developments in Manchuria and, after the fall of Chinchow, he knew that the game was up and that nothing could long delay the Communists from sweeping south. He knew, too, that, like himself, the Communist leadership set great store by Peking as the historic and cultural capital of China. To have to fight through it and risk destroying it would have left a black mark on their record among educated Chinese everywhere in the world, which would have taken many years to erase. At all points, his timing and exact calculation of the strength of his bargaining cards appear to have been faultless.

For the second time within three years, Lobsang found himself taking part in a surrender at short notice. One difference was that Fu Tso-Yi gave his officers rather more warning than the Emperor Hirohito. Four days, to be precise.

'I think that most of us had secretly realised for a long time that the Communists would win in the end, but none of us had expected that it would happen so fast.'

4

CHANGE-IDEA COLONEL

In the four days before the formal surrender, all the officers of the Hupei command – the north-centre army – had it explained to them that, if they agreed to surrender, they would be transferred to the People's Army without loss of rank. This was an extraordinary concession by the Communist leadership, but the possession of Peking and the province of Hupei was, politically and militarily, beyond price. Fu Tso-Yi knew this and had been able to bargain on behalf of his officers as well as himself. He had also calculated correctly that, like himself, they would swallow the ideological pill and count themselves lucky to save not only their skins but their jobs.

Lobsang cannot remember a single instance of an officer not accepting the transfer. Other ranks were simply informed that they would be integrated into Communist formations. The day before, the Communists, who were outside Peking at Pei-Men-Wei, sent a delegation to make arrangements with the KMT command and distribute flags for the public to wave when the Liberation Army entered the city. On the morning of the ceremony, the troops were paraded with their rifles stacked in front of them. When the Communist officers made their appearance, they clapped dutifully in welcome. The whole operation was carried out with the smooth precision of a business merger after a successful takeover bid. The minimum face-saving courtesies were extended to the higher executives, but the humiliation of the old management was none the less complete. Surprisingly, Lobsang says that there was no acute sense of fear among the officers that they would be individually or collectively victimised. 'This may seem extraordinary, considering the violence with which each side had denounced the other in their Civil War

47

propaganda. Some of the hard-core KMT officers may have been apprehensive about the Communists sticking to their bargain, but we were, after all, all Chinese, and surrendering to your own people is never quite the same thing as capitulating to a foreign power. The Communists often used soft words to win people over, until they were sure they were in full control, and then discarded them but, in the case of Fu Tso-Yi's army, I do not personally know of a single case where they did not honour their contract.'

Naturally, some adjustments were necessary. All the KMT officers above the rank of captain and below the rank of General were sent in batches to officers' political training centres for crash courses in Communist theory and practice. Lobsang's 'change-idea' school was housed, somewhat ironically, in the buildings of the old French racecourse at Tientsin – a monument to nineteenth-century western imperialism at its most spacious and uninhibited. The school was organised in an atmosphere of earnest endeavour. There was instruction from four basic textbooks on the history of Communism and the actual process of 'change-history' but what mattered most were the remorseless discussion sessions in which the trainees were exhaustively cross-examined about their ideas and beliefs, with the instructors pointing out the errors of their thinking and doing their best to determine how adaptable individual officers were to the new ideology, and how sincere in their readiness to accept it.

'I must say the instructors at Tientsin were very intelligently chosen for the job. Most of them were veterans of Mao's famous Long March. They showed infinite patience and great ingenuity in provoking discussion. If an officer seemed to accept their arguments too easily, they suspected him of concealing his real thoughts and tried everything to get him to reveal what was really in his mind. When they realised that they were not going to be bullied or penalised for challenging their instructors on facts or ideas, some of the older KMT officers became quite obstinate and argumentative, and we had some amusing set-to's with reactionary old majors in full cry, laying down the law and getting hot under the collar like officers of the old school in regular armies all over

Lobsang, 1973

Lobsang's Bhutanese wife, Rinzi Om, and their four children, 1974

the world. On the whole, our instructors took it surprisingly well, but presumably drew their own conclusions about what use these hard cases could be put to in the People's Army.'

Lobsang himself quickly decided that the only thing to do was to conform. He worked diligently at his set books and found no difficulty in picking up the Communist jargon. Some of it was already familiar from his sojourn in the Soviet Union and his contacts with Red Army officers. What was not so easy was to decide how much he could reveal about his own past. He carefully avoided any mention of his service in the Japanese air force and this also meant that he had again to suppress the whole chapter of his years as a prisoner of war in Siberia. On the other hand, his engineering qualifications were an obvious asset. For one thing, they explained, to some extent at any rate, his remarkable seniority in the KMT army. For another, they were exactly the kind of qualifications that the People's Army was going to need now that it was to become the National Army of a united Communist China. He therefore gave a full account of his birth and education in Japanese-occupied Kwan Tung Chou up to the point of his graduation at Tokyo University. In the searching discussions with his instructors, which tended to range over a trainee's entire experience and background, it must often have been a tricky business to avoid verbal slips or unguarded revelations which would have led to awkward questions. Luckily, by simply advancing his age of arrival at the university by a couple of years, he was able to fill most of the time-gap between his graduation and his joining the KMT army. Fortunately, he had told the same story when he joined the KMT army, so that his service record revealed no discrepancies. The fact that his service with the KMT had been so short was in his favour. It meant that he had not had much time to acquire what the Communists regarded as the corrupt mentality of the nationalist leadership.

One of Lobsang's instructors he found particularly helpful and sympathetic. He was a full colonel named Li Kuo-ya, a veteran of the Long March who had joined the Communists at the age of twelve. He explained to Lobsang how, in those days, the army had given him whatever education he possessed. He realised perfectly well the limitations of such a rough and ready school and told Lobsang that, with the responsibilities of power, the People's Army were going to be in desperate need of young, educated people with university qualifications. 'He was a sincere and open-hearted man and encouraged me to believe that I could have a very bright future in the service of the new China. When he was pleased with my progress, he would offer me cigarettes and we would smoke together and discuss the future and the kind of opportunities that might come my way. In spite of his long and gruelling career, he had preserved all his youthful enthusiasm and idealism. Unlike so many of the Communist theorists and bureaucrats, he remained a warm human being who was always thinking of the welfare of ordinary people and not of his own advancement. I believe he was later promoted and became a Brigadier-General, but his lack of formal education must have prevented him reaching the top. In any case, he was not ambitious enough to push himself up the ladder. He was always perfectly happy doing his best in whatever job was assigned to him.'

So, for Lobsang at any rate, life at Tientsin was busy and bearable. The KMT trainees were treated as officers in the People's Army and, although their courses did not leave much time for anything else, they were allowed to circulate freely whenever they were off duty. The people of Tientsin have always had the reputation of being hard-headed cynics and in these first months of the Communist take-over, they and their new masters watched each other guardedly. Outwardly, life was allowed to go on without any violent interruptions or changes. The citizens of Tientsin showed no sign of being cowed and continued to crack local jokes at the expense of both the Communists and the Nationalists.

About three months after the declaration of the People's Republic, the Chinese New Year was celebrated with most of the traditional festivities. Besides the processions and special New Year meals, it was customary to decorate the doorways of houses with gay paper banners, bearing seasonal inscriptions. One daring humorist hung two vertical ones on either side of his front door which read 'BANDIT MAO, GANGSTER CHIANG: WHO IS

THE BANDIT? WHO THE GANGSTER?' Across the top of the doorway, to complete the triumphal arch, a single streamer proclaimed 'THE PEOPLE SUFFER'. Lobsang explains that it was typical of the Communists' tactics during periods of consolidation and transition, that, as far as he knows, the householder in question was not rebuked or penalised.

By the summer of 1950 Lobsang was passed out of the 'change-idea' school as ready for service with the People's Army. His instructors' reports, both on his technical skills and ideological outlook, must have been excellent. It was natural, in view of the inevitable shortcomings of the improvised Communist army, that it should be most interested in the younger and more highly qualified officers. Even so, Lobsang's posting, when it came, was something of a prize award.

He was sent to the new Tank Training Centre called Chan-Cheh Hsueh-Shiao in the Peking region as a senior instructor. The People's Army during the Civil War had fought almost entirely without armour. Consequently, everything at the Tank Training Centre had to be done from scratch. At first, the only tanks available were American tanks captured from the KMT. They were all light tanks, from ten to eighteen tons. Later, a few Russian thirty tonners were added.

As Lobsang himself had no first-hand experience as a tank officer, although he was an expert on armoured vehicles, he took the line with his trainees that they were all engaged together in an adventure of discovery. Using whatever knowledge they had of cars or troop-carriers as a starting point, he invited them to work out, in theory and in practice, the characteristics that were peculiar to tanks and the problems involved in their use and maintenance. He improvised his technique as an instructor as he went along, encouraging his trainees to put forward their own ideas and suggestions for discussion. This democratic approach, besides being in line with the ideals of the People's Army, was both popular and effective.

Lobsang is always happiest when confronted with a solid job that he can get his teeth into, and it must have been a relief to be back in the world of practical things. For someone brought up in

Japanese standards of military efficiency, the complete absence of the corruption which had surrounded him in the KMT army and the high-pressure programme of military duties must have been quite like old times, with the additional advantage that Lobsang himself was given a very free hand to work out his own rather informal and personal methods. The Tank Training Centre had no established traditions or routine. What counted was results, and there seems to be no doubt that Lobsang, for all his youth, was an outstanding success.

Towards the end of the course, his first batch of pupils, who were all middle rank officers, were asked to make an assessment of his qualities as an instructor and as a leader. Their findings were so flattering that he was awarded two medals for meritorious achievement.

'They were some of the first medals given by the Chinese Communists. During the Civil War, there were no decorations in the People's Army. It was all part of the image of equality and austerity. But once the whole of China was united, it was decided that medals were a useful way of rewarding veterans for past services and demonstrating to newcomers that, if they gave loyal service, they could expect the same recognition as anyone else. My two medals were for efficiency and zeal in training my men and working out training programmes which gave rapid and satisfactory results. It is true that I worked very hard, but above all I learnt a great deal myself about how to get people to work for me with as little fuss and red tape as possible; and this was to come in very useful later on in quite different circumstances.'

During the year and nine months he spent at the Tank Training Centre, Lobsang was almost wholly occupied with his work. The mechanisation of the People's Army was one of its most urgent tasks and China's involvement in the Korean war in 1950 made it more urgent still. Lobsang lived at the Centre itself, but his wife, Li Chin-Fung, was allowed periodically to visit him there. She stayed in the Centre's women's quarters, where Lobsang was allowed to spend Saturday nights with her. Even this rather restricted married life put him in a very privileged category. No officer in the People's Army under the rank of lieutenant-colonel was allowed any married life. This hangover from the puritan discipline of the Civil War days was later relaxed – Lobsang thinks towards the end of 1952 or the beginning of 1953 – but while he was at the Centre Lobsang remembers a tragic old major, who was passed over in the promotion lists, shooting a successful rival out of envy and exasperation, and then blowing his own brains out.

'There were many sex problems in the Communist army at that time. Even nurses in army hospitals who committed misconduct with patients were given prison sentences for their first offence, and were summarily shot if they persisted in their errors.' Lobsang's rank, though it sometimes excited the jealousy of older officers who were junior to him, did at least spare him this sort of frustration and enabled him to concentrate on his work without being entirely cut off from his family.

Considering his background, and taking into account his temperamental inclination to periodic outbursts of self-assertiveness, against which his mother had often warned him, Lobsang at this time seemed set for a promising and honourable military career. Suddenly it was interrupted by a shattering blow from an entirely unexpected quarter. Like most of the events which have dislocated Lobsang's life, it was not even directly concerned with himself.

He received a letter from Mukden informing him that his eldest brother – the same who had talked him into joining the KMT army – was under arrest. The charges against him were very grave. Under the KMT, he had been responsible for taking over former Japanese factories and plant, and incorporating them into the new nationalist Chinese economy. These had included munitions factories and, after the Communist takeover, he was still manager of what had once been an important Japanese munitions factory. Now he was accused of being a KMT agent, in the pay of the Americans, and more specifically, a saboteur. It was alleged, among other things, that hand-grenades manufactured in his factory had had their regulating mechanism systematically tampered with so that, when used by Chinese Communist troops in the Korean war, they had failed to explode.

Lobsang points out that as there were Communist inspectors and supervisors at every stage in the production line, this charge was, to say the least, not very plausible. Owing to the Communist procedure of interrogating prisoners and pronouncing them guilty without making any of the evidence for the prosecution or the defence public, Lobsang has never been able to establish the real reasons for his brother's disgrace.

By the time he had obtained permission to visit him and arranged leave, the interrogation was over, and his brother was awaiting sentence in Mukden. Lobsang found a broken man and is convinced that he must have been very roughly used during his interrogation, if not actually physically tortured. Prison guards were present during his visit, so that his brother had no chance to tell him the whole story. He took the line with Lobsang that, since he had been pronounced an 'enemy of the people', Lobsang should not waste his time or compromise himself by coming to see him again. He urged him to think of himself and his own future, but Lobsang got the clearest impression that he was trying to warn him that there was no future for him within a Communist society and that, if he got an opportunity, he should try to leave the country.

The sentence passed on his brother, which was announced not long after Lobsang's visit, was twenty-five years' corrective detention. He was forty-five at the time, so that it was the equivalent of a life sentence. Lobsang heard that he fainted when told of the sentence. He has never been able to discover where he was sent to serve it, or whether he is still alive.

Lobsang took his brother's disgrace very hard. Since his father's death, he had been the head of the family and, traditionally, the eldest brother occupies a very special place of respect in China as the personal symbol of a family's honour and reputation.

Even in a Communist society, and with his own career at risk, Lobsang is not the sort of man tamely to abandon a friend, still less an elder brother, in a tight corner. He went to the military authorities to make representations against the way his brother had been tried and treated during his interrogation. They were

not unsympathetic and were inclined to agree that the Secret
Police might in certain respects have handled the case by methods
which a military court would have hesitated to employ. They
made it clear however that they were powerless to reopen the
case.

It can easily happen that a man can come to terms with a
political system – or at least can close his eyes to its injustices –
until the moment when someone in his own immediate circle is
victimised. For Lobsang, his brother's disgrace was a signal for
revolt so powerful that it swept aside all those considerations of
self-interest which his brother himself had recommended him to
obey. When he reported back to the Tank Training Centre, he
told his commanding general that he felt it impossible to continue
to carry out his duties as an officer in the People's Army.

The general did his best to dissuade him from taking any rash
decision. He urged him to think of how much more insecure and
uncertain his future would be as an ex-KMT officer in civilian life.
Ironically, he used very much the same sort of arguments that his
brother had once used to persuade him to join the KMT army.
'He was perfectly right. Later, I often bitterly regretted my
decision to leave the army, which had accepted me on my merits
in spite of my past connections. I agreed to my commanding
officer's suggestion that I should postpone a final decision for a
couple of months, to give me time to think it over, but my mind
was already made up.'

At the end of two months he made a formal application for a
civilian assignment and was given an honourable discharge from
the army. For the next eight years, his discharge papers were his
only official proof of identity and the nearest equivalent he
possessed to a passport to take him across provincial or international frontiers.

5

A CIVILIAN'S LOT IS NOT
A HAPPY ONE

One advantage of the Communist victory and the extension of Chairman Mao's authority over the length and breadth of China was that it had again become possible to travel to those parts of Manchuria which had been inaccessible to Lobsang during his KMT days. Now, for instance, he was able to go home to Dairen, where his mother was still living. Of course, there was no longer any family mansion, and the old spacious style of life had long ago disappeared. But his mother still had a house of her own. The fact that his father had died before the defeat of Japan, and that she had stayed on in Dairen throughout the whole of the Soviet occupation as a widow with no personal political past probably explains why, as a former capitalist, she had been so relatively lucky. Her new home was a three-story house, modest by former standards, but still roomy enough to accommodate Lobsang and his wife and their two-year-old daughter. One of his married sisters lived in a street not far away and was in her mother's house with her own children on the day when Lobsang arrived home after leaving the army.

'My daughter, who was only two, was not old enough to remember me. My wife, Li Chin-Fung, had taken her to my mother's soon after the Communist victory and had left her there when she came to visit me at the Tank Training Centre. When her little cousins called to her to come and meet her father, she was coy, and hid her face behind her hands.'

Lobsang and his family were installed on the top floor of the house. His mother had furnished her own first-floor rooms from what she had managed to salvage from their old family house, but in these surroundings, it struck Lobsang as heavy and oppressive and he redecorated his own rooms with simpler contemporary furniture. Lobsang is an accomplished handyman and, wherever he takes up new quarters, enjoys giving them the stamp of his own personality and making or repairing whatever is needed. There was a piano in his mother's drawing-room and also a sort of harmonium, made in Japan, of a kind that had been popular in Manchurian middle-class families in the old leisurely days. Li Chin-Fung was able to practise, and Lobsang considers that, although her studies had been interrupted, she was both a talented musician and a competent pianist. He enjoyed her playing, and with little more than a keen ear to guide him, used himself to strum on the harmonium. He had been made to take piano lessons as a social accomplishment as a small boy, but regarded them with little more enthusiasm than his compulsory Chinese tutorials. To this day, when he thinks he is out of earshot, he sings to himself in a musical, rather melancholy voice, usually snatches of melodies which, to a Western ear, have a curiously haunting and nostalgic ring.

Lobsang, besides being the youngest child, had always been his mother's favourite. From his earliest years, she had lectured him on the dangers of being over-impulsive and strong-headed, but less out of reproach than out of concern that his impetuousness might prejudice him in what she clearly hoped and expected would be a brilliant and distinguished career. During the first weeks after his homecoming her pleasure at having him with her again was tinged with worry about the future. There were interminable discussions about the wisdom of his decision to leave the army, and soon Lobsang began to feel impatient to find himself some suitable civilian employment which would enable him to support his family and repay his mother for her solicitude and good counsel.

The gradual discovery of the realities of civilian life for an ex-KMT officer in these early days of Communist rule was a bitter disappointment. To someone of Lobsang's temperament, eager for instant results, it quickly became intolerable. His search for employment produced nothing but a series of demoralising rebuffs. All worthwhile jobs were in the gift of the Party and public authorities. His discharge papers were in perfect order; his military record in the People's Army was impeccable. But the discrepancy between his age and his rank, and his inexplicable resignation from the army made him virtually unclassifiable in the eyes of the bureaucrats who allocated civilian employment.

'The real trouble, of course, was that I had been a KMT man. With the war in Korea now in full swing, there was a new wave of suspicion about the loyalty of former Nationalists. Many ex-KMT officers had got themselves into jobs by concealing the fact that they had been in the army. When the authorities discovered that they had lied about their past, they were frequently dismissed and even arrested. There was a general atmosphere of mistrust. By leaving the army, I had forfeited the protection that I had enjoyed under the bargain struck between the Communists and Fu Tso-Yi. Then again, I was not a member of the Communist party. If I had been, they would always have found me a job. As it was, the employment authorities were afraid that, because my situation was so unusual, there must be something ideologically wrong with me. They preferred not to take a risk and so all my applications were fobbed off with futile excuses about the difficulty of finding a job corresponding to my rank and my qualifications.'

Opportunities for private enterprise were almost non-existent. Where they did exist, they were in very humble sectors like the fish and vegetable markets, in which Lobsang had no experience. In any case, in his own home town, considerations of prestige probably prevented him from trying his luck in such a lowly field. He still had a roof over his head and had not yet acquired either the habit or the outlook of the true adventurer.

More and more, he found himself condemned to sit at home, with nothing to do and nothing to look forward to. Already his brother's disgrace had thrown him into a severe depression, and this spell of enforced inactivity was the very worst medicine. He had been away from Dairen so long that most of his boyhood friends had vanished. The acquaintances he did bump into were, more often than not, reserved and suspicious about renewing old ties which might compromise them under the new order. Even old friends had to be careful. In public they would greet each other by inquiring 'No one in your family, I trust, is suffering from stomach trouble?' which was the discreet way of saying 'Do you at least get enough to eat?' Even for those who still had some money, there was nowhere congenial left to go to relax or forget one's troubles.

At home, Lobsang grew moodier and more frustrated. He found himself getting impatient even with his mother and his wife. Everything had been said so many times that their sympathy began to irritate him. At the best of times Lobsang is not a placid or patient man. The fact that circumstances have often compelled him to exercise immense control for long periods has not affected his naturally quick temper. When anything is worrying him or obstructing his plans, the need to blow his top boils up until he is incapable of hiding his feelings, even with his closest friends.

Eventually, he became seriously ill. How much this illness was part of his nervous depression is difficult to say, because he was never told the exact diagnosis of the hospital to which he was taken in Dairen. He thinks he was either delirious or completely unconscious for long spells during his twenty or thirty days in hospital. Doctors to whom he has described his symptoms suggest that he may have had cerebral meningitis. Whatever it was, it left him physically exhausted and even more depressed than before.

'I felt useless and lonely and overcome with guilt at having to live off my mother instead of supporting her and my family. Also, I began to be afraid that the Communists might have stumbled on to something in my past that I had concealed from them, and that, like my brother, they might suddenly arrest me. I worried myself into a really desperate state. Convalescing at home after I came out of hospital became a nightmare. In the end, I felt that I had become such a burden that one day, when I was alone in the house, I suddenly decided to put an end to it all. The Japanese stick a knife on the wall, run on to it with their full weight and then suddenly twist so that it disembowels them. I was in no state to do anything so calm and collected. Quite apart from the element of physical courage, trying to kill yourself isn't as simple as it sounds. Either I wasn't scientific or determined enough. I made a bloody mess of it.'

The long, straight scar that runs across the whole breadth of Lobsang's stomach hardly tallies with lack of determination, but he points critically to several minor scars, today scarcely visible, and explains 'I just took a knife and slashed away three or four times. The main incision probably looks so professional because the doctor who sewed it up made a tidy job of it.' Lobsang is not proud of the whole incident and talks about it only when pressed. In Communist China, suicide is officially regarded as a cowardly and shameful act – cowardly because it shows that a person is afraid to face life; shameful because it implies that socialist society is not worth living in. 'When the poor old major blew his brains out in our mess because he hadn't been promoted and wasn't allowed a wife, we were all expected to revile him as a disgrace to the People's Army.'

To rush Lobsang to hospital would have involved too many awkward questions, and not every doctor would have been ready to accept the case. It was several hours before his married sister was able to find a doctor she knew could be relied on for sympathy and help. Luckily, Lobsang is blessed with astonishing recuperative powers, both from illness and wounds. Asked how long it took him to get back on his feet after his attempted suicide he says, as if it were perfectly normal, 'Oh, I don't know. Some days I think.'

Not long after he was up and about again, another macabre incident occurred which not only coincided with Lobsang's own mood of morbid introspection but throws a curious light on contemporary social conditions and taboos in Communist China at the time. One day, to get away from home, he wandered into a public park and spent several hours on a bench in a quiet corner at the foot of a little mound enclosed by trees. When he got home, towards evening, he discovered that one of the two medals he had been wearing on his tunic was missing. It was one of his awards from the Tank Training Centre – a bronze medal plated with silver, depicting a soldier of the People's Army brandishing a rifle in a heroic posture. Lobsang occasionally sported his medals, partly to relieve the drabness of the blue Mao-style tunic which was the Communist civilian uniform and partly to boost his own morale against what, in his depressed condition, he felt to be the contempt and indifference of his fellow-citizens.

Having nothing better to do, he went back to the park to look for his medal. It was late summer, and the light was already beginning to go by the time he reached the secluded wooded corner. As he approached the bench where he had been sitting, he was aware of two figures on the grass, apparently locked in an amorous embrace. They showed no sign of having noticed him and, not wishing to disturb them, he made his way as quietly as possible along a narrow path between the chairs and benches and a small hedge at the foot of the trees. From there, as discreetly as he could, he searched between the chairs for the lost medal. Suddenly, while he was still groping with his eyes on the ground, he found himself pinioned. The loving couple turned out to be two stalwart members of the Secret Police who had pounced on him and were now asking him what he was doing. Lobsang explained that he was looking for something and had tried to warn them of his presence by coughing, but that they had ignored him. Even when he showed them his remaining medal and his army discharge papers, they were not satisfied and insisted on him going with them to the nearest police station. When he protested that this was a public park where everyone had a right to be, he was curtly told, 'Not at this hour or in these circumstances.'

At the station, after hearing Lobsang's story, the officer-in-charge became visibly embarrassed. He ended by admitting that his men had made a mistake and offered Lobsang a grudging apology. Lobsang returned the compliment by asking him to explain why two young security policemen should be impersonating lovers in such obscure circumstances.

'Well, you see,' explained the inspector, 'as you know, before the Liberation, relationships between men and women were severely restricted by bourgeois conventions. Our policy since Liberation has been not to interfere in people's private affairs, whether they were or were not legally married. Unfortunately, some young people took advantage of our tolerance and boys and girls began making love freely in public parks. What was worse, certain hooligan elements began the practice of spying from behind trees and afterwards following the girls in order to blackmail them. They threatened to denounce them unless they allowed the hooligans to make love to them, and there were many cases of girls being victimised in this way. That is why we have had to use special agents to expose these bad elements. It is generally assumed that since Liberation, sex problems and sex crimes have disappeared. But, as you see, this is regrettably not always the case.'

Lobsang himself thinks that many of these problems were bound up with the return to urban life after the upheavals of the Civil War. In the great towns, like Peking or Tientsin, no amount of Communist puritanism could altogether eradicate the long-established tradition of organised vice. During the Civil War, the Communist soldiers in rural China had to satisfy themselves with the Party slogan 'Healthy fatigue and political thought control your sex urges' but, for the civilians who now flocked back to the cities to enjoy the fruits of peace, the problem was not so simple.

It was about this time that the Communists launched the movement for the emancipation of woman, or the Fu Nu Fan Shen. It challenged the old Chinese social order by campaigning in a general way for equality for women, and specifically against child-marriage and arranged marriages, and in favour of marriage by consent. Lobsang, whose approach to sex and marriage has on the whole never been complicated by intellectual, social or political ideology, found the whole Communist preoccupation with these problems as boring as it was to him irrelevant.

The incident in the park, however, left a bad taste in his mouth, and suddenly decided him to get away from Dairen. What, he asked himself, had he to do with a society which was driven to take its sex so furtively, and whose guardians of public morality were reduced to such ignominious and squalid practices? He felt almost relieved that this grotesque incident had provided him with a concrete focus for his discontent.

At any rate, it was now clear to him that he had to get out of Manchuria and make a new start somewhere else. Even his mother and his wife agreed that this was probably the only solution. The question was, where? Lobsang had no passport and precious little chance of persuading the Communist authorities to issue him with one. 'When I was young, very few Manchurians ever thought about leaving Manchuria. It is such a vast territory that I myself never imagined I would go to any of the countries I did. But in times of trouble circumstances decide things for you. If I'd been born earlier or later, I would probably have never found myself in the situations which drove me from place to place. As it is, I have been made to move so far and so often that I sometimes feel I have lived several quite different lives.'

Since foreign travel seemed out of the question, what about the remoter provinces of the Chinese People's Republic? Gradually, Lobsang's plans began to focus on Sinkiang. This remote north-west frontier province had been proclaimed an autonomous republic, and to reach it no national frontiers, involving exit permits or passports, had to be crossed. At the same time, it was the area farthest removed from the Central Government in Peking. Communications from China proper were still primitive or non-existent. The Communists were developing Sinkiang's limitless natural resources and colonising its vast, under-populated territory with Chinese administrators, technicians, soldiers and a growing labour force of political prisoners.

Sinkiang in the early 1950s can be compared with the Middle or Far West of the United States in the mid-nineteenth century, when the railroad was pushing its way into Indian territory, and men were drawn westward by the urge to make a fresh start beyond the reach of central authority and prying officialdom, or by the ambition to make a quick fortune. Chinese Communists might indignantly reject this comparison, but it serves to give a rough notion to Western readers of the sort of adventure Sinkiang represented.

Lobsang had started to toy with the idea of Sinkiang after hearing snatches of a radio programme about minority nationalities on a public loudspeaker in a department store. His attention had been caught by the local songs and dance-music, and he had later seen documentary films which left him with the impression that, because Peking was still busy cultivating the good will of the turbulent local Moslem population, the Communist yoke still sat fairly lightly on Sinkiang.

His mother, when he discussed the idea with her, was filled with maternal apprehension. For her generation, Sinkiang was still a country where Chinese only went if they were outlawed or exiled, inhabited by wild nomadic tribes, speaking outlandish languages and perpetually fighting. Even when Lobsang had made up his mind, she continued to urge him to be careful, and insisted on giving him some of her remaining jewellery as the most portable and easily realisable kind of security. Lobsang felt as wretched about taking it as he did about leaving her and his family behind in Dairen unprovided for. In retrospect, his remorse at abandoning his mother has increased with the realisation of what her feelings must have been at saying goodbye to one of her children, almost certainly for the last time. So much so that he is reluctant to dwell on the details of his last days at home. Perhaps something in his traditional upbringing makes him shy away from discussing his feelings at moments of intimate personal emotion. Instead, he confesses that he himself is sometimes at a loss to understand his own emotional reactions. In talking of his own children, he reflects with genuine astonishment: 'When I am with them, I worry about them and their problems like any normal parent. But when I am away, they sometimes vanish from my thoughts for days on end. My wife teases me about it, saying "out of sight, out of mind", and I am bound to admit that she is right. But if you ask me to explain it, I can't.'

What is certainly true is that, at the time of his departure from Dairen, his strongest feeling was a compulsive desire to escape from the prison of inactivity and frustration that his own country had become. For the moment, only the prospect of being free to move and do something active brought him any relief. Even the idea of parting from his family could no longer hold him back.

Mao swims the Yangtse: the swimmer in the top left hand corner is General Fu
Tso-Yi, in whose army Lobsang served in the Chinese Civil War. Below, Mao
Tse-Tung receives the Dalai Lama, right, and the Panchen Lama in Peking, 1954

In Sinkiang Lobsang witnessed the spread of Chinese communist control. New methods were introduced in the Sinkiang cotton fields, above, and on a rural commune near Turfan

6

LOBSANG HEADS WEST

One autumn morning, carrying a single suitcase, Lobsang boarded the train to Mukden, where he stayed for a few days to find his bearings. Apart from the clothes he stood up in, he had packed his old army uniform and one spare suit. His entire wardrobe was in a sense an expression of his refusal to conform with the existing order. Both his suits were tailored in what, in the early 1950s, was the cream of Soviet fashion, with wide-bottomed trousers and double-breasted jackets, with heavily padded shoulders. 'After I left the army, I got tired of wearing the blue high-collared Mao-style tunic which had become the civilian uniform. Sometimes I wore my army uniform, without badges of rank, partly because the material was much better than any cloth available to civilians and partly because it helped my self-respect at times when I felt particularly low. People could tell I had been a person of some standing and treated me accordingly.'

Lobsang had already learnt the art of travelling light and, in spite of the lateness of the season, refused to take the bulky bedding roll which most Chinese still regarded as indispensable on any long journey. Instead, he carried a warm greatcoat, together with an old-fashioned full-length Chinese travelling robe made of superb black face-cloth and lined throughout with expensive fur. It had belonged to his father and was, in its own way, a thoroughly practical garment for the adventure upon which he was embarking.

Lobsang stood out in any Chinese crowd by reason of his height, and his bizarre accoutrements made him doubly conspicuous. In Mukden, he noticed that he was being unobtrusively followed every time he wore his Russian suit. Before going to catch his train to Lanchow, he thought it advisable to change into his uniform. 'The police fellow still followed me, but he could never seem to make up his mind actually to question me. Anyhow, at the time, I was still feeling a bit light-headed. I didn't really care a damn what people thought of my appearance or my behaviour.'

His train stopped at Tientsin, but he felt no inclination to tarry there or pay a sentimental visit to the French race-course and his old 'change-idea' school. In Lanchow, the busy provincial capital of Kansu, at the junction of traditional trade-routes, he spent nine or ten days picking up useful information and working out plans for the rest of his journey into Sinkiang. Here he also made his first experiment in earning his keep by private enterprise in a Communist society. Noticing a display of accordions at a counter in a department store, he picked one up to try it. It was out of tune and the store-manager explained to him that the whole consignment was defective in the same way. Lobsang quickly discovered that some of the tubes through which each individual note was blown had been crushed and distorted. He asked the manager whether he was interested in having them put right. Given a true ear and a few simple tools, the actual adjustment was easy enough. The manager was delighted, and a bargain was struck. Lobsang was paid ninety yuan, the equivalent of one-and-a-half months' salary for a skilled factory worker in China at the time. This ability to turn his hand to any kind of repair, small or heavy, was to become Lobsang's passport to free transport, free lodging and a full belly in the months and years ahead. It was also the only alternative to regular employment which, because it would have involved him in the whole rigmarole of Communist bureaucracy, was too complicated and too risky to contemplate.

From Lanchow Lobsang pushed on north-westwards by road to Wuwei, a border town which at that time was literally the end of the road. From there, to get into Sinkiang, the only way was to attach himself to one of the convoys of trucks which bumped their way across the arid tracts of almost unpopulated territory which lies to the north of the mountain range of Nan Shan. It was absolutely necessary to travel in convoy. As there were no roads, any truck which broke down was in danger of being marooned without help, and since all supplies, including water, had to be carried, this made driving alone a foolhardy risk. When anything went wrong with a lorry, the entire convoy, often of thirty or forty, came to a standstill until it was repaired or its crew decided to abandon it.

Lobsang had signed on as a mechanic and was quickly accepted as something more than just a useful passenger. He was beginning to be in his element and found himself easily slipping back into the kind of gipsy existence to which he had become accustomed as a prisoner of war in Siberia.

His journey to Urumchi, the capital of Sinkiang, took nine days. Getting a truck and its load to its destination was a full-time job. It was autumn, and the nights were already cold. By day, driving winds engulfed the convoy in clouds of dust or sand as it picked its way over the rough terrain. Lobsang wrapped himself in his fur-lined, ankle-length travelling-robe and slept warmly and snugly. Most of the time talk was of the business in hand – of diesel engines and creature comforts and how to get one's lorry and its load safely to Urumchi.

The last staging-post before the final run into Sinkiang was the town of Hami, just south of the frontier of Inner Mongolia. From there the convoy rolled down into the great Turfan depression which, at its lowest point, falls to over 500 feet below sea level. Suddenly, the heat was intense. The surrounding mountains form a sort of oven. 'From below, they seemed to be on fire, and the heat scorched down on us as if it had been reflected by mirrors.' The word 'Hami', in the local Uighur language, means 'honey', and the town gets its name from the legendary sweetness of the melons for which the region is famous. They grow in such profusion that they are left stacked in piles for the use of travellers and provide cool refreshment in this waterless wilderness.

Just before Hami, as the convoy entered the depression, it passed through a place named Tabanchen, meaning 'high wall'. A fierce, prevailing wind, blowing in from the Gobi Desert to the north, rages down the funnel of the depression with clock-work regularity every afternoon, and the local people have built great walls as windbreaks. 'Our convoy arrived at Tabanchen just as the wind began to blow, and we had to lie up five or six hours in the lee of the wall until it had blown itself out.' To Lobsang, the rigours of the jolting convoy and the freakish changes of climate were positively exhilarating. Depression or no depression, his own clouds were beginning to lift. In Turfan, the cheerful Uighur faces looked as though they belonged to carefree people, still living their lives independently, and free from the constant supervision and restrictions which Lobsang had found so depressing in Manchuria. From Turfan the convoy began to climb again, crawling across the barren desert which stretches right up to the outskirts of Urumchi.

Lobsang's exodus from Manchuria had already given him the physical and spiritual catharsis he needed. His natural resilience had reasserted itself. But, as he rolled into Sinkiang through the somewhat forbidding approaches to the capital, he did not suspect that he was entering a promised land which, for a little while, would offer him everything he required to make him completely contented.

Sinkiang is a country of dramatic contrasts. When Lobsang arrived there in the autumn of 1953, it was still in the early stages of being absorbed by Communist China. The way of life of its predominantly Moslem population – Uighurs, Kazakhs and Mongols – was virtually intact. The Chinese were ruling it on a loose rein as an Autonomous Region, with every show of consideration for the local people. The top jobs at all levels were left in their hands, with Chinese advisers discreetly controlling things as their titular subordinates. This was the standard technique during the initial phase in the absorption of outlying regions into the new People's Republic. It was particularly effective in Sinkiang because Chiang Kai-Shek's Nationalists had adopted exactly the opposite policy during their administration. They had behaved as arrogant overlords, with no regard for local susceptibilities, with the result that, under the KMT, the proud and turbulent local chieftains had been in a continual state of more or less open revolt. During the Civil War in China some of them had formed guerrilla bands and made common cause with the Communists. One of these chieftains,

Burhan, had been appointed to head the Sinkiang provincial government in the dying days of Chiang Kai-Shek's presidency and, in the autumn of 1949, had accepted the Communist peace-terms and remained as Governor of Sinkiang until October 1955, when the Sinkiang–Uighur Autonomous Region was formally established. He was then succeeded as head of government by Sai Fu Din, who had been his deputy, and formerly a popular and successful guerrilla leader.

The Communists quickly recognised Sai Fu Din as a tough and resolute man who could serve their aim of securing rapid and peaceful control over this wild and strategically inaccessible province. They paid him every honour, including the rare privilege of full membership of the Chinese Communist party without any probationary formalities. They even made an epic propaganda film in which Sai Fu Din was portrayed as the national revolutionary hero and which was widely shown in Sinkiang and throughout China. At the time of Lobsang's arrival in Urumchi, he was Vice-Chairman of the regional government and was already actively collaborating in Peking's plans for the development of Sinkiang, which involved sending a large van-guard of Chinese advisers, technicians and labour detachments into the country.

Lobsang's mother had visualised Sinkiang as a brigand-infested desert. On the score of lawlessness, her fears turned out to be exaggerated, but Lobsang had been perfectly right in thinking that it would provide a welcome escape from the claustrophobic atmosphere of Manchuria. In area, Sinkiang is almost a quarter of the whole Chinese People's Republic. Its population of less than six million is under one-hundredth of China's seven hundred million. Lobsang found himself in a country where there was room to breathe, away from the suffocating regimentation that he had left behind him. Even the geography and the climate were in tune with his longing for space and freedom.

In Sinkiang, you can freeze to death in the mountains of the north, bake in the great depressions of Dzoungrai and Tarim, or bask all the year round in the winterless zone round Kashgar in the west, where the spectacular barrier of the Korakhoram range separates Sinkiang from the north-western extremity of Kashmir. You can travel for a hundred miles across waterless plains without seeing a house before reaching one of the oases at the foot of the Tien Shan mountains which form the northern boundary of Sinkiang.

Urumchi, the capital, lies in one of these oases. Lobsang's convoy approached it across the barren desert which stretches from the Turfan depression almost to the edge of the town. If a lorry breaks down on this stretch, its crew abandons it immediately for another truck in the same convoy, or, if it is alone, tries for a lift from any passing transport. To be stranded at nightfall means almost certain death. 'I have seen a man sitting in the cab of his truck, with a smile frozen on his face in the middle of a sentence, staring idiotically out of wide-open eyes. In a vain attempt to restart his engine, he had pulled all the wadding out of his quilted jacket and dipped it in kerosene to use as a flaming torch.' In winter, if a man spits, his spittle is frozen into an icicle before it reaches the ground.

In an otherwise arid landscape, Urumchi is watered by a great artificial lake, fed from the perpetual snow on the peaks which are clearly visible in the distance. The water is channelled from this reservoir, which is just outside the city, into Urumchi itself, giving it the agreeable feeling of having running water everywhere. During KMT days, the Chinese had renamed the capital Tihwa, meaning literally 'assimilation', in order to underline China's sovereignty. The Communists had tactfully reverted to the local name, and were actively encouraging the preservation of Sinkiang's national personality within the framework of the great Chinese socialist experiment.

A fellow traveller in Lobsang's convoy had directed him to a shop in Urumchi, owned by a Chinese from Amdung, where Lobsang's mother's family had their estates. It turned out to be a humble place, built in the unfired sun-dried bricks which are used in the Urumchi area, where the negligible rainfall makes it possible to use them without danger of disintegration. The shop was open to the street and specialised in the repair of Chinese typewriters, primitive adding machines of the kind that were in common use in the shops, and bicycles. The proprietor welcomed Lobsang as a fellow-countryman and allowed him to do some repairs in exchange for his lodging. He explained that, for a Chinese, getting a regular job would be difficult because he had come to Sinkiang on his own initiative and not on government orders. However, he recommended Lobsang to an address in the western outskirts of the town where, after listening to his plans, he thought he might find a suitable lodging.

Urumchi at this time was a town of only 120,000 inhabitants, a walled city about a mile across, with an imposing Soviet Consulate-General in the southern suburbs which lay between the city and its airport. The only Chinese landmark was a park on the western outskirts – a replica of a rock-garden, with willows and a pond – which had been built by Ling Tse-Hsu, who was banished from Peking to be Governor of Sinkiang for his part in China's disastrous anti-British opium war. It was past this park and out through the great western bridge that Lobsang now drove in a local horse-drawn cart, which he describes as a 'wooden box on four wheels', and which was then still the usual form of public transport.

The family he had been recommended to had an interest in a brickworks which made the local sun-dried bricks from which most of the smaller traditional houses of Urumchi were built. Near the brickworks was a rambling complex of buildings – a family farmhouse to which had been added several compounds of bungalows which were let out in two-or-three-room units, mainly to Chinese.

The head of the family, Yan Nai-Ching, came from Shantung. He was a jolly, easy-going fellow who bred pigs and hens on his small-holding, with a sideline in market gardening. Lobsang took an immediate liking to him because of his warmth of character and open-heartedness. It was agreed that he should move in at once to one of the bungalow apartments.

Yan Nai-Ching had a half-Russian, half-Mongolian wife whose first husband had been a white Russian refugee from the Bolshevik Revolution who had found asylum in Sinkiang. By that marriage she had two daughters who both worked in the general hospital at Urumchi, one as a doctor, and one as a senior nurse. This inter-marriage of immigrant Russians with 'overseas' Chinese was common in Sinkiang. The people of the country, being pre-ponderantly Moslem, were still polygamous in their attitude to women, and the Chinese had a reputation both of respecting women more as equal partners and of making better husbands. Although most of the overseas Chinese had arrived in Sinkiang in quite humble circumstances, they generally worked hard and became prosperous and were able to offer a prospect of family security that attracted the Russian women. 'Overseas Chinese' is the convenient all-embracing term which the Chinese themselves use to describe any person belonging to a Chinese community outside China proper. It applies indiscriminately to people in America, Europe, Africa or Asia itself.

In spite of its Sino-Russian background, there was something about the household in which Lobsang now found himself installed that belonged unmistakably to Sinkiang itself. The generosity of the welcome it extended to strangers was typical of an underpopulated country which accepts foreigners and travellers without inquiring too closely into where they come from, or why. Lobsang was delighted by the feeling that no one seemed to count or calculate the cost of things too carefully.

'At that time, Sinkiang was still a marvellous country for a foreigner. Outside the towns, you often came across a farm and found no one at home because everyone was out working in the fields. But the door was always open and it was an accepted thing for a stranger to help himself to a draught of mare's milk from the big vat that stood by the door of every farm. This *Khermiss* is allowed to stand and ferment. It has a powerful kick and at first it used to make me gasp. I think in the long run it might rot your guts, but when you are tired and dusty it is wonderfully re-freshing and somehow goes with the spirit of these gay, devil-may-care people.' Inside the farmhouses there were great ovens, built into the thickness of the wall in the Russian style, where a hungry traveller could always find a loaf of freshly baked bread, often still warm.

The best surprise at Lobsang's new lodgings came when the

two daughters of the house returned home at the weekend from the hospital. Both, besides being charming and intelligent, were authentic beauties. Nadjka, the doctor, was a tall girl, with her mother's raven hair and her father's blue eyes. Besides Russian, she talked Uighur which was the most widely spoken language in the Urumchi area. Lobsang was immediately attracted to her and felt that his time in Siberia had not after all been wasted since it had given him a common language with Nadjka.

A few weeks after their first meeting, he took her out dancing. All the peoples of Sinkiang are passionate dancers, and the Chinese Communists, who always paid great attention to cultural relations, invariably included three or four dances a week in the programmes of their various clubs, recreational centres and Sino-Sinkiang friendship societies. It was a useful way for the younger Chinese officials to break the ice and establish contact with the local people. The dancing itself was an odd mixture of national styles and influences. Usually the proceedings opened with everyone joining hands in a circle in the manner of most of the local dances. The girls were dressed in what Lobsang describes as 'rather Western style', with flared skirts, full-sleeved blouses, tight embroidered waistcoats, worn with Russian boots and shallow, round caps embroidered with flower designs if they were Uighurs, or round fur hats if they were Kazakhs.

At his first dance with Nadjka, the local folk-dancing soon gave way to waltzes and what Lobsang still calls the 'fox-dance'. Not everyone knew the steps, but the fact that you held your partner and danced close together and that the band played Western-type music gave the occasion a sophisticated and rather exotic appeal. At the grander dances there was an orchestra whose main instruments were Russian balaleikyas and piano accordions.

Sometimes the local people would demonstrate their own dances. One of the most popular was a sort of eightsome reel – a square-dance in which the men and the girls held hands and danced intricate figures to quick, exhilarating music. Neat, rapid steps alternated with measures where the dancers stood with their feet completely still and made undulating movements with their arms or necks. There were also Russian dances, with the men squatting on their heels with folded arms and kicking their booted legs straight out in front of them.

As many of the people who came to these dances were good Moslems, refreshments were usually limited to soft drinks, but these evenings were high-spirited affairs, and the various nationalities' more or less clumsy attempts to perform each other's dances added to the merriment. On the first Sunday they went dancing together, Lobsang proposed and Nadjka accepted him. Their engagement met with no objections from her family. Lobsang had been fairly frank with Nadjka's stepfather about the circumstances which had brought him from China to Sinkiang. He had left out some things which might have made Yan Nai-Ching hesitate to accept him as a permanent lodger, for example his former KMT connections. The Nationalist army had been even more unpopular in Sinkiang than it had been in Manchuria.

Now Lobsang felt obliged, in all honesty, to fill in some of the details. Yan Nai-Ching admitted that, if he had been told everything, he might have been less ready to take Lobsang in. As it was, when the happy couple broke the news to him, neither he nor his wife seemed seriously upset at the prospect of acquiring Lobsang for a son-in-law.

The marriage itself was completely informal. 'There was no religious or civil ceremony. We just invited all our friends to a splendid wedding-feast. We had music and dancing and everyone was very happy. I did exchange a formally worded document in Chinese with my father-in-law. After that Nadjka simply moved into my bungalow. She continued to work at the hospital and we lived together at weekends.'

His lodgings had led him to a wife. Now his wife led him to a steady source of well-paid employment. The general hospital at Urumchi had been built in pre-KMT days, when the Russians were still the dominant foreign influence in Sinkiang. It was equipped with its own medical schol, where Nadjka had trained and qualified, and was in most respects fairly up-to-date. But all its equipment had had to be humped into Sinkiang in the sort of trucks and over the sort of tracks in which Lobsang had arrived in the country. Whether it had been imported from the Soviet

Union or from China, it had been jolted and manhandled and had not always received much skilled servicing afterwards. So the hospital authorities were delighted to discover an all-round engineer and mechanic who could diagnose defects and straighten them out in record time without going through any of the bureaucratic formalities and delays normally involved if things were done through official channels.

Starting with operating tables and X-ray machines, Lobsang quickly made himself a reputation as an invaluable Jack-of-all-trades. His work at the hospital enabled him to see a lot of Nadjka but, after some time, it was not a full-time job. Every town in Sinkiang of any size had its own hospital, whose equipment was in no better repair than at Urumchi. The grateful hospital staff introduced Lobsang to these other hospitals and so provided him with a round of respectable work, none of which involved making an application for employment through the Chinese authorities. It also gave him an opportunity to explore the country.

Sinkiang is fantastically rich in natural resources. In places, there is more oil than water. Its minerals are inexhaustible and still largely untapped. Teams of Chinese experts were busy carrying out geological surveys up and down the country, and mining of every description was already in full swing, including such exotic deposits as jade and rose-quartz. Development in agriculture was being pushed forward as energetically as on the industrial and geological fronts. In many hitherto desert areas, the only thing lacking was water, and the soil, when irrigated, was suitable for a large variety of crops. Irrigation projects went hand in hand with experimental farming, and already large areas were under cotton, and textile factories were springing up in the nearest towns. Local agronomists had developed methods of growing cotton on the bush in four distinct colours, and their discovery was given wide publicity as an example of the ingenuity and industry of the new generation of native technicians. 'It was astonishing to see, for the first time, whole fields of blue or red or green standing cotton, reaching almost as far as the eye could see.'

Everywhere Lobsang went, there was a sense of discovery and

opportunity. Usually he was able to hitch a lift from the fleet of trucks used by the local authorities and the Chinese army and technical assistance missions. Most of the drivers were Chinese, often former KMT army drivers who had simply been kept on after the Communist takeover. Travel in Sinkiang, before the arrival of motor transport, had been based on staging posts, each roughly corresponding to a day's journey on horseback. Because of the rough terrain, these were rarely more than twenty or thirty kilometres apart. For anyone travelling by truck, this meant that there was plenty of choice of places to stop for a meal or to spend the night.

Lobsang found that the drivers, like all long-distance haulage men, had become very fastidious about their favourite halts. Often he had to stay several days at a staging post waiting for a truck that was going to his destination and, if he was in a hurry, he sometimes pushed on by horseback in order to make a connection. Between hospital jobs, he was able to pick up plenty of freelance repair work along the route and almost always found his clients ready to pay handsomely and to show him their gratitude in the quality of their hospitality.

Occasionally, in the great tracts of open country between the towns where his work took him, Lobsang stayed with the nomadic herdsmen who follow their cattle from one grazing ground to another, living in elaborate tents and trading their beautiful red and blue Sinkiang carpets for cash or barter. In appearance, these dashing horsemen, with their tall fur hats and long, supple leather boots – worn like stockings with overshoes that can be kicked off at the entrance to their tents – looked fierce and unapproachable. In fact they turned out to be as friendly to strangers as the rest of the population. They would always give a traveller a night's shelter, but their sleeping arrangements sometimes posed problems of etiquette which even Lobsang, with all his experience and natural aplomb, had some difficulty in resolving.

'Once I was shown into a tent in which one whole side was occupied by a long, continuous seat, covered in rugs and cushions. By day, there was no indication to a stranger of who slept there when it became a bed. I was invited to put my things down on this settee, but as I did so, a roar of laughter went up. My hosts then explained that I had chosen that part of the bed which was used by the women of the family. I hurriedly made to pick up my traps, but my hosts were absolutely firm. I had, so to speak, made my bed, and it was up to me to lie on it.' Lobsang was not sure whether the whole thing was meant in jest, or whether it was an advanced exercise in pastoral hospitality. He concludes the story by demurely recollecting, 'The girls were very good-looking and very sexy . . . but they smelt terrible – ugh! I don't think they had a chance to wash very often.'

Lobsang's favourite part of Sinkiang was its western extremity, where it reaches out between the High Pamirs and the Korakhoram range of the Himalayas. This is a well-watered and fertile plain which enjoys a gentle, winterless climate, in which Lobsang loved to relax after the harshness of the deserts and the mountains. His work at the hospital at Kashgar, the western provincial capital, gave him a pretext for fairly frequent visits. Kashgar was altogether more sophisticated than Urumchi, and there were many signs of Russian influence – large, modern buildings and all sorts of small amenities of life unobtainable anywhere else in Sinkiang. The local people also struck him as more Westernised, gentler and more civilised, and he liked to spin out his visits by picking up any extra repair jobs that were going. Almost always these came by recommendation from satisfied clients.

Without any particular effort, he now found he was making an excellent living. 'This was the only time in my life when I felt entirely free from cares about money or work, or even anxiety about the future. I had fallen in love with Sinkiang and, if it had been left to me, I would willingly have made it my home for life.'

Quite soon after his arrival, Lobsang made contact with some Chinese officers who had been his pupils at the Tank Training School. They had been sent to Sinkiang to act as technical advisers for various development schemes. They were quartered at Liu Klingtze, a few miles outside Urumchi and, although they still officially belonged to the army, they were living civilian lives in private quarters with their families. Most of them were fairly senior officers and they were genuinely pleased to see Lobsang, even when he told them of the irregular situation in which he now found himself.

'When I was an instructor, I had never adopted the attitude of a teacher towards my pupils, with the result that my relations with my trainees had nearly always been very friendly and informal. In any case, the officers I remet in Urumchi, when they heard my story, asked if I needed any help and seemed genuinely prepared to do whatever they could for me. By then I had already done quite well with my hospital work, and I was able to explain to them that I had everything I needed. At the same time, I remember thinking how lucky they were. They all stood a good chance of being seconded to permanent civilian jobs in this new and fast-developing country and that, to me, seemed a very enviable prospect.'

For the best part of a year, Lobsang's luck held. His wife was expecting a baby and he was earning surprisingly good money. Living was cheap and his overheads were negligible. He would work intensively for a spell and then take a break, enjoying life with Nadjka and the family circle, and spending freely. She was quiet and serene by temperament, but she had the Russian gift of enjoying herself with gusto, which Lobsang found charming and irresistible. But, to anyone as conditioned as he had become to be on the look-out for storm signals, it was beginning to be obvious that difficulties were looming ahead. As the tempo of the Chinese development programme was stepped up, a huge new labour force was required to keep pace with the ambitious planners in Peking. Sinkiang was far too under-populated to supply the necessary manpower and the Chinese, with their countless millions, solved the problem in the simplest and the most logical way. Anyone sentenced to more than ten years of corrective labour was liable to be sent for service in Sinkiang. 'You saw them everywhere where a big government scheme was in progress. They were easily recognisable by the square patch sewn on their backs, but in reality they needed very little supervision from the point of view of security. There was nowhere for them to escape to.'

As the Chinese population in Sinkiang grew, the Communist

party machine extended its methodical web. In and around Urumchi, a population census was taken, house by house. This gave the Party a chance to pry into everyone's private affairs and the authority to ask a lot of searching questions. Since Lobsang's arrival, Chinese attitudes towards contacts between Chinese immigrants and the local population, the so-called 'minority peoples', had also undergone a change. Too much mixing with minority peoples was now definitely discouraged. Intermarriage between Chinese men and local women, particularly if they were Moslems, was only allowed in special circumstances and even then both parties had to secure official permission. Unauthorised extra-marital relations were punished by a mandatory sentence of at least six months' imprisonment for the offending Chinese man. Any Chinese who had come to Sinkiang from China proper without being deported for corrective labour or officially posted as a technician or adviser was automatically suspect. Lobsang was vulnerable on both these counts. While he was away from Urumchi, local Chinese security officials had come to the house and told Nadjka's stepfather that they wanted to question Lobsang on his return.

When he called at their office, he was interrogated at length, first by one officer and then several together. Their questions were in themselves fairly trivial, but their manner suggested that they were meant as calculated pin-pricks. Lobsang sensed that they were deliberately trying to provoke him into losing his temper and saying something which would give them an excuse for further action against him. Eventually he was allowed to go home, only to be summoned again after a couple of days and made to go through an almost identical performance. This was repeated at intervals over the next two or three months. Finally he decided to go to the People's Civilian Affairs Bureau, where he made a formal demand for an explanation of why he was being harassed. He even made an application for some officially approved civilian work, only to be told the old story about a long waiting-list. 'It was the same vicious circle as in Dairen. I had been forced to leave Manchuria because I had left the army, yet my old army rank was constantly thrown up at me as a reason for not being able to provide me with a civilian job. Nadjka clung to the hope that, because of my qualifications, I might in the end get a steady job as an engineer in one of the new factories, but when the local party officials and the Secret Police began prying into my affairs, I realised that they had got their knife into me and were determined to make life intolerable for me by one means or another.'

Lobsang made up his mind not to allow a situation to develop again where home became a prison of gloom and self-reproach and he worried himself into another nervous breakdown. He talked things over with Nadjka and her stepfather. Miserably, they had to agree that things looked too ominous to risk staying indefinitely in Urumchi, or, indeed, even in Sinkiang. Lobsang could not bear the idea of leaving Nadjka and her baby daughter. He told her and her stepfather that he would go back to Manchuria and try to arrange a separation from his second wife, to put himself on a more regular footing with the Chinese authorities and be able to come back to Sinkiang or send for Nadjka to join him, according to how things worked out. He hardly dared admit, even to himself, that in fact the only thing for him to do was to push on farther away from China proper.

Two young Chinese who also lodged in one of the bungalows and whom he had employed as handy-boys in some of his repair work, were in much the same predicament as himself. They were in their early twenties and had found their way into Sinkiang, one from Shantung and one from Honan, in search of a livelihood and, if they were lucky, some training which would improve their chances of worthwhile jobs. They were called Liu Tin Tew and Siu Mo Te and were both simple, uneducated fellows from poor homes. They had proved themselves willing enough workers but had no experience in anything but the simplest manual tasks. It was they who first put into Lobsang's mind the idea of Tibet as a possible asylum if he was forced to leave Sinkiang. They had listened to Chinese propaganda broadcasts and gathered from these that Tibet was still a country of free enterprise and. more important, that the Tibetan Government and not the Chinese army of occupation had the last word in deciding whether foreigners should be allowed to live and work in the country. Gradually, Lobsang found himself coming to the conclusion that, taking everything into account, Tibet probably was his best option. Reliable information about conditions there was hard to come by, and a final decision might have to be postponed until he could find people with up-to-date knowledge. Meanwhile, the two Chinese boys decided to go with him when and if he left Sinkiang.

Anxiety and agonising moral decisions seem always to affect Lobsang physically. As his plans for his departure hardened, he developed a swelling and acute pain in the throat, which made it difficult for him to swallow. After he had set a date for his journey, his father-in-law had sold some pigs in order to provide a nest-egg for Lobsang. To this he added an extra 200 yuan for his return fare if and when he found it possible to come back to Urumchi. Lobsang's conscience smote him as he accepted it, but to have refused would have meant finally admitting that he saw no likelihood of return, and this he could not yet bring himself to do, even to himself. 'I am ashamed to say that I had nothing to leave Nadjka. During our life together, I had always spent freely as I earned my money. Perhaps, even in the early days, I realised in my heart of hearts that things were too good to last, and I wanted to make Nadjka happy and to enjoy every moment together to the full.'

Two days before he left, the gland in his throat played up so badly that Nadjka had to give him penicillin injections. 'Our last night together was the saddest I have ever spent. I was overwhelmed with bitterness that I was once again being forced to abandon everything I loved – my family and a country which had treated me so well and had captured my heart.' But a place had been booked on a truck leaving next morning. He left with scarcely more luggage than he arrived with, except for a bag of essential working tools.

PART II

Tibet

7

LHASA

It took Lobsang and his companions something like four and a half months to get from Sinkiang to Tibet. The truck in which they left Urumchi took them safely all the way to the railway junction at Lanchow by more or less the same route as Lobsang had taken on his way into Sinkiang. From there, he headed south by rail to Chengtu, in the province of Sechowan. He had hoped to continue by the shortest route, but it was reported to be far too wild and dangerous. He therefore took the longest, easier route using the road under construction from Chengtu to Lhasa, passing through Yaan, Kantsi and Kangting.

In Kangting, Lobsang made what turned out to be an invaluable contact with a former KMT captain named Kuo Chou Fung. He was a burly, jolly, middle-aged buccaneer who, in his KMT days, had been a military administrator in the Sikang province. This had given him a thorough knowledge of the border country between China and Tibet, and of the habits of its people. Shortly before Lobsang met him, he had been in Lhasa and had brought back a consignment of Swiss watches, imported from India, which at that time fetched fancy prices in western China. Unfortunately the captain had run into trouble with the local customs authorities who had confiscated something like a thousand watches pending payment of the official import duty. As he did not possess such a sum, he was waiting for his wife to send him enough money to reclaim them so that he could restore his fortunes. He turned out to be a mine of practical information about conditions in Tibet. He was a likeable companion, as well as useful, and Lobsang decided that it would be a good investment to invite him to meals and, in due course, to settle his hotel bill which was becoming pressing. In return, Kuo Chou Fung gave him some introductions to Chinese friends in Lhasa. He was a

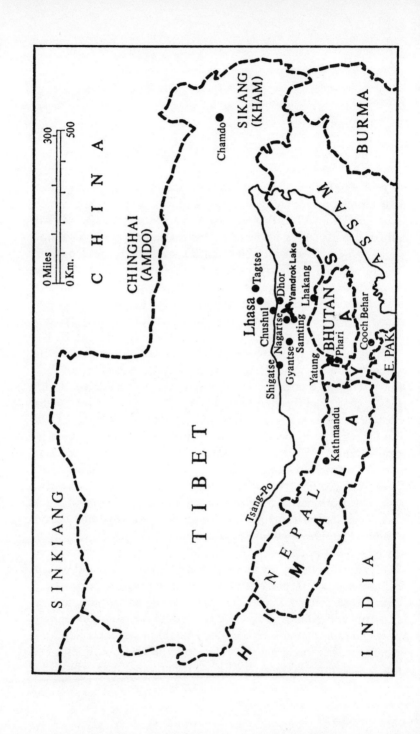

native of Honan, and there were enough Chinese from that province in Lhasa to start a Honan association. The Captain gave Lobsang a letter of introduction to one of its members, a Chinese photographer named Tung Wha.

The Captain also gave Lobsang encouraging accounts of the opportunities for private enterprise in Tibet. To judge by his own activities there, few trading restrictions existed and the country still seemed to enjoy considerable administrative autonomy, and offered plenty of scope for an enterprising foreigner.

The last stage of Lobsang's journey into Tibet took him up into the great Kham mountains. Most of the labour force on the motor-road that was in course of construction was drawn from the Chinese army, although some local Khambas had also been recruited. During the winter the Chinese suffered terribly from the cold and the altitude. They lived in improvised camps, and the whole region was treeless and barren of any natural shelter. The Chinese army in Tibet at this time consisted of three divisions – one in Lhasa itself and the other two spread out along the highway from China. Almost all the transport using the road belonged to the Chinese army. Officially, it gave no lifts to stray travellers, so that a good deal of Lobsang's travelling had to be done on foot. To compensate for this, there were virtually no police or security controls beyond Kangting. As far as Yaan and Kantse they were lucky in getting lifts, but from there virtually all motorised traffic stopped, and they spent the last eight or nine days of their journey to Lhasa on foot.

It was almost summer when they entered the Holy City. Following the Tsang-po river towards the bridge leading into Lhasa, they saw the great monasteries of Sara and Chopen towering up and dominating the rest of the town. These are the two biggest monasteries in Lhasa. At that time they housed 7,700 and 10,000 lamas respectively. A bend in the road had concealed the Tashi Gompa, a smaller monastery which was the first important ecclesiastical monument which Lobsang passed on his way into Lhasa.

He confesses that, while he was impressed by the size of these buildings, the first thing that struck him about the Holy City was not so much its grandeur as its squalor. The actual town of Lhasa is built around the Lhasa Chokang, or Holy Temple, where devout Tibetans from all over the country come to perform their devotions. Around this great temple are crowded thousands of houses, huddled in innumerable tiny intersecting lanes. The mansions of the nobility and the rich merchant classes had a certain dignity, but Lobsang was taken aback by the stench of the smaller houses and the streets which divided them. At that time, only the grandest houses boasted indoor lavatories or any form of sanitation, with the result that the front and back of most dwellings resembled dung-heaps and offended Lobsang's fastidious nose. On the other hand, nearly all these small houses were ready to give accommodation to travellers who, if they had no friends to lodge with, had little difficulty in finding food and lodging at prices they could afford. Around the temple were one or two lanes of crowded houses, then a broad outer circle in which there was always a throng of devout Buddhists, perambulating slowly, spinning their hand prayer-wheels as they made their pilgrimage to the Chokang. Even more picturesque were the penitents who made the same circuit by prostrating themselves at full length on the ground, springing erect with a jack-knife motion and immediately flattening themselves again on their arduous way. Lobsang recalls that it was quite a normal penance to make forty-nine circuits of the outer perimeter in this way.

Towards five o'clock in the evening, the crowds of pilgrims were joined by a throng of shaven-headed lamas in their deep mulberry-coloured robes. This was the hour when their monastic duties left them free and, to Lobsang, they seemed to outnumber the lay population and take over the entire city. He could not yet talk any Tibetan and so made no attempt to find a lodging in the city centre. Instead, he crossed through to the far side of the town to look for Tung Wha, the photographer from the Honan province to whom the Captain's letter of introduction was addressed. As Lhasa was in fact a very small town, he did not have far to go. He found a cheap booth in the more open outskirts of the city with a sign reading 'China Photos'. It appeared to do a thriving fairground trade in instant portraits, for Lhasa at this time was full of visitors. Apart from the usual pilgrims, the coming of the Chinese army and the opening-up of communications had turned Lhasa into something of a boom town. There were Chinese soldiers and truck-drivers from Kham and the South as well as peasants and farmers bringing in their produce to market, and itinerant traders of every kind. Studio photography was still enough of a novelty to pull in a steady flow of customers wanting a souvenir of their visit to Lhasa.

The proprietor gave Lobsang a warm welcome as a friend of the smuggling Captain. He was short-staffed and overworked and was delighted to give Lobsang a shakedown in exchange for help in developing and printing. Lobsang stayed with him for about a month. Besides his work as a photographer's devil, he became the assembler-in-chief in the establishment of a flourishing Chinese bicycle merchant. Cycles, imported from India, were the latest rage in Lhasa. To make transport easier, they arrived in detached pieces, and so brisk was the demand that Lobsang found he could command seven silver Tibetan coins for each bicycle he assembled.

His work made it necessary for him to be up and about early. This led to the discovery that every morning, at dawn, Lhasa was invaded by an army of donkeys. 'The smallest donkeys I've ever seen. Some of them no bigger than a tall dog. But they were very strong and carried unbelievably heavy loads.' The task of this dawn-patrol was to supply Lhasa with its domestic fuel. The surrounding country, for forty or fifty miles, is almost totally barren of trees, and firewood was a rare luxury. For cooking and heating, most of the population still relied on yak-dung, dried and flattened into round pancakes which were loaded in great pyramids on wooden frames with long sloping sides, carried saddle-wise by the tiny beasts of burden. 'So you see,' says Lobsang, 'my first memories of the Holy City are indelibly of lamas and donkeys – and smells.'

Among Lobsang's earliest Lhasa acquaintances, again by introduction from the Captain, was Yutung Lama. He was a Chinese from the Shansi province, and Lobsang has a suspicion that he had entered holy orders less from any sense of vocation than in order to benefit from the protection of the special ecclesiastical courts which dealt with lamas as opposed to lay-offenders. Rumour had it that he had killed someone in a brawl and had alertly opted for the monastic life in time to avoid a jail-sentence from a lay court. At any event, he had settled down in Lhasa and, like many lamas, successfully combined commercial and financial transactions with his religious duties. Lobsang explains this link between the cloth and trade in Tibet in two interesting ways. First, the Buddhist Church, as in medieval Europe, was extremely rich. The monasteries, apart from owning property and land, often acted as money-lenders. It was customary for borrowers of large sums to pledge land or houses as security and, if they defaulted, these went to swell the monastery's holdings. Poorer Tibetans, with no possessions worth pledging, paid interest on their small loans by giving labour or services to the monastery, often over periods of many years.

Individual lamas also had a personal interest in making money to meet the considerable expenses of their religious education and preferment. In order to advance in the monastic hierarchy, a lama had to take a series of stiff theological examinations. The most important of these took the form of public scholastic debates conducted in one of the major monasteries. These often lasted for several days, during which the examinee had to pay for refreshments and butter-tea for the assembled monks. In a debate in the Chopen monastery, for instance, with its 10,000 lamas, the expenses involved could be truly formidable. Unless a lama had family resources, his only hope of footing the bill and so climbing the ladder of promotion was to accumulate some money through private enterprise. A colour film of the 14th Dalai Lama's three final examinations, which is in the possession of the Tibetan Society, gives some idea of how elaborate and lavish these occasions could be, with the huge audience-hall packed at floor-level with purple-robed lamas and galleries, decked with silk hangings, filled with members of the lay nobility in all their finery.

Yutung Lama, who belonged to the minority of the priesthood, perhaps ten per cent, which embarked on these higher theological examinations, possessed a well-developed business instinct and had managed to finance several enterprises of his own in Lhasa. One of these was a Chinese-style restaurant called the Snowy Mountain. It was housed in a Tibetan house in the middle of the town, but organised in the Chinese fashion, with dining-rooms on the first floor and a separate kitchen from which the food was served by waiters. Besides his other duties, Lobsang at times helped out in the kitchen of the Snowy Mountain during his early days in Lhasa, and this led him, almost by accident, into a new and unexpectedly lucrative venture of his own.

'Most of the people who came to eat in the restaurant were lamas. There were no proper Tibetan restaurants, so the Chinese cooks simply served whatever food they could lay their hands on. As practising Buddhists, the Tibetans will not take life on principle, but they always seemed quite willing to eat anything in the way of meat, fish or poultry that was actually set before them. Tibetan chickens ordinarily only found their way to the table after dying a natural death and were often not fit to eat. In exploring the countryside around Lhasa I discovered a pretty little river which was teeming with fish. There was one particular spot where passing Tibetans used to throw scraps of their local barley-bread to the fish, which Buddhists regard as propitious creatures. The result was that the fish there were unbelievably guileless and were quite undisturbed by human beings. I made myself some big nets, each about twelve feet long, and used to bicycle out in the evening and wait until dark, or at any rate until everyone had disappeared. Then, in no time at all, I would haul out anything up to thirty or forty fine big fish. At the Snowy Mountain, each of these fetched five silver coins – the big silver dollar with the head of Huan Shi-Kai which was then in common currency in Lhasa.'

If fish, then why not fowl? The landlord of 'China Photos' was the magistrate of the Tatse Dzong, about forty miles outside Lhasa. These dzongs played a key part in the organisation of the old Tibetan way of life. Their nearest equivalent in Europe was the medieval fortified monastery. Originally, they combined the functions of a fortress, a religious centre and the administrative and judicial offices for an entire district or region. The official in charge of the dzong was usually a lama, with a lay assistant, who exercised, among other things, the function of magistrates.

The success of Lobsang's fishing expedition prompted him to ask the Tatse magistrate whether there was any objection to his buying poultry for the Snowy Mountain from the farmers in the area administered from his dzong. 'That', said the magistrate, 'would be difficult for a mere stranger, but I see no reason why I should not tell the village headmen that you are an agent buying chickens for some government department.' So Lobsang was introduced, sometimes as representing a branch of the Chinese Army, or the Sino-Tibetan Information Department, or any other plausible-sounding official body. So many of these had sprung up as a result of joint Chinese-Tibetan planning for the new Autonomous Region of Tibet that no village headman was likely to be surprised or to question Lobsang's *bona fides*, particularly as he was introduced by such an influential patron.

The magistrate and the village headman, between them, fixed the price of a chicken at one *thanka*, a small coin worth fifteen cents of the silver dollar. At the Snowy Mountain, the same chicken fetched between four and five silver dollars. There were roughly a thousand small holdings in the area administered by the dzong and soon Lobsang was collecting several hundred chickens at an outing, and the money was rolling in. He had sometimes to take seven or eight horses to carry the chickens slung on poles across the horses' backs.

Most entrepreneurs in Lobsang's position would have experienced a feeling of triumph at promoting such an outrageously profitable piece of private enterprise under the noses of the Communists while they were in the process of diligently laying the foundations of a socialist Tibet. Yet, in recounting his Lhasa catering enterprises, Lobsang allows a note of self-deprecation, amounting almost to melancholy, to creep into his story. 'It used to depress me to think that yesterday I had been a lieutenant-colonel and today was nothing better than a chicken-poacher.' A poacher with panache, admittedly, but it rankled all the same.

'It was also against Tibetan religious law and Buddhist scruples to treat animals in this way – trussing them or hanging them head downwards. If any of the lamas had seen me, I could easily have been in real danger of being stoned. So I had to move my poultry in the dark. Sometimes it was a ghostly business. When I heard voices behind walls or buildings I had an eerie feeling that a lama might jump out and scare me. I remember pressing myself against the horses to keep them out of sight. The touch of dead fish or the muffled squawkings of the hens was curiously disconcerting, particularly when I was feeling cold and tired. There were even times when I could imagine that bad spirits were lurking in the shadows, waiting to pounce on me. We Chinese, whatever we pretend, have a superstitious streak somewhere. It is part of our folklore, and it bobs up when you least expect it. I used to try to cheer myself up by telling myself that this was only a temporary expedient until I could get myself organised in some worthwhile activity.'

8

A SILVER HIGHWAY

Lobsang has always remained, at heart, an engineer. Except when he was in prison, there was never any long period during his adventures when he was not exercising his professional skills in one way or another. By 1955, he had saved up enough capital to start a mechanical workshop. He began by renting a house in the Thebunkong area, about a kilometre outside the centre of Lhasa. His living quarters were in the original farmhouse and the workshop was in the garden, which was conveniently large.

With the new road communications, it had become comparatively simple to get things like lathes, drills and other basic workshop equipment. The coming of the Chinese army of occupation and the consequent shake-up of the economy had brought trade and a new market to Lhasa. The Chinese were not yet making any attempt to interfere with private trading. In fact, when it suited them, they positively encouraged it, so that small traders were making fortunes importing from India things in short supply in China, like watches or penicillin, and selling them to the Chinese army.

Lobsang's mechanical workshop was the first of its kind in Lhasa. The demand for every sort of mechanical repair was growing but Lobsang managed to recruit staff, mainly of Chinese, which enabled him to keep pace with it. Once his workshop was equipped and launched, it was almost bound to be a success. He also became a sub-contractor to the Chinese army, which provided his workshop with regular employment and a steady income.

Feverish preparations were in progress for the arrival in Lhasa of a very large all-China delegation, headed by Marshal Chen-Yi, which was to come for the formal inauguration of the Tibetan Autonomous Region. Something like 10,000 delegates were expected. Many of these, technical advisers and administrators, were due to stay on after the inauguration to help with development schemes under a seven-year plan of Chinese technical assistance to Tibet. The accommodation of this number of visitors placed a heavy strain on Lhasa, whose total population at that time was only 150,000. Lobsang contracted to manufacture component parts for temporary buildings for the Chinese delegation. This government contract greatly simplified his problem of getting the necessary import licences for additional plant and machinery to equip his workshop and the necessary transport priority to get it quickly to Lhasa. Finally, it gave Lobsang a semi-established position in the eyes of the Chinese army authorities.

The Chinese army in Lhasa consisted almost entirely of the political branch of the 18th Army. It was under strict orders to limit its role to providing friendly advice and collaboration in the work of the Preparatory Committee for the new Autonomous Region. As Chairman of this Autonomous Region, by agreement with Peking, the Dalai Lama still exercised sovereign powers and the civil administration of the country was still in the hands of his government.

Lobsang confirms, with some reservations, that the aim of Chinese policy at the time of this 'honeymoon' period of Sino-Tibetan relations was to win friends and influence among Tibetans at every social level. As a non-Communist Chinese on the spot, he is in a good position to give an objective account of where this policy succeeded and failed during these critical early years. He insists that the accounts given to the western world by Tibetans who left their country at the same time as the Dalai Lama in 1959 represent nothing more than a minority report – made by a minority which, for obvious reasons, was neither impartial nor representative.

Lobsang's work brought him into contact with Tibetans of every degree as well as with the Chinese authorities. He admits that the picture, as he saw it, was full of paradoxes. Many of these he attributes to compromises reached between the Chinese authorities and the Dalai Lama and his administration which, because they were based on misunderstandings and contradictory interpretations, were bound in the long run to produce confusion and resentment both among the Tibetans and the Chinese.

Back in 1950, when the Chinese Communist Liberation Army was advancing towards the borders of Tibet, the Dalai Lama's government had sent eight *debens* – Tibetan military detachments of about 800 men each – to check its advance into the province of Kham or, as the Chinese call it, Sikang, over which both Lhasa and Peking claim territorial sovereignty. This Tibetan force stood no chance whatsoever against the modern professional army of China and was duly routed near Chamdo. The eight commanders of the *debens* were all captured. They were taken to Peking where, for four months, they were reasoned with and politically indoctrinated. The most convinced convert to the Chinese point of view was Apeh Awang Jigme. In 1951 he was sent back to Lhasa to convince the young Dalai Lama that further resistance would be not only futile but against the best interest of his country.

The Chinese also sent the second-ranking dignitary in the Tibetan lamaistic hierarchy, the Panchen Lama, back into Tibet with the advance guard of the Chinese 18th Army, the political unit which was to prepare for local autonomous government. Relations between the Dalai Lama and the Panchen Lama had been strained for years owing to rivalries over questions of ecclesiastical and temporal authority. The Panchen Lama's stronghold was actually outside the political confines of Tibet, in the Chinghai province of China. While he remained there he had become increasingly identified with Chinese policies. His return to Tibet in the train of the Chinese Liberation Army was an unwelcome surprise to the Dalai Lama, but the Chinese did their best to convince him that the situation demanded that they should treat each other as brothers and co-operate in building the new order in their country. Both lamas were eventually invited to Peking in 1954, where they were received with every mark of respect and courtesy. They were photographed sitting on either side of Chairman Mao – 'like his sons', as Lobsang says. He considers that this had an important effect in reconciling many Tibetans to the new Communist experiment. In retrospect, Chinese policy during this period appears cynical in the extreme. Lobsang's view is that it was also astute and, broadly speaking, effective. Its immediate aim was to control the levers of power without upsetting the existing machinery of administration, while at the same time preparing the Tibetan people for the long-term integration of the Autonomous Region into greater Communist China.

In their contacts with the Tibetan upper classes – high government officials, noblemen and the influential merchant class – the Chinese Communists quickly divided them into those who were not worth cultivating and those who looked likely to prove useful and co-operative. To these, they offered impressive-sounding posts in the new joint Sino-Tibetan institutions and planning committees. They not only sounded prestigious, but were often handsomely paid. The Chinese consulted these officers deferentially and explained that, because of their limited knowledge of Tibetan religion, language and culture, they valued the advice of such experienced and respected Tibetans. In this way, many of the Dalai Lama's high officials and advisers were soon drawn, willingly or unwittingly, into a situation where they were so dependent on Chinese goodwill, or so publicly identified with Chinese policies, that they were effectively neutralised as possible leaders of an organised opposition. Lobsang believes this is why, when the Dalai Lama eventually broke with the Chinese in 1959, only a fraction of these high officials and merchants – he puts it at not more than ten per cent – made common cause with him or followed him into exile. It was, after all, the Dalai Lama himself who set the example of collaboration with the Chinese during this period. Apart from being Chairman of the Autonomous Region of Tibet, he was made a member of the Central Committee of the Political Consultative Assembly in Peking, while the Panchen Lama was made a member of the Assembly. Peking, in this way, acknowledged the Dalai Lama's hierarchical pre-eminence. At the same time, by firmly installing the Panchen Lama as their man in Tibet, they provided a constant reminder to the Dalai Lama that, if he resisted Peking's wishes, Chinese support could always be transferred to his rival.

At the popular level, Chinese policy was less transparently

opportunist, but no less effective. After 1952, when the Chinese 18th Army moved in to garrison Tibet, officers and men were under the strictest orders to cultivate the good will of the peasants and the common people. Tibet, under the 14th Dalai Lama, was still not just a theocracy but a feudal aristocracy in the fullest sense of the term. In the presence of their superiors, common people had to bow low, lifting their eyes to the sky but never daring to look straight into their master's face. Even this servile deference was probably less burdensome than their exploitation by the monasteries. Besides having to offer their sons for lifelong service as monks, they had to supply out of their own meagre resources all the lamas' needs in food and fuel. To all intents and purposes, they were often little more than serfs, and were constantly reminded of their lowly estate by the arrogant and contemptuous manner adopted towards them by their social superiors.

When the advance guard of the Chinese army moved into Tibet, its soldiers proclaimed themselves the servants of the people. More extraordinary still, they acted as if this was really the case. When an ordinary Tibetan called at a local Chinese army headquarters, he was invited to be seated, and was offered tea before getting down to business, which was then discussed as between equals. Another eye-opener was the Communists' behaviour in procuring their own needs. Anything they took in the way of food and supplies was paid for at honest, agreed prices. Later, after two or three years, when 'productive units' of the Chinese army had set up their own model farms, they shared their surplus produce with the local population. The role of the Army of Liberation was, in fact, essentially the same as it had been in China itself during the heroic days of the Long March and during the Civil War.

When the army started its model farms near Lhasa, the Tibetans were introduced to all sorts of vegetables which they themselves had never tried or bothered to cultivate. To their staple diet of potatoes and a kind of beetroot were now added cucumbers, cabbages, lettuces, radishes and other green vegetables. The Chinese, instead of merely scratching the surface soil, in the

Tibetan manner, dug deep and used fertilisers and animal manure. They even started a service for the methodical collection of human manure in the cities for use on their farms, and if the Chinese purchasing agents, when they bought barley or oils from the peasants, traded a bit of propaganda along with their silver dollars, few of the humbler Tibetans resented it. The army also organised social gatherings and shows of documentary films showing life in the other Autonomous Regions, Sinkiang or Mongolia. All in all, the peasants were duly impressed.

The wooing of the peasantry was, however, a long-term project. It was still too early and too dangerous for the Communists to antagonise the Tibetan establishment. It would have been particularly risky to offend the monasteries and, for the time being, the Chinese authorities not only made no attempt to interfere with monastic privileges but showed complete tolerance towards monastic abuses. Lobsang quotes one example of how crude these abuses could still be and how supple and machiavellian Communist reactions to them were during this 'honeymoon' period.

During the twenty-one days following the Tibetan New Year, a lama is elected to the office of Chaso Lama. This title, which means Iron Rod Lama, makes him a glorified festival king. He is invested with a rod of office which can inflict a lethal blow and whose origins Lobsang thinks date back to pre-Buddhist times when the worship of the human phallus was still part of Tibetan religious practice. During his term of office, the Chaso Lama wielded virtually absolute power. The Dalai Lama retired to his summer palace and kept well out of the way. During this brief annual reign of terror some of the more unruly lamas committed all sorts of excesses. They extorted money with threats of violence from debtors and waylaid girls who ventured out into the streets. 'I remember', says Lobsang, 'one occasion in Lhasa when they abducted and raped some Chinese girls who worked as counter-hands in a state-run emporium for Chinese goods. As far as I know, the Chinese authorities never took any action against the lamas or even lodged any formal protest. Certainly they did not try to have the Iron Rod Carnival abolished or

the arbitrary powers wielded by the Chaso Lama curtailed.'
Lobsang gives this as an example of the lengths to which the
Communists' permissiveness and non-interference in Tibetan
domestic affairs was carried at this time. He adds a very Chinese
comment of his own. 'It bore out what I had already seen in
Sinkiang – that Peking regarded the Tibetans as just another
backward minority people who had not advanced to a sufficiently
civilised state to be treated as Chinese. It was therefore politic
to humour them until conditions were ripe for their complete
absorption into the Chinese system. Meanwhile, the Chinese
were prepared to put up with their quaint customs and, if a few
Chinese were inconvenienced as a result, that was just too bad.'
In softening up Tibetan public opinion, the Communists did
not overlook the merchants. As a class, they were far less
numerous than either the peasants or the religious and lay
officials, but at this time of rapid economic expansion, they had
an important role to play which the Chinese were anxious to
exploit for their own ends. Where goods were in short supply,
importers were often given a fifty per cent subsidy and capital
was made available on easy terms for business ventures which
fitted into the overall pattern of economic development. Even
where this was not the case, privileges were often granted simply
as a means of ingratiating the new order among the influential
merchant class.
Lobsang himself benefited from this policy of mercantile
laissez-faire. His workshop, and particularly his work as a sub-
contractor for the Chinese army, were considered useful and progressive activities, and he fulfilled his contracts with gratifying
punctuality and efficiency. How he managed to recruit and train
a staff capable of meeting the demands of state and private enterprise is something of a minor managerial miracle. In Lhasa at
this time there was a community of some 1,800 non-Communist
Chinese. A few of them were ex-KMT officers and men or established traders, but for the most part they were humble people
who had drifted across the borders of the frontier provinces into
Tibet, in search of a better living or, if they were lucky, of making
a modest fortune. Out of this miscellaneous and not very prom-

ising material, Lobsang formed a team of surprisingly efficient unskilled or semi-skilled artisans and mechanics. Around the nucleus of the two boys who had travelled with him out of Sinkiang and a young Chinese partner who had come to him without experience but had shown natural aptitude for the office and business side of the enterprise, he built up a workshop staff of nearly forty.

'The main thing was to understand their personal problems. I paid them well by local standards, but generally money was not the most important consideration. I took great trouble to see that everyone got the kind of food he liked. When a man is feeding well and regularly, particularly in a strange country, he is halfway to being contented. For others, what mattered most was to be able to send money back to their families in China. With the growth of road transport to Chinghai, and through Kham to Sechowan, it was nearly always possible to get a few hundred or a few thousand yen to most parts of China. I got to know most of the truck drivers, and at that time to have friends on the road was a key to many problems.' Lobsang himself is a really first-rate cook in the north Chinese style. He knew just what to buy for the boys in his workshop, whatever province of China they came from. In his business deals, if he discovered that someone was going to the home-town of one of his workers, he usually managed to see to it that a message or a remittance reached its destination.

By this time he was talking fluent Tibetan. Lobsang is not the sort of linguist to be daunted by the pitfalls of a language which, besides its complicated and archaic forms, requires that people in different social categories should be addressed in what almost amount to separate languages. He had made acquaintance with people of every rank and now conversed with them all in Tibetan which, if not always socially impeccable, was at least lively and intelligible.

'I used to watch the Chinese community in Lhasa. Most of them went about with bowed heads and a meek, rather apprehensive look, keeping themselves to themselves and doing their best not to be conspicuous. I am not at all like that. I like to get to know people of all kinds, to talk with them freely and join in their everyday lives. If they are gamblers, I like to gamble with them.'

People soon got to know that the tall Chinese in the Russian-style suit could play an excellent hand of Mah Jong in the Tibetan style, which by all accounts is a pretty cut-throat school. 'Every time I played, it meant three more acquaintances – or rather, four, because in a real Tibetan Mah Jong session, which can last for days or even a week, there are always four players and one person sitting out, sleeping or resting or amusing himself. At a high-class Mah Jong party, in the house of a nobleman or a rich merchant, there was always plenty to eat and drink. There was music and dancing and it was an understood thing that if the player sitting out fancied one of the girls who was serving refreshments or entertaining the company, it was quite in order for them to disappear together into a bedroom. I have seen wealthy Tibetans at these parties gamble away their castles and their estates. One of my close friends and neighbours, who lived near the workshop, had lost his family home in this way. In Tibet, and as long as I stuck to Mah Jong, I was pretty lucky in my gambling. In other places, and particularly at cards, it has been a different story.'

These reflections of Lobsang on himself and his fellow country-men, when they were tape-recorded in conversation with a Mandarin-speaking Chinese scholar in London, moved him to comment: 'For me, what Lobsang has just told us is worth a thousand pages of classical Chinese history. There, the chroniclers tell us of the great travellers and ambassadors who went out into the corners of the earth and won fame and influence for their imperial masters. They would have us believe that these successes were due to their superior diplomatic skills and the magnificence of their style and rank. I have always known that their triumphs had nothing to do with conventional diplomacy but were achieved through that rare ability to behave entirely naturally with everyone they encountered and to get themselves accepted as human beings wherever they happened to find themselves. That, of course, is Lobsang's real secret too – to be able to throw himself with gusto into the life of whatever society he is in. That, and those long legs and seductive eyes which make him irresistible to women at first sight. He is in the great Chinese tradition of knowing what living is all about.'

Lobsang's first impression of Tibet had been that people were less sincere and open than those he had left behind in Sinkiang. To this day, his feelings towards Tibetans are distinctly mixed. At first, he was too busy picking up the language and organising his own life to waste much time on such invidious comparisons. Bursts of hard work began to alternate with periods in which business and pleasure could be agreeably mixed. As his circle of acquaintances widened, he discovered that Tibetan hospitality could be warm and lavish. Beneath a surface of elaborately artificial manners and etiquette, well-to-do Tibetans were mostly a pleasure-loving lot. Behind the walls of their solid mansions, they could afford to relax and live like lords. Lobsang has memories of days or weeks spent with business or gambling acquaintances when his work took him outside Lhasa.

He discovered, too, that Tibetan ladies were as fun-loving as the men. Society demanded that women of rank or wealth should put up a formal display of decorous manners. This apparent modesty, however, seldom turned out to be more than skin deep. Demure protestations were liable to be accompanied by quite unladylike provocations, so that even a philanderer of Lobsang's calibre was sometimes taken aback by the goings-on in this permissive society. Lower down the social scale Tibetan girls were frankly promiscuous. 'It was the usual thing in Lhasa if you passed them on the street, to shout outrageous compliments or propositions. Usually, they retorted with good-humoured ribaldries. Only the youngest and shyest of them giggled and ran away.'

For his first two and a half years in Tibet, Lobsang worked and, by and large, prospered. His workshop had become almost a Lhasa institution, and his restless energy began to demand new outlets. Since his arrival, the road on which he had travelled from Sechowan across the wastes of Sikang-Kham had been completed and the other highway from Chinghai-Amdo to Lhasa was steadily opening to motor-traffic along its whole length. China's purpose in building these two roads was both strategic and political. Without them, it would have been impossible to maintain and supply a modern army in Tibet or to control the country effectively with such a comparatively small force. Without them, too, the crash-programme of economic development, with all its implications for a gradual Communist takeover, would have been an interminable business.

The road through Kham, as Lobsang had seen for himself, runs through the roughest sort of country between high mountains and deep river gorges. Quite apart from the engineering problems involved, the work of road-building on some of its stretches was very rigorous. The passes to be negotiated commonly ran up to 12,000 feet and more. In one place an attempt was made to push the road up to an altitude of 18,000 feet, but the casualties among the mainly Chinese labour force were so heavy that it had to be abandoned.

As the highway ran deeper into Tibet, increasing numbers of local Khambas – the natives of the Kham province – were lured into working on the roads by the exceptionally high rates of pay offered by the Chinese. During the building of the Chamdo-Lhasa section, they could earn 100 silver dollars a month, compared to a normal wage of fifty or sixty. It was said that if this entire section of some hundred miles had been completely paved over its average width of three to four yards with a layer of silver coins one yard deep, that would have accurately represented the cost of building it.

With truly Chinese ingenuity, the Communists devised a special currency operation to finance this formidable project. All Tibetans, and particularly Khambas, set great store by silver in any form. The Chinese therefore methodically collected all silver sacrificial vessels and religious ornaments in China proper and in the border provinces for melting down into bullion. They set up a mint in Chengtu, on the Chinese side of the border, where faithful replicas of the popular old 'Republican' dollar were turned out in large quantities. Besides supplying the currency for the highway labour force, these heavy, picturesque coins came in useful for financing trade between Tibet and India and in buying the good will of selected Tibetan aristocrats, lamas and merchants.

The Khambas, for all their eagerness to get their hands on the silver dollars, soon began to view the highway project with deepening suspicion and concern. Their whole traditional way of life revolved round a combination of yak-herding and caravan trade. Following the routes dictated by the seasonal pasturing of yaks, which can only live above a certain altitude and below a certain temperature, they carried tea and other portable wares from China and moved slowly towards Tibet, selling yak-butter and other produce wherever they could along the way. With what they made, they bought whatever personal belongings they needed at either end of their trading circuit. As long as Tibet remained without roads or rapid transport, this time-honoured system brought them in a decent living. They alone were tough and energetic enough to put up with the cold and the altitudes which it involved, and so were able to keep a monopoly of their particular trade.

The highway, they realised too late, not only brought competition of the most serious kind, but, in the long run, threatened the whole free-and-easy pattern of Khamba existence. Like all itinerant people, they resented controls and bureaucracy of any kind. They were also fiercely independent and had always shown themselves jealous of Chinese attempts at suzerainty. These were the sparks from which the great Khamba rebellion – the only effective resistance movement against the Chinese takeover of Tibet – gradually burst into flames.

This revolt against Chinese authority started and reached its dramatic climax during Lobsung's five years in Tibet. He agrees that one of its underlying causes was the Chinese road-building project, and that, as its political, military and economic implications unfolded, the tempo of Khamba resistance quickened. About the rebellion itself Lobsang takes a detached and critical view. If the Khambas' way of life was rooted in the Yak Age, Lobsang's whole outlook was bound up with everything that the highway stood for. He was a trained engineer, and his entire military career, even including his prisoner-of-war years in Siberia, had been more or less directly linked with problems of transport and communications.

So, at the beginning of 1956, with his workshop business running smoothly and profitably, he branched out into road-haulage. In many ways, it was a natural extension of what he was already doing. His private repair work and government contracts provided him with plenty of ready-made customers. He had enough capital in the new Chinese bank in Lhasa to make him anxious to invest it in something more productive than a Communist deposit account. His first step was to order three two-and-a-half-ton Dodge trucks from an Indian merchant named Motilal, who was doing a flourishing business in imports from India into Tibet. Drivers and mechanics, both Chinese and people from the border provinces, were by now fairly easily available, and he began plying his trucks between Yatung and Lhasa, six hundred miles along the road that carried all the main trade to and from India.

Lobsang now really had scope to use his skills and satisfy his energy. He enjoyed holding together all the technical and organisational threads of his various enterprises, jollying along the members of his team and ready himself to dash off at a moment's notice to straighten out mechanical or business problems that only he could handle.

It was during the hey-day of his trucking enterprise that Lobsang became the hero of one of his most entertaining escapades. In one of the provincial towns, he agreed to give a lift in a lorry he was driving to a Tibetan matron who wanted to go to Pari. Her daughter was to accompany her, and sat between Lobsang and her mother. As the journey proceeded, and the old lady dozed, the girl made unmistakable advances to Lobsang which set him wondering whether there was anywhere on their route where he could conveniently break their journey and spirit her out of her mother's vigilance. But the remaining distance was through inhospitable country, with no obvious stopping-places.

Lobsang had just reluctantly come to the conclusion that the situation offered no hope of accepting the girl's pressing invitation, when they came to a long hill, the last major descent before

Pari. Seized by a desperate resolution, Lobsang suddenly slammed on the brakes, bringing the lorry to a grinding halt. He gravely explained to the old lady that something had happened to the underneath of the vehicle, which made further progress impossible until he had inspected the damage. He would have to crawl under the lorry and the problem was to make sure that it would not run away downhill while he was carrying out any necessary repairs. To guard against this danger, he asked the mother to sit astride the handbrake and pull the brake handle back towards her with all her strength. At all costs, Lobsang earnestly entreated her, she must not relax her hold for an instant. Their lives, as well as her hopes of reaching Pari in time for her appointment, were in her hands. Meanwhile, perhaps her daughter would be obliging enough to give him a hand by passing his tools to him as required. Duly impressed with her responsibility, the old lady took a firm grip of the brake and assumed a look of ferocious determination. Fortunately, the lorry had a high road-clearance and was equipped with plenty of soft furnishings to cushion the hardness of the road surface. When Lobsang climbed back into the driver's seat, flushed with his exertions and brandishing a spanner, he complimented the old lady on her steadiness in emergency and on her daughter's unexpected handiness as a mechanic's mate. The girl blushed modestly at the compliment, the mother resumed her outer seat with dignity, and the party freewheeled contentedly down towards Pari.

This story illustrates, more seriously, the impact of the new roads on the whole pattern of Tibetan life and the habits of its people. Before the road, the journey to Lhasa from Pari would have taken anything up to two months, by yak or on horseback. By truck, it could be comfortably managed in one and a half days. Until the Chinese army came to Tibet, no motor roads had existed between China and Lhasa, and there were only the roughest of caravan tracks over virtually the whole country. No wonder that the old lady considered it a privilege to ride in Lobsang's thunder-box. No wonder, too, that Tibetan merchants and businessmen were prepared to pay handsomely for freight space on lorries that could bring them their goods, particularly if they were perishable or urgently required, so fast and so dependably.

It was in the same year, 1956, that Lobsang embarked on another new venture of a completely different kind. Perhaps it can best be described as an investment in political reinsurance. For a time, it paid an interesting dividend, but eventually led him into waters so deep that even such an intrepid swimmer as Lobsang almost submerged. At first sight, it appeared innocuous, if highly improbable. He was invited to become co-secretary of the Buddhist Society.

This was a Communist front organisation started by the Chinese for the purpose of cultivating goodwill among influential ecclesiastical dignitaries. It had offices in the headquarters of the Political Division of the Chinese Army in Lhasa, but was under the most illustrious Tibetan patronage. The Dalai Lama was honorary President, and the two vice-Presidents were the Panchen Lama and Tibet's only female living Buddha, the Dorji Paghmo, whose title, literally translated, means the Thunderbolt Sow. She is also known as the Diamond Sow-Faced Goddess because she is supposed to be the human incarnation of the source of energy which, in Buddhist mythology, is symbolised by the productive sow who, together with her consort, the Horse-necked Tamdin, a sort of centaur, was given the task of defending Buddhism against its enemies. She is traditionally depicted as a goddess with a small excrescence behind her ear in the shape of a pig's head. Like the Dalai Lama himself, she ranks as a Khutuktu or phantom body and is the only woman Khutuktu among these most revered incarnations in the lamaistic hierarchy of priesthood.

Lobsang was genuinely mystified at being asked to join such an exclusive organisation. He was not an obvious choice either on religious or cultural grounds, but the Chinese officer in the Political Division who first suggested the job – a fellow-Manchurian with whom he had become friendly – explained that there were already plenty of theological experts among the Society's members and that Lobsang would be very useful because, apart from his fluent Tibetan, he appeared to have more friendly contacts with Tibetans than almost any member of the Chinese community in Lhasa. He assured him that the secretarial duties involved were not exacting and would not interfere with his own work. They would involve attending a few meetings and issuing invitations whenever the Society organised functions or goodwill trips. As all invitations were issued in the name of the Society's patrons, there would in any case be no likelihood of complications or refusals.

The job, in fact, looked like a sinecure. It also had the great advantage of giving Lobsang a respectable official identity in Communist eyes. Bitter experience in Manchuria and Sinkiang had taught him that nothing aroused suspicion so much as failure to fall into an immediately classifiable category. From Lobsang's point of view, the invitation was made more acceptable by the fact that the Chinese side of the organisation was, like everything else in Lhasa, controlled by the army rather than by civilian Party officials. After carefully weighing the pros and cons of the offer, he decided to accept.

One of his early duties as an official of the Society was to attend upon the Dalai Lama when he left Tibet on the first stage of his journey to India in 1956. He had been invited there to attend the Buddha Jayanti, the 2,500th anniversary of Buddha's birth, as the guest of the Maha Bodhi Society and, very reluctantly, the Chinese authorities had finally agreed to his going. Apart from one long visit to China in 1954–5 this was the first time the Dalai Lama had left Tibet, and convention demanded that he should be seen off by a very large delegation of his own government and senior Chinese officials. With other officers of the Buddhist Society, Lobsang was present in Yatung, the last town in Tibet on the route into India, to pay their respects and bid him farewell. The Dalai Lama has given his own account of this fateful visit to India, during which he met Nehru for the first time, had discussions with Chou En-Lai in New Delhi, and received news of a serious revolt by the Khambas against the Chinese Army of Occupation in Tibet.

As Secretary of the Buddhist Society, Lobsang had access to some of the confidential reports which the Chinese Communists in Lhasa received during the Dalai Lama's visit to India. Lobsang's own opinion is that the Dalai Lama was badly advised in India, particularly by his two elder brothers. Lobsang believes that one of these was unduly influenced by the Americans, and the other by the Chinese Nationalists in Formosa. What is certain is that it was during this journey that the Dalai Lama became convinced that his best course was to leave Tibet – a decision which Lobsang still thinks was fatal to whatever chances Tibet might have had of resisting or delaying a total takeover by China.

The younger of the two brothers had left Tibet for China in 1947, and had a long history of association with the Chinese Nationalists. Even the Indian authorities regarded him as heavily committed to Kuomintang policies and interests. At the time of the Dalai Lama's visit to India, the Chinese Nationalists were still interested in the possibility of encouraging anti-Communist movements in the north-west frontier province of China. The Dalai Lama's elder brother, before he lived in the United States, had been the head lama of a monastery in the Chinese border province of Chinghai, in a district whose population was, however, predominantly Moslem. Lobsang recalls rumours that, because of this Islamic connection, Chinese Nationalist attempts to foment trouble in Tibet and on the Tibetan border were at one moment actually subsidised by one of the Arab monarchies.

From secret Communist Party reports, which Lobsang saw in Lhasa, he says that Peking at any rate was convinced that the two brothers had gone to meet the Dalai Lama in India with the firm intention of influencing him in an anti-Chinese sense. Chinese suspicions were confirmed after his return to Tibet. Whereas before his visit China had had no reason to complain about the Dalai Lama's willingness to co-operate in their plans for the Autonomous Region of Tibet, his attitude subsequently changed. The reports that Lobsang saw also made it clear that the Chinese Communists suspected that India was now, in practice if not openly, pursuing an anti-Chinese policy over everything connected with Tibet. Once they had come to this conclusion, Lobsang believes Peking began to take every opportunity to test Indian intentions by trying to force the Indian government to declare whether it was supporting the government in Peking or the Chinese Nationalists in Formosa.

Only a few weeks after the Dalai Lama left for India, accompanied by the Panchen Lama and a retinue of ecclesiastical advisers, another party of lamas prepared to leave Lhasa on a goodwill tour of China, organised by the Buddhist Society. As Lobsang's friend had predicted, there had been no difficulty about the invitations. These had been sent to forty lamas at their respective monasteries. According to Lobsang, the Chinese Communists had infiltrated agents into the monasteries even before they took over power in Tibet. In this way they had a clear notion of which lamas might be susceptible to progressive ideas. The invitations for the Chinese trip went partly to lamas who had shown themselves sympathetic to the new order and partly as a sort of consolation prize to high-ranking monks who were disappointed or resentful at not having been included in the Dalai Lama's delegation to India.

Lobsang found himself drafted as conducting officer and assistant organiser of this expedition.

9

TO PEKING WITH A GODDESS

Having taken such trouble to get out of China, Lobsang naturally had reservations about returning. He reasoned, however, that since he was performing a useful function and was an official member of the delegation he was unlikely to be bothered by the police inside China itself. In any case he had not much choice in the matter.

'Although I had some good friends in the monasteries and among the lama-officials, I was not in a general way very sympathetic to lamas as a class. I had seen too many who took advantage of their privileges without any thought for the spiritual life or the welfare of the common people.' Nor did Lobsang much care for his role as conducting-officer. It smacked too much for his liking of the overseer and informer, and he was determined to avoid anything that would lead the lamas to think that he had been sent to spy on them. So he made up his mind in advance to do what was necessary, but to show as little zeal and curiosity as possible.

The first stage of the journey from Lhasa was by road to Sining, the capital of Chinghai. It was a road that Lobsang had covered many times in his everyday business, and so he found the journey quite uneventful. At Lanchow the party transferred to the railway, and the rest of the trip consisted of fifteen-day stops in the important cities of China.

There was another reason why Lobsang's attention was not always concentrated on his duties as tour-manager during his four months in China. By far the most important delegate in the party was the incarnate lady lama, the Dorji Paghmo. Besides being one of the official patrons of the Buddhist Society, she was the only female Living Buddha in the Tibetan hierarchy. She was also being assiduously cultivated by the Chinese authorities. Although at this time she was only twenty-two, she had been to Peking before, in 1954-5, at the same time as the Dalai Lama.

A tallish, slightly built, serious-looking girl, she had received the thorough theological education given to important incarnate lamas from the moment of their discovery in infancy. She was also naturally intelligent and, by Tibetan standards, quite progressive in her ideas and grasp of contemporary politics. On the journey down from Lhasa to Chinghai, Lobsang had not had any opportunity to get to know her. The delegates had travelled in jeeps, and she had been in her own party with her travelling-companion, a middle-aged nun, and her father. Lobsang in fact had only gradually realised how important she was when he noticed the reverence in which she was held, even by other senior incarnate lamas.

On the train, the Dorji Paghmo had her own suite, which she shared with her attendant and her father. Lobsang had been given a berth in a first-class compartment with three Chinese officials attached to the Yumen oilfields. They had been intrigued by the dress of the Dorji Paghmo when she had passed along the corridor on her way to the restaurant. She was wearing a bright yellow silk sash as a belt over her travelling robe – a colour only worn by members of monastic orders in Tibet. Lobsang explained that she was a Lady Living Buddha, unique of her kind. The Communist officers had been amused and intrigued and had remarked jokingly that she was a striking-looking girl and asked why she wasn't married. They had then gone to the restaurant car, leaving Lobsang alone in the compartment. On her way back, the Dorji Paghmo had come and sat with him and made small-talk of a perfectly conventional kind.

It was the first time they had exchanged anything more than formal greetings. Finding her natural and easy in conversation, Lobsang had told her of the Chinese officials' curiosity about her dress and rank, and their astonishment at her remaining single. The Dorji Paghmo laughed, and the conversation imperceptibly took a more relaxed and personal turn. With something approaching consternation, Lobsang suddenly became aware that the Diamond Sow was behaving very much like other Tibetan girls of her age. 'I think', he reflects, 'it is very hard for a young girl, even in her position, to control her sexual urges.' He found himself fondling her breast, and asking her why she was teasing him. Their tête-à-tête was interrupted by other passengers returning from the restaurant along the corridor to their own compartments.

'It's easy to understand why she chose a journey abroad and a foreigner for a flirtation. It would have been unthinkable, in her position, to have conducted an affair with a Tibetan. Morals in the monasteries were often pretty lax, but incarnate lamas of her eminence were expected to lead exemplary lives. There have, of course, been cases of even Dalai Lamas falling from grace. The 9th Dalai Lama is known to have been notoriously promiscuous. But there is a convenient theological explanation in lamaistic Buddhism for such occasional lapses. In the long cycle of their reincarnations, throughout which they strive to achieve perfection, the Living Buddhas must face all the temptations of an ordinary mortal. Carnal desire being natural to the human condition, it is held inevitable that spiritual progress should proceed through carnal experience towards that perfect state of grace achieved by the Lord Buddha himself. In monasteries you often find a statue depicting a Living Buddha in the act of sexual intercourse with a female figure with several heads and pairs of hands.'

This presence of 'positive' and 'negative' elements is used to account for any sexual indulgences of the high incarnate lamas during their life-span on earth. The Dorji Paghmo, besides being the only recognised female Living Buddha, was also the only nun in Tibet not required to shave her head. This symbolised her assumption of the complete characteristics of human kind, with all its attendant positive and negative elements.

This sort of theological quibble, however, did not provide Lobsang with any easy way out of his immediate predicament. He was apprehensive enough already about the risks of being on Chinese territory again, and the last thing he wanted was complications of a kind with which, even in his most cautious calculations, he had not reckoned. That night, while he was sleeping in the upper berth of his compartment, he was woken by someone gently but insistently tweaking his toe. The Dorji Paghmo's companion, decorous as ever in her nun's habit, was unmistakably beckoning him to follow her. Hastily pulling on some clothes, he made his way to the door of the Dorji Paghmo's suite through which he could see the two ladies inviting him to come in. His only comment on his actual seduction is that when it came down to brass tacks, the Celestial Lady did not differ very much from ordinary Tibetan girls, except that her travelling robe was more complicated to remove than the lay dresses with which he was familiar and that, when it came to the point at which Tibetan convention demands that the lady, however willing, cries 'Stop thief', the Dorji Paghmo appeared to be unaware of the convention.

'She was, in reality, a very innocent girl – learned but, in worldly ways, little more than a child. I felt guilty at taking advantage of her, but overwhelmingly sorry for her in her predicament as a woman. She wasn't pretty, but had an interesting face with a very sweet expression when she allowed it to relax from the rather stern look that she was normally required to assume. She had a beautiful body and was a very passionate girl. She didn't talk too much.' And that, in women with whom he has had serious love affairs, is a quality which Lobsang professes, not always entirely convincingly, to rate very highly.

Fascinating as it would be to know in detail more about the amorous or psychological problems of being the lover of a Living Buddha, Lobsang prefers not to dwell on them. Later, in Tibet, he came to know the Dorji Paghmo more intimately and discussed their relationship in greater depth but, of his Chinese adventure, he merely says 'we never discussed politics or anything like that. I don't think at this time she yet understood very much more about the outside world than most other Tibetans. She liked China because everything was new and exciting, and, partly no doubt, because the Communist authorities paid her such flattering attention.'

The Buddhist Society's goodwill tour of China took it to Peking, Pukhow, Nanking, Wuh Sien, Shanghai, Hangchow,

Hankow and back to Peking. On the final stage back to Tibet, the lamas were taken to visit the important monastery at Sanshi.

Everywhere they were treated as honoured guests and given the best available accommodation. In Peking they stayed at the Peking Hotel, which had just been entirely renovated and was regarded as the last word in government hospitality. In Shanghai it was the skyscraper International Hotel, with its magnificent view over the city. Besides the obvious cultural set pieces, the lamas were taken to communes, factories, universities, chemical plants and mining enterprises. They were overawed by the great textile machines which could spew out seemingly unending rolls of fine cloth at a speed which seemed miraculous to men who were still used to thinking in terms of the single hand-spun robe-length from which their monastic habit was made, and which took four or five months to weave.

Very few of the delegates had ever been out of their country before. They had been brought up in the belief that Tibet, the Holy Land, was in every respect superior to China, which they thought of as a materialistic, inferior world. The scale and grandeur of China, as it was now presented to them, and its technical achievements were something they were quite un-prepared for. No trouble was spared to make them feel honoured guests of the People's Republic. They were formally received by regional authorities and local People's Committees and, in Peking, by national leaders such as Chang Ching-Wu, Personal Secretary to Chairman Mao and Special Representative for Tibet, Prime Minister Chou En-Lai, Deputy Prime Minister Chen Yi and Liu Shao-Chi. They attended sessions of national and regional committees and were entertained at countless receptions, banquets and theatrical performances. At most of the factories they were presented with commemorative gifts.

Lobsang says they were model guests, sitting out the most long-winded speeches or expositions with perfect patience and dignity, even when they understood not a word. They did full honour to the banquets, enjoying the Chinese delicacies which they found so much more varied than their own Tibetan cuisine. They allowed themselves to be bear-led through their exhausting programme without ever showing boredom or impatience. To the Chinese who entertained them, they must have appeared as fascinating relics of a bygone age, with their shaven heads and flowing robes and solemn, unhurried courtesy.

Before leaving Lhasa, Lobsang had borrowed a handsome Tibetan *chiru* from one of his neighbours. This was a light purple robe of the kind worn by the Tibetan lay upper-classes. Lobsang sported it occasionally during the tour and was aware of attracting as much attention in the streets as he had before he left Manchuria in his Russian suit or his father's fur-lined travelling-robe.

As the tour proceeded, Lobsang became more and more aware of its real purpose. Under the seven-year plan for the gradual transformation of Tibet, which China had worked out with the Dalai Lama, the gradual transition from private to state ownership was one of the most delicate issues. As the monasteries owned something like half the land in Tibet, it was vital gradually to convince the most influential lamas to accept the evolution towards the new socialist order. The visit to the great monastery at Sanshi, for instance, was clearly designed to convince them that the Church had nothing to fear from a socialist society. Although Sanshi had only a limited number of monks, it was in some respects stricter in its religious observances than many monasteries in Tibet.

The delegates, in spite of their dignified appearance and seniority were, according to Lobsang, a pretty gullible lot. He became more and more disagreeably aware of how each item in their programme had been carefully calculated to drive home some particular point which Peking was trying to impress on the people of Tibet and their leaders. All the achievements of Chinese art and industry were somehow presented as triumphs of the Communist regime, as if nothing worthwhile had existed before. At his change-idea school in Tientsin Lobsang had been taught by his Communist instructors that the whole pattern of socialist society grew spontaneously as an expression of the will of the people. Now he was treated to a daily demonstration of how Peking was imposing its ideas and policies from the top, leaving neither the Chinese nor the Tibetan people any say in the matter.

Even in Peking Lobsang found it difficult to share the lamas' enthusiasm. He had already seen many of the treasures of this capital. When he was serving in the KMT army during the Civil War he had been quartered in one of the imperial parks – Peihai – where, in the declining days of the Manchu Empire, the wicked old Dowager Empress Tzu-Hsi had squandered the price of a new squadron of warships or a double-track railway linking Peking with Canton on fantastic landscape gardening projects which survive to this day. When he had left home in Dairen, Lobsang remembered regretting having to abandon the centre of Chinese civilisation for the cultural wilderness of the border provinces. But now, on his return, he had little stomach for sentimental pilgrimages. During the visits to cultural monuments he was made to feel a hypocrite by being associated with such a palpable confidence trick on the guileless Tibetans. He took as little part as he decently could in these set excursions. 'When occasion demanded, I made all the right remarks in the right Communist jargon and, if any of the delegates asked me for advice or help, I did my best for them. But apart from that, I became less and less interested in the so-called goodwill aspects of the tour.'

His return to China did, however, enable Lobsang to make one interesting discovery. Peking at this time was officially still on polite and even cordial terms with Moscow. Yet everywhere he detected an undercurrent of anti-Soviet feeling. There is a Chinese saying, 'only two with perfect understanding can co-exist; only two willing to suffer together can be true friends.' The Russians and the Chinese, Lobsang felt, had no longer any basis for sincere friendship. During the Korean war, the Russians had shown by their grudging and mercenary attitude towards aid to their Chinese ally how unwilling they were to share the sacrifices of the Chinese Communists. During Mao Tse-Tung's experiment in liberalisation – the so-called period of the Hundred Flowers – the Chinese people had for a short time been encouraged to speak their minds. The result had been that everyone had begun to criticise the Russians and their policies. China was not yet strong enough, militarily, economically or politically, to do without Soviet support. So Mao had decided that, for a few more years, he must clamp down again and silence the critics of Moscow. These included some famous contemporary figures.

General Chien-Chin, the man who had once been Mao's tutor and had founded the Communist Republic after capturing Nanking in 1948, had made a violent anti-Soviet speech in the People's Consultative Assembly. The editor of Communist China's most important daily newspaper, the *People's Daily*, Hsiao Chun, had published a slashing leading article attacking Moscow's arrogant and patronising attitude towards China.

He used the story of some starving boys gazing through the window of a restaurant where Russian officers attached to Technical Aid Missions to China were eating off the fat of the land, and of how the Russians had them chased away because they thought they were putting out their tongues at them. In fact, the boys were licking the window-panes at the sight of the banquet which the Russians were devouring. The *People's Daily* commented: 'Our friends should at least observe the minimum decencies. The hammer and sickle on the Soviet flag is supposed to symbolise respect and not contempt for the struggling working-classes.' China's most famous lady novelist and poet, Tin Ling, who had been awarded a Stalin prize for her translations from the Russian classics, was another former pro-Soviet leader of Chinese opinion who now railed against Moscow under Mr Khruschev. She had been a disciple of Lu Shun, who had been called the Chinese Maxim Gorki, but now she became so strident in her denunciation of the Soviet Union that she was disgraced on Chairman Mao's orders.

During their stay in Peking, the Dorji Paghmo was received twice by Chairman Mao himself. The Dalai Lama has written his own account of how agreeable Mao could make himself to his distinguished Tibetan visitors. With the Dorji Paghmo, he seems to have been even more cordial and positively gallant. During one reception, he seated her next to him and told her she should be given a new name – the *Cho-Lang*, or Holy Maid of Peking. The Chairman, as a good atheist, may have had his tongue in his cheek. Even so, he was paying her an honour which he cannot have conferred on many of his guests and which brought her immense prestige, both among the Chinese and Tibetan members of the delegation.

Either Lobsang was simply not curious, or she herself was deliberately discreet about her relations with the Communist authorities. Even about such momentous occasions as her audience with Mao, Lobsang does not recall that she talked at any length and, in a general way, she seems to have kept her official and private lives in severely watertight compartments.

In the VIP hotels where the party stayed on their tour, it was easier to conduct a secret affair than on the train, but it continued to have about it an element of French farce. The delegation had been divided into two groups. The Dorji Paghmo was in one, Lobsang in the other. Their programmes were often different, and the accommodation allotted sometimes made it difficult to share the same bedroom without attracting attention. The faithful nun, far from being an encumbrance, turned out to be a godsend. She was always available to take a telephone call, arrange an assignment, carry a message or run out to buy cigarettes when her presence was not required. Even so, she must have witnessed some pretty compromising goings-on, both for her mistress and herself as a lady in Holy Orders. Asked whether he had never found her presence embarrassing, Lobsang replies philosophically, 'Not really. You see, the Dorji Paghmo is so exalted in Tibetan eyes that no one is allowed to lift up their countenance in her presence. Ani-la always had to keep her eyes discreetly downcast.' Ani-la, in Tibetan, is the affectionate form of address for any nun, just as a lama is sometimes affectionately addressed by his friends as 'lama-la'.

Lobsang often asked himself why, of the Chinese members of the delegation, the Dorji Paghmo singled him out for her attentions. 'Perhaps because I was the only one who was not an official. The Tibetans thought of me as just a businessman, and I never used all the boring Communist jargon and conventions in conversation, either with Tibetans or Chinese.' She can scarcely have chosen him because he was unlikely to attract attention. Even for the official goodwill tour of China, he stuck to Western-style suits, which he had had run up for him by a Chinese tailor in

Lhasa. Occasionally he wore the Tibetan *chiru* he had borrowed, but never the drab blue tunic with its stand-up collar which all the other Chinese members of the party affected. His only concession to socialist democracy was to replace the bourgeois tie by a loosely knotted scarf, worn with an open collar and tucked inside his shirt. To their Chinese hosts and passers-by in the street, he must have appeared an odd man out, an unaccountable character strangely miscast among the medieval ecclesiastics and the Maoist zealots, yet with a precarious foot in both camps.

Total discretion was almost impossible under the circumstances. Lobsang admits that he confided in one of the lamas during the journey, and that, after an initial reaction of awe-struck incredulity, he had laughed uproariously. Lobsang also suspects that one of the senior Chinese organisers, a Mr Cha, who worked in the United Front Organisation in Lhasa, knew or guessed a good deal more of what went on between him and the Dorji Paghmo than he realised at the time. It was Mr Cha's business to keep himself informed of delegates' movements. When he began to find it frequently impossible to contact the Dorji Paghmo in her own room, he may have started his own inquiries and drawn his own conclusions. As Lobsang had discovered in Sinkiang, affairs between Chinese and members of 'minority' races were frowned upon except under very special circumstances. In this case there were obvious objections. The Dorji Paghmo was being groomed for an important role as a collaborator in the Chinese plan for Tibet. Anything which might damage her reputation or her authority among her own people was undesirable; and to have her name linked with a person as dubious in Communist eyes as Lobsang, with his former KMT connections, was very undesirable indeed. In retrospect, Lobsang thinks that their affair, which can hardly have failed to reach the ears of the authorities, may well have been one of the reasons for his subsequent troubles.

The only person who seems to have been quite unconcerned was the Dorji Paghmo's father. He belonged to one of the eight great merchant families of Lhasa, which played a special role in the conduct of government under the Dalai Lama's administration. The official treasury was often short of funds, and these eight families were called upon by the government or by the Dalai Lama himself, in his capacity as head of state, to finance policies and enterprises which they were financially unable or politically unwilling to underwrite openly themselves. Lobsang claims that the Khamba rebellion was financed almost entirely in this way, with the knowledge and connivance, but not with the official blessing, of the Dalai Lama. In return for services rendered, these families often accumulated titles and official positions, but their collective function of enabling the administration to act without its right hand officially knowing what its left hand was doing remained unaffected by these promotions. The Dorji Paghmo's father was, by Lobsang's account, a thoroughly likeable fellow. Lobsang says he is not sure whether his daughter ever told him about their affair, but that he always found him affable and relaxed and that, during the mission to China, they became good friends.

For Lobsang, the visit to China was dominated by his relationship with the Dorji Paghmo. He had in any case to be careful about trying to make contacts with friends or relations and, perhaps fortunately, the itinerary did not take him anywhere near his native Manchuria. The rarefied and artificial atmosphere of a conducted propaganda tour did not provide much opportunity even to study the changes in general conditions in China during the four years since he left. On the economic front, things were passing through a difficult period. When he had left Manchuria for Sinkiang, there had been shortages of food and goods which varied from district to district. But food rationing had not been general, and the major experiments in nationalisation of industry and collectivisation of agriculture had not yet begun. Now even the lavish government hospitality and the conducted visits to show projects and enterprises could not conceal, at any rate to a Chinese with Lobsang's background and experience, how uniform and drab life had become for ordinary people.

Halfway through the tour, in Shanghai, he ran into his eldest brother's wife. She was a doctor working in one of the factories his party visited but, apart from the bare news that his brother was alive and still serving his prison sentence, he had no opportunity of seeing her alone or learning any detailed news of the rest of his family. He had known Shanghai well in his KMT days and was able to see for himself that Peking's boasts that this former sink of capitalist iniquity and imperialist decadence and squalor had been transformed into a model socialist city were not quite so justified as the Chinese would have their visitors believe. In the poorer parts of the city there was still great poverty. The night-life of this once pleasure-loving international port had, admittedly, disappeared or been driven underground but for those who knew where to look, it was still possible for anyone who could afford it to entertain himself, if not in the old style, at least in a more agreeable and worldly way than the face of Maoist Puritanism suggested.

These fleeting and rather depressing observations did not close Lobsang's mind to the achievements of the regime. It was a period of intensive building and industrial planning and expansion. 'You have to admit that the Communists can be very efficient at carrying through a project rapidly if it has high priority in the overall national plan. For instance, immediately after the Korean war, it was decided that the dense concentration of industries on which the defence of the country depended was too vulnerable to air attack. Within a few years, half the plants and factories had been moved – lock, stock and barrel – to safer places, often in areas as remote as Mongolia. The necessary skeleton labour force, complete with families, was dispatched to the new site and local workers were recruited and trained to help man the new factories by the time they were complete.'

Lobsang considers that Chairman Mao made several blunders in his attempts to rush through development plans against the advice of more experienced and better educated experts. All the same he acknowledges the tremendous sweep of the Communist plan and the determination to lift the country up through its own efforts. He criticises the timing of individual policies and the ruthless disregard for the feelings of ordinary people. But he doubts whether any regime less dedicated or dictatorial could have accomplished what Mao did to unite the country and consolidate the central government's effective authority over the length and breadth of China and its outlying provinces. He shows surprising detachment in weighing methods he detested against aims he often respected. At heart, Lobsang remains very much a Chinese patriot, glad to see his country strong and restored to the front rank of world powers. As long ago as 1968, when he was in London, he predicted how quickly the other great powers, including the United States, would change their attitudes towards China and acknowledge the reality of her growing military strength and self-dependence upon her own resources. He also recognises the difficulties which the regime faced as the quarrel between China and the Soviet Union deepened and Moscow began to obstruct China's material advance by every means at its disposal. In his wanderings he saw much evidence of Soviet malevolence. From the earliest days after the Communist takeover in China he had been disgusted by Moscow's unscrupulousness in making Peking pay out of her own inadequate resources for all the much publicised Soviet technical aid.

'They took all the food and all the raw materials they could lay their hands on. And for everything they supplied in return they drove a tough bargain. When the Americans gave aid to the Chinese Nationalists in Formosa, they at least wrote off debts which would have crippled Chiang Kai-Shek's government in exile and backed their political support with many outright gifts.'

As the Buddhist Society's delegation wound its way back towards the frontiers of Tibet, Lobsang was more interested in such considerations about the new China and her destiny than in the impressions of his fellow delegates of what they had seen during their trip. None of the lamas seem to have drawn the conclusion that the place of religion or the power of their monasteries in Tibet was directly threatened by the Chinese takeover. 'Perhaps they didn't confide in me because they were uncertain to what extent I was acting as a spy for the Communists. And I confess that I never tried to raise the subject with them.' When the party got back to Chinghai, Lobsang was glad enough to say goodbye to the lamas, shed the mantle of co-secretary of the Buddhist Society and turn his attention to his own neglected business.

In the provincial capital of Sining, most of the delegates stayed in a government guest-house until transport could be organised to take them back to their various monasteries in Tibet. Lobsang had contacts among the road haulage community in town and, through one of the drivers, heard of a big ten-ton Canadian truck, belonging to a co-operative society, which was for sale. Like most of the lorries in this part of the world, it needed putting in order, but it would enable him to extend the scope of his trucking business and he decided it was a good buy. The negotiations for its purchase gave Lobsang a pretext to detach himself from the delegation. He moved into the home of one of his driver acquaintances who had a workshop of his own and had agreed to help him overhaul the big truck.

This sudden outburst of activity enabled Lobsang to escape the tedious business of formal farewells and to cut short his leave-taking from the Dorji Paghmo. To tell the truth, the strenuous manual work into which he now plunged helped to take his mind off troublesome speculation about his relationship with the Dorji Paghmo and the disturbing unanswered questions it posed for both of them. She too had urgent business to attend to, and in the end they parted with nothing more dramatic than mutual promises to meet in Lhasa where, in the normal course of things, both of them expected to be before long.

IO

A CHAPTER OF ACCIDENTS

After the charade of the goodwill mission to China, Lobsang enjoyed the company of the rough, uncomplicated fellows who helped him get the big Canadian truck ready for the road. He knew many of these Chinghai drivers, and had often traded watches and lengths of cloth from India with them against mechanical spare parts or tools which were more easily available from the Chinese side. They addressed him familiarly and affectionately as *Ta-Keh* or Elder Brother. After three weeks in Sining, everything was ready and a crew of five recruited. This was necessary not only for relief at the wheel of such a heavy truck across the rough country between Sining and Lhasa, but also for security in the wilder and more desolate areas and to provide the necessary manpower for all the hazards of camping along the route. It was already autumn. The weather was crisp and clear, and the truck was fast, strong and ideally suited for the expedition.

Their journey took them through the Kunlun Mountains, the great barrier which separates the province of Chinghai from Tibet. Perhaps because he had always had other preoccupations when travelling, Lobsang rarely volunteers anything more than the most perfunctory description of the landscape, architecture or local flora and fauna of the places through which his adventures have taken him. But in recounting one particular day in the high Kunlun plateau, he becomes almost lyrical.

'Up there, the valley is so broad that it is almost a plain. It is a great open space between the high peaks. Everything was covered with snow and there was in any case no regular track. The reflection of the sun off the hills and the ground made everything sparkle; it was like driving along a dazzling hall of mirrors. Suddenly we saw a herd of wild asses. It was the first time I had seen these animals which are, I believe, very rare. They live always at high altitudes in uninhabited areas and are very shy. I have never heard of anyone catching one or keeping one in captivity. They were magnificent animals – bigger than a big horse, with a long deep body and a low-slung back between a high arched neck and very strong prominent hindquarters. Although in fact their coat must be very thick to keep out the cold, it gives the appearance of being short and glossy. In this bright light, they gave off a high sheen, at once velvety and almost metallic. The colour was unlike anything I have ever seen – between grey and purple, but always changing and glinting in the sunlight. As soon as they saw us, they started to gallop.'

Lobsang's whole face lights up as he describes the excitement of the chase. 'Our truck could do seventy miles an hour on a road. In the snow, over rough, trackless ground, we of course did less than that. But we chased them flat out, on and off, for over an hour without managing to close with them. I've never seen an animal with such speed and stamina, although the wild bison and rhinos I saw later in Bhutan take some beating as strong runners. I am satisfied that the wild asses were incomparably faster than the fastest horse. Their legs are very thick and must be as strong as steel. The sight of them streaking away from us gave me an immense longing to possess one. I tried to reckon the chances of running one down, making rough calculations of our height off the ground, our speed, the weight of the asses, and the strength of the bodywork of the truck. Even with such a solid vehicle the impact of one of those animals at full stretch would have been no joke, but I decided we could just about get away with it. I put my foot right down, convinced that sooner or later, as long as the herd stayed on the plain, their wind must give out. But it never did. If we stopped, the entire herd would stop too. The other drivers were as excited as I was and, as we roared down the valley, they whooped and shouted at the top of their lungs. In the end, the herd just wheeled away to the right up into the mountains, apparently by no means exhausted.'

More than once in his life, Lobsang has lost everything he possessed. In terms of material things he is not particularly

acquisitive. But he confesses that, for a moment, he passionately
coveted 'just one skin' of those wild asses of Kunlun. There was
something about their magnificent strength and independence
that particularly appealed to him. At the end of the chase, he
admits that he would have been disappointed if they had allowed
him to catch up with them. But he would still treasure a Kunlun
rug to remind him of the exact colour and texture of their
glistening coats.

After dropping his crew off in Lhasa, Lobsang headed straight
on southwards in the Canadian truck to Phari, an important trading
post near the junction of the frontiers of India and Bhutan. He had
business in Yatung at the bottom of the Chumbi valley, the
triangular spit of Tibetan territory that points down between
Bhutan and Sikkim and through which the old caravan trade
route between India and Lhasa used to pass. As there was not yet
a proper motor road between Phari and Yatung, Lobsang left the
big ten-and-a-half tonner in Phari, to be loaded with locally consigned goods or freight that would be sent up from Yatung by
jeep or in a lighter truck. By the time he had finished his business
in Yatung and got back to Phari, the big lorry was loaded and almost immediately Lobsang saw it off on its journey to Lhasa
with five passengers, the driver and his assistant.

The weather had been bad, the road was in poor repair, and the
rivers along the route were swollen and dangerous. Only fourteen
miles out of Phari the road runs parallel to a small torrent, with
nothing but a low retaining wall dividing them. At this point the
river runs through a deep, rocky gorge. The wall, made of
unbonded stones, had been undermined by the unusually high
flood, which had caused a bulge of loosened stones on the roadside of the wall. The rear wheel of the truck, which was only
fitted with single tyres, struck the bulge with such force that the
wall collapsed. The weight of the heavy lorry caused the edge of
the road to crumble and the truck slowly keeled over and toppled
into the river. The two passengers nearest the riverside were a
well-to-do old lady and her nine-year-old granddaughter, dressed
in their ceremonial best and wearing all their jewellery for a visit
to the Panchen Lama in Shigatse. At the moment of impact they

were immediately flung into the river. The other three passengers managed to cling on to the bodywork of the truck. In the narrows through the gorge the stream ran deep and exceptionally fast. The fall of the truck was broken by a large boulder a little way out in the stream. The side of the truck hit it a shattering blow which loosened some of the freight and pitched it into the river.

The driver and his assistant managed to scramble out to safety. Seeing no sign of the old lady and the girl, they ran frantically almost a mile down-stream, thinking that they must have been carried away. In fact they had been sucked down by a swirling race round the big boulder on to which the truck had fallen and pinned by the downward current under submerged rocks which prevented them either from being carried downstream or floating up again to the surface. They must have drowned almost immediately. When their bodies were recovered two months later by searchers paid by Lobsang, the local people told him that, with the river in spate, rescue would in any case have been out of the question. It was even impossible to salvage the truck itself. For three months it lay in full view of every driver and pedestrian using the road.

The death of the passengers and the loss of the freight, which was made up mainly of flour in sacks and sealed wooden and steel crates, was serious enough for Lobsang. To make matters worse, the impact of the fall had smashed open some of the crates and spilled their contents into the stream. There, on the river bed, plainly visible but impossible to reach, lay a collection of rifles, pistols and automatic arms. A consignment of rifles would not have particularly surprised the Tibetans. Many of them went armed as a matter of course, and Lhasa at this time was a lawless city. Robbery with violence was common and many people carried a gun. Under the Dalai Lama's administration firearms were not forbidden and could be bought freely on the open market.

Chinese who passed the scene of the accident, however, certainly saw this miscellaneous collection of weapons in a different light. The Khamba uprising was now in full swing, and for the

Chinese gun-running on this scale could only be intended for the guerrillas. Much later, Lobsang learnt that within days of the accident a full report was sent to the Chinese central government and that, as a result, photographs of himself as a wanted person were publicly displayed in several Chinese cities. One of his brothers in Mukden had tried to send a warning message to him in Lhasa but, by the time it was delivered to his workshop, it was already too late.

At the time of the accident the truck was in charge of a Chinese from Shantung named Wu Han Ting. He had come to the workshop soon after Lobsang opened it, looking for a job. He had no mechanical qualifications, but was young and willing to learn. Gradually he had become Lobsang's right-hand man. He turned out to have an excellent head for business and was absolutely honest and reliable. First he took over most of the office work and, when the trucking business took Lobsang more and more out of Lhasa, he left Wu in charge with growing confidence. He grew to respect him as a partner and a real friend. 'We were like brothers.'

After the accident, Wu Han Ting stayed with the lorry to continue the search for the missing passengers, and sent an urgent message to Lobsang in Phari. Lobsang insists that neither of them knew the contents of the sealed crates. They were boxes of a type commonly used in Tibet, both for caravans and road transport. The man who had consigned them and travelled with them was the agent of Shanwang Surkhang, a senior minister in the Dalai Lama's government and one of the moving spirits behind the Khamba uprising. He was himself a man of some distinction, and had received a special award for meritorious service from the Dalai Lama. He was accompanied by a courier who also turned out to be a Khamba guerrilla of some importance.

The whole incident illustrated the increasingly confused situations which stemmed from the compromises which the Dalai Lama made with the Chinese authorities. On the one hand, he had committed himself to co-operate with the Chinese in the planning of the Autonomous Region; on the other, the fact that he continued to control the internal administration of the country meant that the Khambas, more often than not with the connivance of some of his officials, were able to continue to organise resistance and supply themselves with men. The Chinese army was still thinly spread, and then only in the most strategic places in Tibet. There were, for instance, no Chinese administrative officers in Phari and months after the accident Tibetans were actually able to salvage arms from the truck when the river subsided and sell them on the open market.

Lobsang's first concern was for the driver of the truck. He was a Chinese who had migrated to Chinghai from Manchuria. He was thoroughly scared and desperately anxious about what would become of his wife and family in Chinghai if he was put in jail in Tibet. His immediate anxiety was that the relations of the drowned passengers might blame him for their death and take the law into their own hands to punish him. Lobsang gave him a pistol and told him to make his way to Lhasa, collect some money and his own belongings from the workshop and take the first safe opportunity to return to Chinghai. He seems, in fact, to have helped himself liberally to Lobsang's clothes from the workshop before making himself scarce.

The next priority was to to settle the case of the old lady and her granddaughter with the local Tibetan authorities. One of Lobsang's first calls was on the responsible official in the provincial capital of Shigatse, some seventy miles to the north-west of Phari. This official explained that the proper procedure was to report the affair in Gyantse, in whose administrative district the accident had taken place. There the appropriate authorities would deal with any claims arising out of the accident and, if necessary, report to him as their superior in due course. The inspector in Gyantse dealt first with the claim of a small trader who had lost some boxes of watches and luxury goods. He put their value at thirty to forty thousand silver dollars. Luckily for Lobsang, the inspector had an accurate idea of this merchant's resources and the scale of his business. He knew the claim was grossly inflated and made him accept three thousand silver dollars as fair compensation.

The case of the drowned passengers was much more protracted

and complicated. The standard rate of compensation for deaths in accidents involving Chinese army vehicles had been fixed at five hundred and fifteen silver dollars. Under Tibetan law, there was no such fixed limit. The lady in question was a person of considerable standing and witnesses were able to establish that, apart from her usual ornaments, she was wearing for the occasion a necklace of valuable *zhis*, the curious brown and white striped lozenge-shaped stones which Tibetans prize so highly. A funeral befitting her position would also be a costly affair.

During weeks of complicated litigation, which kept Lobsang shuttling between Phari, Gyantse and Shigatse, he bumped into a most useful acquaintance. He was a high-ranking Tibetan lama in his early thirties named Chunsin Losang Yishi. He had entered a monastery as a poor man's son, but had won a valuable scholarship which was only awarded every twelve years, and had shown such brilliance in his theological studies that he had been promoted to the high ecclesiastical rank of *Chunsin* while still in his twenties. He had then blotted his official copybook by leaving his monastery without asking permission from the Tibetan government and going to China. In Peking, he took a course at the School of Nationalities. Both he and his wife learnt excellent Mandarin but, after three years in China, they separated. He returned to Tibet, but his wife remained in China and became the first Tibetan woman to broadcast on Peking Radio's Tibetan language service.

Back in Lhasa, Losang Yishi had been cold-shouldered by the Dalai Lama and had not been given any official appointment corresponding to his rank. He had then paid a longish visit to India and was on his way home when Lobsang met him. He admitted quite openly that many Tibetans suspected him of being a Communist agent, but Lobsang is convinced that he was a loyal Tibetan. This is supported by the fact that, in the great exodus from Lhasa after the Dalai Lama's flight to India in March 1959, he was shot down by the Chinese army in the act of filming the massacre of unarmed Tibetans who were trying to escape from Lhasa.

Losang Yishi was a friend of the senior Tibetan magistrate in

Phari, with whom the compensation for the old lady's death had to be agreed. He helped Lobsang to reach a settlement of eighteen thousand silver dollars to cover all claims for loss of life and possessions. Lobsang was naturally anxious to get the case disposed of with as little fuss and public attention as possible. He accepted the Phari magistrate's valuation without quibbling. Even so, it took something like a month to complete the necessary formalities.

With the Tibetan claims officially settled, Lobsang was still apprehensive about how the whole affair would affect his standing with the Chinese authorities. Immediately after he had reached the scene of the accident, Wu Han Ting had suggested that they should take whatever money they had and make for India without delay. 'I made a great mistake not to take his advice. We had plenty of money and we could still have got away without trouble. We were very near the India border and there were almost no Chinese security forces in the area. Looking back, there is no doubt that it would have been the wisest thing to do.' Looking back, too, Lobsang is tempted to detect a chain of bad luck dating from his association with the Dorji Paghmo. In spite of his real affection for her, he still had pangs of conscience about their relationship. 'In China we have an old superstition that an affair with a nun brings bad luck.'

When he eventually did return to Lhasa, things at the workshop looked normal enough. There was plenty to attend to after his long absence, and he was just getting back into the swing of his Lhasa routine when the blow fell. Five days after his return, in October 1957, very early in the morning, Lobsang was seeing off one of his lorries. It was October and the nights in Lhasa were already chilly. To heat the cold engine he needed a blow lamp and, not finding one handy, he jumped on to his motor bike and hurried round to a neighbour's house to borrow one. When he got back to the workshop, he saw five men with bicycles whom he immediately recognised as belonging to the Chinese Army Political Division. Keeping the engine of his motor bike running, he asked the riders their business. 'We've been waiting for you,' answered one of the security men. 'We've got some vehicles which need attention, and we'd like you to repair them.'

Lobsang had no illusions about what they had come for. He tried to gain time by saying that he would come down later when he had finished the job he was doing. 'No, now,' they insisted peremptorily. When they told him to leave his motor bike behind, on the pretext that the road surface was too bad in the place where the vehicles were stranded, Lobsang's suspicions became a certainty. He was carrying a revolver, as he normally did, and did not want it to be found on him when he was arrested. So, shouting that he had to give a friend an urgent message, he opened his throttle and tore around the corner of the workshop. There he threw his gun through the window of a house belonging to a Tibetan neighbour. He was the aristocrat who had fallen on hard times through his passion for gambling. He had been a man of great wealth and social standing but had lost everything, including his family mansion and estates. Lobsang, to whom he also owed gambling debts, had done him many favours and had become a trusted friend. When he came to the window, woken by a noise of broken glass, Lobsang held up his hands with his wrists together, as if manacled, to explain to him why he had hurled his gun through his bedroom window and aroused him at such an ungodly hour.

The security men had run after him and heard the crash of the window. Lobsang explained it by saying that, in order to deliver his message, he had had to throw a stone through the window to wake his friend. Most of the workshop hands who were already on the job appeared unaware of what was happening. Presumably they knew that Lobsang had connections with the Chinese Army Authorities and assumed that there was nothing sinister in this early morning call. 'But there was one old blacksmith, from Shantung, who realised that I was being taken away for good. He looked at me despairingly and I could see that he was in tears. I was moved by his compassion, but it also brought home to me chillingly that this was indeed probably the finish.'

He followed his escort the short distance to the headquarters of the Preparatory Committee of the Tibetan Autonomous Region. The army intelligence and political departments were now housed in a new building in which Lobsang's office as secretary of the Buddhist Society had been before he left on his Chinese tour. He was led into a room where a Chinese intelligence officer was waiting for him, flanked by two Tibetan officials who were working with the Chinese army. This officer informed him that he was under arrest. Lobsang asked him on what charge, and was told, 'It is too early to say. I am sending you to jail to give you time to think things over. Then you must tell us what you have done.'

Lobsang knew all about the Communist technique of forcing prisoners to be their own accusers but, for want of anything better to say, he began to protest that he had done nothing to warrant arrest. 'We know, we know,' the officer replied in a voice that stung Lobsang into retorting, 'Well, if you know, there is no need to ask me.' The officer gave him such a cruel look that Lobsang judged further argument inadvisable. 'In Communist China, once they put you in prison, you're finished. It doesn't matter whether you're guilty or innocent. Even if they eventually release you, you remain an outcast and cannot hope to rehabilitate yourself.' He had already been searched for arms, to the visible chagrin of the officer when nothing was found on him. Now everything was emptied from his pockets and his belt and shoelaces were removed. He was taken to a building in the centre of town in which the officers belonging to the Political Branch of the Chinese Army were billeted. Behind the main building the Chinese had rebuilt an old house as a jail with barred windows. On the ground floor fifteen or sixteen other prisoners were detained – mostly Tibetans, as far as Lobsang could see. He was locked in a separate cell, where he was to spend three months contemplating his errors before he was paraded again before his interrogators.

Once again, the new world that Lobsang had built so laboriously for himself had collapsed around him like a pack of cards. This time, from the look of things, there was no way out.

II

❦

TRIBULATIONS WITHOUT TRIAL

Of the thirteen months that Lobsang was to spend in the Chinese jail in Lhasa, the first three were much the worst. To begin with they were spent in solitary confinement. This, and being suddenly reduced to total inactivity, would have been demoralising enough for someone as restless and energetic as Lobsang in any circumstances. He reproached himself for what he now realised was his folly in refusing to listen to Wu Han Ting's advice to leave Tibet immediately after the accident and in imagining, even for a moment, that the Communists would overlook the whole incident. How could he have been so naive and so reckless?

What tortured him even more was the nagging uncertainty about the real reason for his arrest. He asked himself endlessly which the Communists were likely to regard as the worst offence – the death of the passengers, the discovery of the arms or his association with the Dorji Paghmo. When he had spent hours trying unsuccessfully to resolve this riddle, he found himself wondering whether it might not simply be that his old KMT connections had led them to the conclusion that he was, after all, still an active Kuomintang agent.

It was already autumn, but he had been given neither a mattress nor blankets. He had to sleep on straw on the wooden floor in the clothes he was wearing when he had been arrested. His guards were soldiers from Sechowan, whose attitude towards prisoners was uncompromising. They were simply 'enemies of the people'.

'A Communist jail is worse than a Communist pigsty. You make one mistake and they throw you into prison. Then your whole life is finished.' Lobsang was too agitated about the nature of the charges which he would have to answer to try to come to terms with captivity. In the event, he could have saved himself the trouble of beating his brains out trying to think of the best way to deal with specific charges. None were ever formally preferred against him.

On his admission to prison he had been interrogated about the truck incident and its immediate sequel. He was asked why he had not immediately reported it to the Chinese authorities in Lhasa, and why he had paid nearly three times the regulation Chinese army indemnity for the death of his Tibetan passengers. The implication was that, by agreeing to the Tibetan magistrate's assessment, he had deliberately tried to make the Chinese authorities appear mean and heartless; alternatively, that he had agreed to such inflated compensation because he was trying to hush up something suspicious.

They had asked him point-blank, 'Why were you selling arms to the Khambas?' and he had replied, 'I am a businessman. As you know, I work as a subcontractor for the Chinese authorities and they are my main source of income. If I were really in the gun-running business on the scale that you suggest, I would not have needed to accept work of that kind.' 'How do you come to have so many Tibetan acquaintances? And why are you on such intimate terms with Tibetan officials?'

'My sort of business brings me into touch with people of all sorts and I am naturally on friendly terms with some of them.'

This first interrogation convinced Lobsang that the Communist authorities had kept a very close check on his movements ever since he had left the army. In his more hopeful moments, he tried to persuade himself that the fact that they had not made any charges against him meant that they had no really damaging evidence. Their questions, he argued, had been framed in an attempt to trap him, by some slip of the tongue, into betraying some complicity in encouraging the growing mood of Tibetan opposition to China. In 1957, posters, printed in Tibetan and Chinese, had appeared on the walls in Lhasa, stating that the Dalai Lama was the head of a sovereign Tibetan state, and not merely the representative of a Tibetan republic forming part of China. This and other demonstrations of discontent had led the Chinese army to crack down hard for the first time on all signs of dissidence. Lobsang now wondered whether they had uncovered some KMT influence in spreading anti-Communist propaganda and whether, because of his contact with Tibetans of all classes, he had come under suspicion of being part of a systematic network.

By his own admission, he must have been an awkward prisoner. This was a military jail and, as a former lieutenant-colonel, he knew the Communist military regulations and the rights they gave to prisoners. He has a natural authority and a quick temper and is not an easy man to browbeat or intimidate. Army regulations set a limit to the time a soldier could be detained without trial. Lobsang took every occasion to remind his jailers of these theoretical rights.

After some weeks, bedding and blankets arrived mysteriously from outside. He guessed that they must have been brought by his workshop staff, but was never told who was his benefactor. He had already put in a demand to be allowed to collect a change of clothing and now made a formal request to be taken before the competent authority and told at least of the reason for his detention. After three months he was taken to the new building just outside the centre of Lhasa, which housed the main offices of the army's Political Division. He was taken before an elderly major in civilian clothes, who had been seconded to the joint Sino-Tibetan administration. His interrogation lasted an hour and a half, during part of which several other officers came and went. It followed the now familiar pattern, but with some ominous variations:

'May I know what I am being held here for?'

'We think you are working for the overthrow of the Chinese civil and revolutionary government.'

'I am much too unimportant a person to attempt anything like that. You can't put that sort of cap on me.'

'On the contrary, we believe it fits you exactly.'

There followed all the old questions. 'Why did you leave the Communist army? Why did you leave China? Who sent you to Lhasa? Where do your funds come from?' The major always came back to the same point. 'If you wish to get out of here, you must tell us frankly what you have done. We shall find out anyway, but for the moment we have no time to waste on making charges or checking your claim that the money which stands to your account in the bank was earned by legitimate means and mainly through government contracts.'

Lobsang tried to vary his tactics by saying that if the Communists had decided to abolish private enterprise and seize his assets, he would be prepared to accept that he was a capitalist and that his wealth should be confiscated. The major replied that this was not the point at issue and that, as he perfectly well knew, private business was still tolerated for certain purposes. Lobsang protested that he had indulged in no anti-communist activity and that, if it could be proved that he had, he was prepared to face the consequences; but that it was impossible for him to invent some imaginary offence. Did this mean that he would have to stay in jail indefinitely?

'That is so,' replied the major blandly. 'We know you have been very busy in Tibet, moving here, there and everywhere. We shall find out on whose behalf, however long it takes us – unless, of course, you save us the trouble by making a clean breast of it now.' In that case, Lobsang retorted, he wished to repeat his request to be allowed to collect some spare clothing since his stay looked like being a long one, and winter was approaching. To his surprise, the major gave orders for him to be taken, under armed escort, to his home.

He found the whole place ransacked from top to bottom. Floors had been ripped up and the ground beneath the boards dug up, in places to a depth of several feet. His safe had been forced, and the entire premises, both in his living quarters and the workshop, searched with a fine-tooth comb. He was closely watched and so could not verify exactly what had been removed. His fleet of trucks had presumably been commandeered by the Chinese army. While he was collecting a few clothes, he noticed that even the inside band of an old felt hat had been burnt through in several places, presumably as a possible hiding-place of secret documents.

The ruthlessness of the search and the complete disregard for his property confirmed the impression that the Communists had from the beginning decided that there was no question of releasing him. Why else should they have allowed him to visit his workshop? Unless it was one more calculated attempt to undermine his morale and force him into a confession? Another bad sign, he reflected, was that no one at any stage made any inquiries about his personal finances or possessions. In cases of prisoners serving short sentences, he knew it was usual to make arrangements for the settlement of their personal day-to-day affairs during their stay in jail. When, for instance, he had told the authorities that his bank account could be checked, so as to verify his claim that his money had been honestly earned and did not come from sinister outside powers, they had shown not the slightest interest and said that such pointless investigations were a waste of time.

In retrospect, Lobsang sees the comic side of his futile dialogue with the Communist major. 'It's hopeless arguing with Communists,' he says with rueful exasperation. 'You start in the wrong, and remain in the wrong until you say what they want you to say. They can't lose. The funny thing is that, long before my arrest, I once invented a story about it to amuse my workshop boys. I called it 'Confucious and the Argue-Hall', and it went something like this:

Long ago, in the time of Confucius, there lived in the south of China a family renowned for its prowess and sophistry in intellectual debate. Confucius, who was born in the north of China, in Shantung, travelled south to find out about this famous family and see what kind of wisdom they had to offer. At the front-door of their impressive mansion he was received by a youth of sixteen or seventeen. He said he would like to ask some questions to which he or his family could no doubt supply the answers. He was led into another room where he was handed over to an older man who also declined to answer his questions but took him into an inner sanctum where a venerable bearded figure was seated behind a table. 'I have heard', said Confucius, 'that you call your house the House of Challenge-Question or Verbal Duel, or even Argument Hall. I am curious to know what exactly that means.' 'It means', replied the sage, 'that one of us puts forward an idea or proposition, and the other refutes it. Then we see which of us is right. Of course, you have to pay a price for the privilege of putting your idea to the test.' Confucius put down a modest stake of five ounces of silver and, deferring to his host's age, offered him the honour of beginning. 'My contention', said the old man, 'is that although you are known throughout the land as a sage and a saint, in fact you are not.' 'Why?' asked Confucius. 'In your teachings, you have instructed your disciples that, while their parents are still alive, it is an offence against filial piety to travel abroad and desert them. May I inquire after your own parents' health?' 'They are, I am glad to say, both in excellent health.' 'But you', exclaimed the old man triumphantly, 'are here in the south. Yet you are a native of Shantung, a far-away province. You have broken your own precept. So, you see, you lose.' And he pocketed the silver.

Confucius was amused and a little abashed, when there entered Chu Kwai Li, one of the eight Olympians of the old Chinese pantheon. He is always represented as limping with a crutch, carrying a gourd slung over his shoulder, and is often popularly referred to as Lame Li. Having greeted Confucius and asked how he had fared, Li said he would try to win back his loss for him, and put up a forfeit of twenty ounces of silver. Once again, the master of the house opened the debate. 'What is in that gourd you carry?' he asked. 'Medicines and remedies,' answered Lame Li, 'panaceas for every ailment.' 'In that case,' said the sophist, 'I'll say you're a liar'. 'And I', said Li with some heat, 'will say I am not.' 'Indeed you are. Why, you claim to cure everything, but you haven't even managed to make your lame leg whole. So you lose.'

The third customer was a butcher, a great hefty fellow with a pocket full of money he had just taken at market. He came swaggering in, still brandishing his butcher's knife in one hand and the balance he used for weighing the meat in the other. He banged down eighty ounces of silver and said, 'I'll challenge you, master, for the lot.' 'With so much at stake,' replied the sophist mockingly, 'perhaps you would care to open the debate yourself.' 'Certainly,' said the butcher, 'I'll say your head weighs exactly eight pounds, to the ounce.' 'And I say it doesn't, and I defy you to prove it.' 'Easy enough,' smiled the butcher, 'I cut off your head with this knife and then we put it on my balance here and see who's right. Perhaps,' turning to Confucius and Lame Li, 'you two gentlemen would care to assist me?' 'No, no,' cried the Master in terror. 'Then you lose, master, you lose.'

'What I was driving at with my story,' says Lobsang, 'is that no one can argue with people who make their own rules and also have the power to cut off your head to settle the argument in their favour. Not even saints or gods or the wily old Master of the Argument-Hall. At the time, all the workshop boys thought it a great joke, but it proved too prophetic to be funny.'

12

A POEM IN LHASA JAIL

Lobsang's interview with the Major had two direct consequences. It made him finally resign himself to the fact that there was no chance of quick release, but it brought an end to his solitary confinement. He was put in a room which, during the time he occupied it, housed anything between ten and twenty other prisoners. Conditions were in some ways worse than in his single cell and communication between prisoners was forbidden. A single tin served as a common urinal and visits to the prison lavatory were limited to one in the morning and one in the evening, with guards standing watch outside the open door. Still, there was human fellowship of a sort, and after the utter loneliness of his cell, this was a great consolation for Lobsang. The prisoners, nearly all Chinese, conversed in signs and whispers, and new arrivals brought in scraps of news from the outside world.

Now that he had abandoned hope of freedom in a foreseeable future, Lobsang began concentrating on ways of shutting out from his mind the thoughts that drive a prisoner to despair. 'The golden rule', he says, 'is never to ask yourself "how long will I be here for?" Occupy yourself in any way, however trivial or mechanical, to banish that question. Count slowly up to a hundred, then another hundred, then another. For a change, imagine you are preparing and eating a meal. This can be very time-consuming if done conscientiously. Slowly, you cut the pork or the chicken into small pieces and slice the vegetables, paying infinite attention to the exact shape and pattern of the pieces. Then you go through the cooking processes – frying, steaming and stirring, as deliberately as possible. When everything is ready, imagine you are eating, piece by piece, slowly, slowly ... spinning it out, chewing every mouthful, until the bowl is quite

empty. Properly done, this routine has saved you from demoralising thoughts for a surprisingly long time. Better still, make your
mind a complete blank. Don't think of anything at all. Not at all
an easy exercise, but can be done with practice.'

Lobsang has never quite lost this ability to switch off at will.
Years later, in Hong Kong, he remembers occasions when, in a
room full of garrulous Cantonese whose conversation did not
particularly interest him, people asked him what he was thinking
about to make him so silent and pensive. 'And when I answered
"Nothing", they wouldn't believe me, but it was quite true.'

Not that Lobsang was ever in danger of acquiring seriously
contemplative tendencies. His truculent instincts still occasionally
asserted themselves. Soon after he was moved in with the other
prisoners, he organised a protest against the prison food. The jail
shared a kitchen with the living quarters of the political branch
officers, and the prisoners' diet was sometimes supplemented by
left-overs from the officers' mess. Lobsang, in his best military
manner, complained that this was contrary to regulations. The
only result was that the prisoners' food was then strictly limited to
an unvarying menu of the waste material from bean curd, water
and the scantiest possible ration of rice. When the other prisoners
asked to be allowed to go back to the old regime, their request
was curtly refused.

Luckily for Lobsang, during the months he spent in Yatung
immediately before his arrest, he had been living extremely well,
and claims that he weighed around two hundred and forty pounds.
He is six foot two inches, broad-shouldered and big-boned.
Even so, he must have been remarkably well-covered, although
he says that he never appeared really fat. After sixteen months
in prison, he weighed under one hundred and seventy pounds.

What Lobsang found hardest to put up with in his Lhasa jail
was the atmosphere of deliberately sustained tension. 'There was
never any relaxation. Everything had to be done by numbers.
Get up. March to the lavatory. Morning meal. Study Communist newspaper, with room-leader obliged to make propaganda
commentaries on its contents. And so on throughout the entire
day. When the prisoners were not doing anything in particular,

they had to sit in their alloted place with their backs to the wall. There was always an armed guard on duty, watching us and ready to shout at us and abuse us for the slightest departure from the routine that was laid down. This discipline and surveillance was kept up even at night. Evening meal. March to the lavatory. Nine thirty, sleep. We all had to lie in the same position so that, after so many hours a guard could shout "Turn", and everyone had to turn over on to the other side.' Lobsang still speaks bitterly about the Communist habit of treating all prisoners – even those who, like himself, had never been charged or convicted – as outcasts and enemies of the people. What is curious is that he took refuge so much in mental abstraction and never seems to have tried to pass the time by improvising ways of using any of the manual skills he possessed. Even allowing for the fact that the prisoners were given no recreation or facilities, it is extraordinary that anyone with Lobsang's dexterity and ingenuity should not have found some secret way of employing his hands to keep himself occupied. He recalls only one occasion when he tried his hand at anything creative, and that ended in disaster.

It was not forbidden for prisoners to have paper or pencils. They often borrowed a sheet of paper from the prisoner whose duty it was to do the washing for the officers in the adjoining billets and who had a notebook in which to keep his laundry lists. One day Lobsang jotted down a four-line poem in conventional Mandarin form. Like most Mandarin verse, it is virtually impossible to translate satisfactorily. It contains nuances which depend on the exact juxtaposition of characters and the concepts they represent, so that all sorts of allusive meanings are implied. Translated literally, Lobsang's poem reads: 'The sun comes up in the morning. In the evening it departs. The jail is always dark. You never see the sun. Through the iron bars the soldiers watch by day and night.'

The piece of paper on which Lobsang had scribbled his verses was picked up by one of the guards, who handed it over to the officer on duty. This officer was incensed because the word that Lobsang had used for 'soldiers' was an old pre-revolutionary usage dating from the days when the military profession was

looked down upon by cultivated people in China. It conveyed the
idea that soldiers were rough, low, contemptible fellows, as in
English one might say 'the brutal and licentious soldiery'.

Lobsang was duly upbraided, and his poem was read aloud to
the other prisoners and made the occasion for a moral homily. 'In
the days when the people were still the victims of autocratic
education', the officer told his audience, 'there used to be a saying
that "good steel never makes nails and good people never become
soldiers." But we Communists have another saying: "Workers
and peasants are uncontaminated people, and uncontaminated
people join the People's Army." ' Challenged to explain what he
had meant by his poem, Lobsang told the officer that he must
have read some such idea in an old book in his childhood, and
that this accounted for his use of archaic words and concepts. The
officer was not satisfied and asked his assembled room-mates
whether they thought the poem was 'correctly orientated'. Dutifully and unanimously, they had to vote that it was erroneous
both in thought and content. Not that Lobsang was likely to be
much impressed by the literary judgment of prison officers. 'Most
of these Communist officers, particularly the older ones, had only
learnt to read and write after they joined the army. To give the
Communists their due, they did use the army as a great educator
and turned a lot of ignorant bumpkins into more or less articulate
people. During the Civil War, when they came to a new area, they
always used to send an officer to talk to the villagers. He would
begin by saying that he understood their problems because he was
the son of a poor peasant and had been illiterate before he
volunteered for the Liberation Army. They were very clever in
this sort of way at spreading the idea that the army was identified
with humble people and that it was also a civilising force.'

Even the incident of the poem made a welcome diversion in the
deadly monotony of prison life. One of the worst privations for
Lobsang was not being able to smoke. He is normally a very
heavy cigarette-smoker and invariably keeps a packet and a lighter
tucked half under his pillow, with an ashtray within arm's reach
in case he wakes in the night. 'There was no question of smoking
or of receiving a prisoner's tobacco ration. The only thing that

came our way were the occasional fag-ends thrown away by officers or members of the prison staff, and collected by sweepers or laundrymen. These we stripped, rubbed out and rolled in newspaper. Even then it was difficult to find an opportunity to have a lungful of smoke without being found out. It was pretty well impossible in our room, which was guarded day and night. In the end, it always had to be the lavatory.'

As the months dragged on, Lobsang had difficulty in fixing the exact chronology of even those incidents which stick in his memory. But about six months after his arrest at the end of March, 1958, the prison's routine was shaken by a dramatic interruption. Without at first realising it, Lobsang was in a sense the central figure of the drama but, for once, he was condemned to the role of a passive spectator.

During February, 1958, the Chinese authorities had suddenly rounded up and arrested the entire non-Communist Chinese community in Lhasa. Lobsang soon heard of this because a few of the arrested men were sent to his jail. He thinks this wholesale sweep was made as a result of a top-level policy decision by the Chinese central government.

His workshop manager, Wu Han Ting, must have somehow got wind of this decision in time to avoid arrest. He had always been intensely suspicious of Communist intentions and at the first hint of trouble, had left Lhasa and gone into hiding in the surrounding countryside with other members of the workshop staff. Here they hatched a plan of breathtaking audacity. Wu recruited no fewer than thirty to forty men, nearly all of them formerly employed at the workshop, and set about acquiring a veritable arsenal of small arms. He had managed to salvage five or six pistols which Lobsang had kept on the premises for security in Lhasa or when travelling. Members of the team now slipped singly into Lhasa, disguised as Tibetans, and discreetly bought up more arms and ammunition on the open market, in small enough quantities not to attract attention.

The next stage of the conspiracy was to gain access to the prison compound itself. The key to this part of the plan was a shop directly across the road and round the corner from the main gate of the officers' living quarters which, in turn, led to the prison itself. This shop belonged to a Chinese from the Amdo province, who was acquainted with Lobsang and, no doubt, also with Wu Han Ting. As he dealt in firearms, Wu approached him with a tempting order for rifles, making it clear that he would not quibble about the price. The shopkeeper agreed, and it was arranged that Wu would collect the rifles at the shop with some friends. The shopkeeper suggested eight o'clock in the evening and the appointment was punctually kept. Wu and his companions were told that the rifles were ready in an upstairs room but, as they entered it, were confronted by Chinese soldiers, commanded by a major in the Political Division, who had been hiding in an adjoining room. This officer ordered Wu to drop his gun and put up his hands. Instead, Wu fired at the major, killing him outright, and made for the window. He was shot in the stomach by one of the soldiers, but managed to jump into the street, where he was either killed by his fall or dispatched by soldiers waiting in the street below, disguised as lamas and posted at strategic points surrounding the shop.

There followed a gun battle of which Lobsang necessarily has only confused accounts. Of the thirty-odd members of Wu's team, an unknown number were shot, and the rest escaped in the darkness. Several of the small party who had gone into the shop with Wu, also jumped out of the window. Most of them broke limbs in their fall, and all those in this party who were not killed were eventually arrested. Twenty-two of the party outside ran for it, with Chinese soldiers firing with submachine guns which they had kept concealed under their voluminous robes.

At three o'clock in the morning, Lobsang was woken and taken under escort to a room where a row of officers, looking for all the world like a summary court-martial, were already seated, with a colonel presiding over a major and two or three Political Branch officers. 'At first, I thought that I was about to be taken out and shot. The other prisoners in my room obviously thought so too, because as I was being led away, some of them made gestures of farewell.'

Instead, he was asked whether, since he had been in prison, he had been in touch with any of his workshop staff. He truthfully denied this, saying that he had supposed that they had all been recently interned with the rest of the Chinese community. At this point, the gunmen who had been caught were brought into the room. They were all handcuffed and hobbled with ankle fetters, and their chains clanked as their guards prodded them forward with their rifles, Lobsang was told that he must find out exactly what their plan had been, and was then taken back to join them in prison.

He was not yet aware that the shooting affray had been an attempt to rescue him. Like everyone else, he had heard the shots, but had assumed that it was a clash between Chinese soldiers and armed Khambas. Now he realised that his summons in the small hours, before he had a chance of talking to the captured men, was to enable the officers to determine, by his reactions, whether or not he had been privy to the conspiracy. He felt satisfied that they must have realised that he was not, and that that was why they were now trying to get him to worm out the truth about the real aims and scope of the plot.

As he was officially authorised to talk to the arrested men, he quickly learnt the general outline of the story. Wu's death was a terrible blow for him. Not only had he risked his life for Lobsang, but had sacrificed his own chance of escape from the Communist system which he so detested. 'He and the other boys may have thought that they would have a better chance of getting out of Tibet if I was with them, because I had so many contacts and so much experience of the world at large. They had been living rough for some time and must have been physically exhausted. I wept when I heard that Wu had been killed. Poor boy. He was only twenty-four. And now I felt responsible for the plight of all these other brave fellows. They faced the prospect of almost certain execution, either summarily or after interrogation and torture. Yet not one of them ever seems to have betrayed that the real object of their attack was to rescue me from prison. If they had, it would have made my own position even worse than it was already.'

The newspapers in Lhasa published a report which explained

the shooting by saying that a band of hooligans, who had taken to a life of organised armed robbery, had been detected and dealt with by the Liberation Army before they had time to cause serious harm. In fact the conspiracy had been planned with a good deal of care and detailed local knowledge. The conspirators' idea of shooting their way in and out of a military prison was not so scatter-brained as it sounds. Every morning, between six and ten o'clock, all but five of the thirty-six soldiers who performed guard duties at the prison attended study courses at the Political Branch headquarters, outside the centre of Lhasa. During this time, the principal entrance to the officers' building was guarded by only a single sentry. For thirty men dressed as Tibetans to converge on it would attract no particular attention because the ring-road round the temple was always full at this hour. Both the officers' headquarters and the prison formed part of the complex of buildings, inside this circular road, which embraced the main temple. The passers-by were normally Tibetans who came to make a symbolic act of worship by spinning one of the heavy prayer-wheels which were placed along the outside walls of the temples, or lamas and laymen who had business in the temple itself. This, incidentally, explains why the Chinese soldiers were disguised as lamas on the evening of the attempt.

Lobsang is still not sure who betrayed the conspirators. The most likely suspect, he thinks, is the shopkeeper. He is known to have had connections with the Political Branch of the army, many of whose officers were, like himself, from the Amdo Province. He would almost certainly have recognised Wu and his companions in spite of their Tibetan clothes. Finally, it was he who had suggested that they should pick up the arms inside the shop and had fixed the time. Another possible suspect is a Chinese doctor who had originally volunteered as part of the jail-break party but who failed to turn up on the night. He may have simply lost his nerve, but the workshop boys who were in prison with Lobsang all regarded him as the most likely informer when they discussed the matter together. Lobsang thinks they were influenced by the fact that the doctor came from the Honan Province, and that most of the Political Branch officers were also Honan men.

He himself thinks that if the doctor had decided to betray the conspirators he would also have told the authorities where the ring-leaders could be picked up and arrested before any fighting began. He would have realised that a gun-battle in the middle of Lhasa was something which the Chinese authorities would wish to avoid at any cost, particularly in the deteriorating state of Sino-Tibetan relations.

Inside the jail, tension between prisoners and guards was naturally heightened. The sight of his workshop boys in irons was a daily reproach to Lobsang. Even if they escaped execution, they faced jail sentences of at least fifteen to twenty years. 'That is no life', says Lobsang, 'better die.' The situation cried out for action, the more violent the better, but that was the one thing that Lobsang was powerless to provide.

About this time, two young Chinese, who had come to Tibet in the Communist army and been imprisoned for very minor offences, were detailed to remove some furniture from the officers' old living-quarters to the new Political Branch headquarters. On their return, one of them told Lobsang that there were only three soldiers on guard duty and that if any of the prisoners could make a break into the street, they would have an excellent chance because a very large crowd was attending some religious festival and would make pursuit almost impossible. Lobsang had no special reason to doubt his good faith but he had often wondered why these two boys had been held so long on such trivial charges, and the thought had crossed his mind that they might be informers. So he preferred not to take any chances.

Some of the workshop prisoners, to whom the boys had told the same story, showed more interest. Having so little to lose, they were more prepared to take a risk than Lobsang. They began discussing among themselves the chances of overpowering the three guards, one of whom kept the keys to the prison, and of stealing their guns and making a break. Before they had a chance to put their plan into action, one of the two Chinese boys who had given them the information was himself denounced.

'He was very young and not very intelligent,' explains Lobsang, 'at the time I was allowed to fetch my spare clothes from the workshop, he had been very envious, and I had told him to choose himself one suit to wear when his release came. He had been expecting it for a long time, and had interpreted his permission to help with the furniture removal outside the prison as evidence that a date had now been set. While he was working in the old offices from which the furniture was being moved, he came across some white ceremonial scarves of the sort that Tibetans give on formal occasions as a token of greeting and respect. They had probably been brought by Tibetan callers at the Political Division and been thrown into a corner and forgotten. These scarves are long and invariably made of some excellent white silk. The boy had taken some of them and smuggled them next to his skin back into the prison. There he had been unable to resist the temptation to boast of his prize. He even began wearing one of the scarves round his neck under his threadbare tunic. The next day he was sent for to appear before the prison officers, and left his room thinking that he was either being sent to do more removal work or perhaps even to be given news of his release. He returned crestfallen, wearing handcuffs and ankle-fetters, to report that someone had told the authorities of his petty theft and, to aggravate things, had revealed that he had been disclosing to other prisoners the disposition of the security guard outside the jail. As a punishment, he forfeited any remission he had earned and was told that he now had no chance of an early release. This evidence that someone was acting as a stool-pigeon and that the authorities already knew that there had been talk of overpowering the guard had decided even the most reckless of the former workshop hands that an attempt at a break-out was bound to end in failure.'

For Lobsang, this was a period of unrelieved misery. Before the attack on the prison, he had had only himself to think of and was almost beginning to come to terms with prison life. Now his situation was more hopeless than ever, and he felt a heavy sense of responsibility for the plight of his companions. In this state of anguish, the petty tyrannies of prison authority became more unbearable than ever. One day he failed to ask the guard's permission to use the urinal tin. The guard, a particularly officious fellow, ordered him outside the room and tried to put him in handcuffs. Lobsang knew that he was exceeding his powers, and resisted, demanding that the officer-in-charge should be summoned. Infuriated by this challenge to his authority, the guard shouted to other soldiers upstairs in their first-floor rooms to come to his assistance. Lobsang's blood was up. In the scuffle that ensued the guard lunged at him with his bayonet, driving it right through his leg. Then, with the help of the other soldiers, he finally secured the handcuffs. The result was a general uproar. The thin round Russian bayonet had caused a painful wound that was now bleeding freely. When eventually two prison officers, a major and a captain, appeared on the scene, Lobsang was still so angry that, in spite of his wound, he insisted on lodging a formal protest against the guard's conduct. For good measure, he took the opportunity to remind the officers that, after nearly a year in jail, he had still not been charged, tried or sentenced. It was time, he shouted, for the government to decide whether he had anything to answer for. If he had, they had better shoot him if they thought that was what he deserved, but they had no right to allow their jailers to treat him with such senseless brutality. The major, taken aback by the violence of this outburst, replied rather defensively that the soldiers of the Liberation Army felt justifiable hatred for prisoners because they were enemies of the people. Lobsang recalls with a certain grim satisfaction that shortly after this incident this particular liberator was promoted sergeant and, within a month, killed in an affray with Khamba guerrillas whom he was in no position to use as unarmed targets for bayonet practice. Even the other prison guards who told him the news had not appeared to waste much sympathy on their former colleague.

When the shouting subsided, it was plain to everyone that Lobsang was seriously wounded. After he had been overpowered, the handcuffs had been fastened very tightly, and he suddenly lost consciousness. He was bundled into a jeep and rushed to the general hospital – the one and only hospital in Lhasa. The senior surgeon was an army doctor whom Lobsang had got to know well because they were both Manchurians. He personally dressed Lobsang's wound, apparently under the impression that he had been hurt in an encounter with Khamba guerrillas. As he was finishing, he asked how it had happened. But, before Lobsang could answer, the major snapped 'He is a prisoner.' The doctor's face, which had been full of sympathy and concern, froze and went blank. Lobsang was driven back to jail and returned to his guards and fellow-prisoners. He was weak from loss of blood and emotionally exhausted by his outburst. He suddenly felt an over-whelming weariness and a desire to be finished with everything. He decided to go on hunger-strike, calculating that, in his weakened condition, this would be the quickest and easiest way out. For fourteen days he refused all food.

On the fifteenth day, one of his workshop boys, who had no business to be in his room, managed to slip in while the guard's back was turned, and entreated him to drink some water. 'He told me that for his sake and his friends', I must get well and live. Because they were in irons, they had no chance of escape and they did not care anyway if they died quickly. But before that they might be able to help me get out.' Lobsang was so touched by his kindness and unselfishness that, to thank him, he took a sip of water. 'I felt ashamed at my lack of courage in the face of their devotion and sympathy. They used to address me as "Elder Brother" and, in Chinese families, next to one's parents, the elder brother has a very special place. In our workshop days, it's true that we had become almost a family. I felt great sympathy for the boys because I knew what it was like to be stranded in a foreign country in such an insecure position with the Communist authorities. I always went on the principle that, while we were free to do so, we should take advantage as a team of everything we were earning. We never worried about fixed salaries. Everyone just came and asked for what he needed. With Wu Han Ting and my closest assistants I had an understanding that they were free to spend what they liked within reason without even consulting me. They were more partners than employees. As a result, every-one worked hard and willingly, and we managed to have a lot of fun as well. Now they were proving to me what loyal brothers they were, in bad times as well as good. If only because they had asked me, I decided that, after all, I must not give up.'

At the same moment, Lobsang made another decision. He was going to get out of prison or die in the attempt. What he could not guess was that fate, in the guise of a new shift in Chinese policy, was about to play right into his hands.

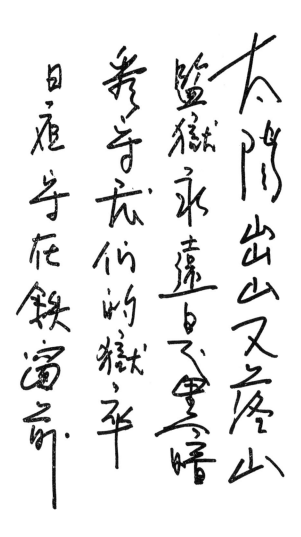

LOBSANG'S POEM

13

ESCAPE

About this time there was a short-lived Chinese project, which never came to anything, to build a railway linking China and Tibet. It was to run from Chinghai to Lhasa, roughly along the same route that Lobsang had taken in his Canadian truck on his way back from the Buddhist Association's trip to China. From an engineering point of view it would have been a heroic undertaking. Lobsang was never told whether the main purpose of the railway was strategic or economic, but, like all Chinese Communist development schemes, it was to be completed at top speed.

Not long after he ended his hunger-strike, Lobsang was taken to see a senior officer who gave him an outline of what was planned and asked him if he was prepared to collaborate. The proposal was to transfer the plant from Lobsang's workshop to the prison compound. It could then be used to manufacture component parts for the railway track.

Taken aback by the scale of the project, Lobsang inquired where the necessary labour force was to come from. The officer told him smoothly that this would present no problem. 'We can easily let you have fifteen to eighteen hundred men. They are in other army prisons in Lhasa.' Lobsang was flabbergasted. At the time of his arrest, the only Chinese jail in Lhasa, as far as he knew, was the one in which he had spent the past year. He had heard news of the round-up of the non-Communist Chinese community, but had not bothered to ask himself where they had been taken. Lhasa itself was a very small town. The Dalai Lama, in his book, mentions that after the arrival of the Chinese army in the 1950s, its population was 150,000, and that it had never been so large.

Lobsang then inquired what his own status would be, and whether it would affect his prospects of release. 'We would expect you', the officer told him, 'to be prisoner-in-charge of the workshop. We know that when you had your own business, you and your men worked extremely hard and efficiently. We want this railway built and running before the end of 1960. If the project succeeded, and you had worked equally hard on your part of it, you would have deserved well. To begin with, I want you to draw up a detailed plan for the new prison workshop. You needn't worry about manpower, or any additional equipment. You will get everything you need.'

Lobsang did not take long to make up his mind. For one thing, he had no real choice in the matter. The officer had been affable, but he knew that this was an order rather than an offer. The idea that the railway could be built in a little over two years, even if Peking and the Chinese army gave it top priority, he regarded as frankly preposterous. From his own experience as an engineer and from his knowledge of the terrain he would have reckoned ten or fifteen years as a more realistic estimate. He had no intention of spending that sort of time as a prisoner-in-charge, working his guts out with no guarantee of freedom at the end of it.

Still, the proposition had obvious short-term advantages. Lobsang managed without much difficulty to convince the authorities that the only part of the compound which could accommodate the necessary machinery was the ground-floor of the building in which the officers who worked on the outskirts of Lhasa at the new headquarters of the Political Division now had their living quarters. The prison building itself, which had been put up by the Chinese, had not the necessary open floor space and was unsuitable in any case for laying the concrete beds which were essential for the machines. The ground-floor of the officers' quarters, like most traditional Tibetan buildings, had continued to be used as sheds and storehouses.

This meant that, in order to draw up his plans, Lobsang would have to be allowed access to the officers' building. This would give him a chance to survey the whole area in detail and perhaps discover something to his advantage in the way of an escape-route. The next twenty days were some of the busiest of his life. After more than a year of inactivity and stagnation, he had a job of work to get his teeth into. That alone was a stimulant which lifted him out of his despondency and set his imagination racing in directions which he had not dared to explore since his arrest.

For the first time since he arrived in Lhasa jail, his service as an officer in the Chinese People's Army began to be a tangible asset. He was quickly accepted by the Political Branch officers, if not exactly as a colleague, at least as someone who was familiar with the Communist military code and was engaged on useful army business. The most important thing, from his point of view, was that they soon came to take his presence in any part of the compound during working hours for granted. 'When they went in for their evening meal, they would tell me it was time to go back to the prison for my own supper. Sometimes, when they were attending a meeting on an upper floor, they would signal through the window that it was five o'clock or, if I was still around after that, would shout to ask if I had forgotten the time.'

When Lobsang started work on his plan, a young Chinese prisoner was attached to him as an assistant. He was a nineteen-year-old lad from Shantung, who had worked as a handy-boy in an army transport unit. He was not qualified as a driver and had got into trouble for driving a truck without permission, and running over and killing a child. Lobsang was told that he was

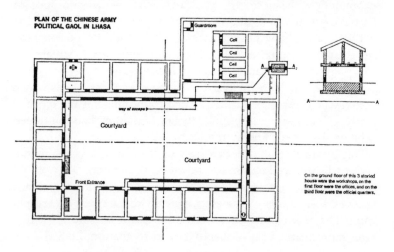

PLAN OF THE CHINESE ARMY
POLITICAL GAOL IN LHASA

Guardroom

Cell
Cell
Cell
Cell

way of escape

Courtyard

Courtyard

Front Entrance

On the ground floor of this 3 storied house were the workshops, on the first floor were the offices, and on the third floor were the official quarters.

mechanically minded and would be useful to him when the projected prison workshop was being installed. His name was Chu Huan Fong. Lobsang was not surprised when he found out that Chu was more of a shadow than an assistant. He took it for granted that he had been assigned to him to keep a check on his movements and report anything suspicious to the prison authorities. He also realised that it would be virtually impossible to conceal from Chu that what he was doing was not wholly connected with the project for installing the workshop plant. An escape plan was already beginning to take shape in his mind, but it required much more detailed reconnaissance in odd corners of the compound and careful observations of prison personnel and routine. Chu stuck to him like a clam and he made up his mind that, sooner or later, he had to take a calculated risk and take him into his confidence.

'I told him that I wasn't going to die in prison and that, as it would probably take twenty years to build the railway, I had decided to escape. I put it to him squarely that, if I succeeded, he was bound to get into serious trouble. If, on the other hand, he reported my intention, he might earn some remission, or even his release. If he said nothing, I was prepared to take him along with me and look after him as far as possible as long as I could. He asked for time to think it over and two days later came to me and said, "I've heard about you in Lhasa, about what you have done and the sort of man you are. I've made up my mind. I'll take a chance with you."

Lobsang's plan revolved around the old-fashioned Tibetan lavatory, situated in the alley between the officers' yard and the jail building. It was to this lavatory that the prisoners went under escort every morning and evening. It was a small, self-contained building, with the lavatory on the first floor above a cesspit, dug out at ground-level. This could only be entered by a trap-door, two foot square, to which the prisoners were allowed no access. From the situation of the lavatory building, Lobsang suspected that the cesspit extended to serve another lavatory in an adjoining building which belonged to a shop with an entrance on a side-street. If his guess was correct, it seemed logical that, in order to simplify the cleaning of the cesspit, it should also be accessible from the shop side – in other words, that it had an exit beyond the prison premises. Lobsang's deduction was supported when he noticed that a dog from the officers' compound regularly met another, presumably belonging to the shopkeeper, which appeared from nowhere in the officers' yard. The timing of the attempt was determined by observations which Lobsang had managed to make during his daily rounds. The first was that, without arousing suspicion, he could use the lavatory before returning into the prison building for his evening meal. The second was that the jail superintendent also acted as canteen supervisor, so that at mealtimes he was busy issuing rations to the prisoners. 'I decided that the moment to make a dash was on our way back to supper. We would pretend to be going up the stairs to the lavatory, as we had now established a habit of doing, but actually stay on the ground floor and try our luck with that little trapdoor.'

On the day of the jailbreak, Lobsang and Chu dressed, as far as was possible without risking detection, in a double layer of clothing. At the end of the day's work they waited for the usual reminder from the officers that it was suppertime, and signalled that they were going to use the lavatory on the way. Then, with a sudden awful realisation that this was the point of no return, and that the gamble of life and death was on, they ran past the staircase leading up to the lavatory and dived through the trap-door. In almost total darkness, they scrambled through the mire, trying to keep to the edges and avoid the place immediately under the lavatory, where the cesspit was likely to be deepest. Lobsang's calculations had been correct. When they struggled to the far side there was a second trap-door and, covered in filth but with bounding hearts, they emerged into the light of the courtyard of the shopkeeper's house. Only a wall now separated them from the street. But it was so high that it was obvious that scaling it was going to be a major operation. They could not be sure that their absence from supper had not already been noticed, or that the guards were not at this moment organising a search.

There was only one thing to do – back to the slough of despond. After making sure that both trap-doors were properly closed in their normal alignment, they each crouched behind one door and waited for the hunt to begin. As their eyes grew accustomed to the gloom, they were able to make out their surroundings in more detail. They were in a lofty, cavernous dungeon. As Lobsang had guessed, it ran under both houses but, to anyone entering from the prison side, the door at the far end was invisible, being in the darkest part of the vault. What light there was came from above. An old-style Tibetan lavatory consists simply of a hole in the floor, shaped like a large letterbox but completely open. When the lavatory was unoccupied, some light was visible from below, but not enough to give a clear view of the whole cesspit to anyone coming in from the light outside. Except when the cesspit was emptied, which was demonstrably very seldom, almost no one can have been familiar with the topography of this insalubrious hiding-place.

The stench, according to Lobsang, was indescribable. He has a highly-developed sense of smell and often, in describing exotic places, mentions how things or people smelt – usually to explain why what would have otherwise been picturesque and agreeable was in fact repugnant to his delicate Manchurian nostrils. He still cannot bring himself to dwell on his thoughts or feelings during the thirty hours which he and his companion spent in the pit, beyond recalling that as they huddled behind their trap-door, every visit to the lavatory put them in peril of getting their heads spattered or splashed by direct or indirect hits. They could hear every word that passed between the prisoners going in and out, and during the morning and evening latrine parades, dared not move for fear of attracting attention. There was always the danger that one of the search party, or simply an inquisitive prisoner, might take it into his head to peer down the shaft. From scraps of overhead conversation, they gradually gathered that the prison authorities had concluded that they had escaped either over the high wall or through the ground floor of the shop itself. 'When any of the search-party were in the lavatory, we had to hide ourselves completely, even our heads. Nobody can ever have been so filthy, but there was nothing for it – to survive, we had to submerge.' What is even more amazing than Lobsang's own determination to stick it out is that he managed to persuade the terrified and disconsolate Chu to stay with him.

In the darkest hours just before dawn, on the second night, all sound of the manhunt had died down. Lobsang and Chu decided that their pursuers must have shifted the search to the town. In almost complete darkness they ventured out again into the court-yard. By standing on Chu's shoulders and working on loose bits of stones, Lobsang managed to get a fingerhold on the top of the wall. It must have required all his strength to pull himself up, but at least there was no longer the paralysing fear of sudden inter-ruption. Once astride the wall, Lobsang removed his belt and, linking it to Chu's, hauled him slowly up the side. The fact that they had belts at all was due to their special work outside the prison building.

They had been as quiet and as quick as possible. Now, after listening carefully for any sound of passers-by or concealed searchers, they dropped into the narrow alley on the other side of the wall. As soon as it was light their tell-tale footprints and the marks where their filthy clothes had been dragged against the wall would give away their escape-route. The urgent thing was to put as much distance as possible between themselves and the prison before daybreak. Long afterwards, Lobsang learnt that the shopkeeper had been able to defend himself against the suspicion of complicity by claiming that, as the escape had been in the middle of the night, he and his household was as unaware as the prison guards themselves of where the escapers had been hiding.

14

THE ORACLE AND THE KHAMBAS

Lobsang and Chu spent their first moments of freedom in a wary reconnaissance of the streets immediately surrounding the prison compound, the temple and some big houses in the broad ring-road where the Chinese soldiers had waited, disguised as lamas, on the night of the gun-fight. They felt certain that the Communists had not yet abandoned their search and half expected hidden soldiers to jump out and challenge them from dark corners. They were also exhausted, physically and emotionally.

After several cautious halts, they decided that the coast was clear, and walked out of Lhasa at a brisk pace to a piece of waste land a few kilometres beyond the city, where yak-herds some-times killed and cut up a beast to sell to Lhasa citizens whose appetite for fresh beef was stronger than their religious scruples against taking life. They were rough fellows who camped in a kind of lean-to. Lobsang and Chu, who had not dared to stop to clean themselves, managed to persuade the butchers to exchange what they were wearing for some tattered Tibetan clothes. Lobsang's outer layer of clothing, which he had collected from his workshop, was of excellent quality. Even in its present state it was an acceptable swop for the ragged yak-herd's robe. To complete their disguise, they smeared their faces and hands with a mixture of butter and earth, to cover their prison pallor. Lobsang, with his height and his rather swarthy complexion, had no difficulty in passing as a Tibetan. In his own family he had been the darkest of the eleven children, and there is something about his rather erect bearing and long, loose-limbed stride which does not mark him as a typical Chinese. Chu was more of a problem and, even under his make-up, did not look a very convincing Tibetan yokel.

They decided to make for Tagtse Dzong, thirty miles outside Lhasa, where, in happier days, Lobsang had come to buy chickens. He hoped to find his old friend the magistrate at the dzong and to equip himself for the next stage of his escape. Apart from proper clothes and advice about safe routes, some money was absolutely essential. Lobsang's plan was to head south-west to the Indian frontier, but this meant crossing territory that was thick with Khamba guerrillas. Even for a Tibetan it would have been a hazardous enterprise. For Chinese without money it would have been suicidal. The Khambas took the line that the only good Chinese was a dead Chinese and, for fear of offending these fierce guerrillas, the local Tibetans might hesitate to give them any assistance unless it was made worth their while.

Lobsang knew the way to Tagtse Dzong blindfold. In his poaching days he had made the trip often enough in darkness. Now he took care to avoid regular tracks where any passer-by could betray their passage to their pursuers. They pushed on without stopping, but when they arrived at the dzong they met with their first set-back. The magistrate, they were told, was away in Lhasa. In these days, at the height of the Khamba rebellion, dzong officials often preferred the security of Lhasa to the hazards of life in their country districts where they were more and more subjected to truculent demands by guerrilla bands and were even threatened with violence unless they provided them with everything they wanted. There had been cases of the magistrate-in-charge being held hostage until his district had coughed up its quota of provisions and supplies. So it had become a common practice for the magistrate to leave a subordinate in charge of the dzong, who could truthfully say that he had no authority to hand over large quantities of stores but that, within the limits of his authority, he would do his best. In this way, with luck, the depredations of the Khambas on the local population were kept within more reasonable bounds, while the dzong magistrate himself could enjoy the comforts of life in Lhasa with a good conscience.

At first, the assistant-in-charge at Tagtse showed great concern at seeing Lobsang in such a lamentable condition but, when he told his story, became visibly apprehensive. When Lobsang asked whether he could spare him some money, he regretted that he simply could not afford to give him anything. A local farmer, whom Lobsang had used as an interpreter in his early days in Tibet, did, however, give him and Chu a square meal. Lobsang remembers it with tender gastro-nostalgia. There was *changpa*, a concoction of barley, butter tea and a sort of Tibetan black pudding, or country sausage, made out of mincemeat and blood.

There was nothing for it but to push on. They kept walking in a wide semi-circle round Lhasa, this time about forty miles to the Pemba Satun Dzong. The magistrate there, an impoverished aristocrat, had been a neighbour of Lobsang's and owed him many favours and a good deal of money. After having served the Dalai Lama as the Master of his stables, he had gambled away his entire fortune. During Lobsang's imprisonment he had travelled to Peking and had taken a training course at the Institute of Minority Nationalities. On his return to Tibet, he was given an appointment as a magistrate at Pemba Satun. Lobsang, when he heard this at Tagtse, had great hopes that his old friend, now restored to affluence, would extend a helping hand to his benefactor of leaner days. They arrived at the dzong at the end of their tether, only to find that he too was away in Lhasa. His half-brother, however, was staying in the dzong and agreed to put Lobsang and Chu up for the night.

Lobsang was still determined not to risk a long journey with no money. He decided that, even at the risk of being spotted and arrested, Lhasa was the only place where he could be certain of finding some friend who would provide him with enough cash to give him a sporting chance of getting out of the country.

As they came down towards Lhasa, they steered clear of the main road which runs parallel to the Gia river, on which Lhasa is situated. This meant making a detour and they found themselves on a small track which branched off up the hillside. They were nearing the Sara monastery, one of the largest and most important in Tibet. Before they reached it, they passed the smaller Chopen monastery and, between the two, came to a third monastic building which also belonged to Chopen. This had been one of

Lobsang's familiar haunts in his early days in Tibet. It was here he used to visit his friend Tampa Sekang, one of the state oracles who played an important role in Tibetan religious and political life.

These oracles were what we should call mediums. They were consulted on affairs of state, including such mundane matters as harvest prospects upon which agricultural policy would be decided, and were even used at meetings of the Cabinet. The essential qualification for an oracle was the ability to enter into a state of trance and transmit coherent prognostications and advice. When not acting as mouthpieces through which divine guidance could be sought and given, the oracles led perfectly normal lives. That they had no special powers of divination or second sight except during their official duties seems to be borne out by the fact that Tampa Sekang had been a regular Mah Jong player in Lobsang's set, and that he was not regarded as a particularly lucky gambler.

Like Lobsang, he was then in his early thirties and, together with *Chunsin* Losang Yishi, they had had many memorable sessions here and in Yatung in the old days. Lobsang knew his way about the monastery and made his way straight to Tampa Sekang's private apartments. His luck was in at last. The oracle was at home and received him like a long-lost friend. He warned him at once that the Chinese army had not given up their search for him and had been systematically combing the houses of Tibetans in Lhasa which Lobsang was known to have frequented. They had not yet come to visit him, but he was expecting them at any time. He therefore proposed that Lobsang and Chu would be safest locked up in his storeroom. His sister, he said, would see to it that they were properly fed and looked after. The warehouse turned out to be roomy, and it was decided that they should lie up there until the search had died down and it was safe to leave.

The oracle's sister was already well known to Lobsang. Her permanent residence in her brother's monastery apartments was, to put it mildly, unconventional. As the only girl in a family of four brothers, and an unmarried daughter at that, she should strictly have been living with her mother. But the oracle had insisted that he was so attached to his little sister that it was essential to his happiness and well-being that she should come and keep house for him. She was even required to sleep in the same room. This eccentric ménage had caused monastic eyebrows to be raised in Lhasa, and had led to malicious imputations of an incestuous relationship which Lobsang retails with a grin, but without giving them his own confirmation. He himself had had plenty of opportunity to get to know the lady. She was always present during gambling sessions in her brother's rooms, because he did not like her going to bed until the game was over. The men often teased her, and Lobsang used to get her to play his hand at Mah Jong while he sat out and rested. Then he would sit beside her and watch her play. The oracle explained to Lobsang that, since he last met her, she had married their friend Losang Yishi. This news did not surprise Lobsang. When the Mah Jong sessions lasted late, Losang Yishi used often to stay overnight and had shared the same bedroom as the oracle and his sister. Lobsang found it easy to understand that his learned and revered friend, whose wife had long ago left him and remained in China, should have succumbed to the charms of this lady into whose arms, so to speak, the Goddess of Chance had literally thrown him.

When the arrangements for hiding Lobsang and Chu had been discussed and agreed, Lobsang's first request, before being locked up as an item of surplus stores, was for cigarettes. Tampa Sekang's sister was sent to buy a supply from a nearby shop, and they were then taken to the store-room for their first night's sleep in safety since their escape. To have walked over a hundred miles with his bayonet wound only just healed had been a searching test for Lobsang after such a long confinement without any systematic exercise whatever. Now, with a good supply of cigarettes and the entertaining company of the oracle's sister, he was glad of this chance to build up his strength, plan his journey and brush up on the latest Lhasa gossip and the whereabouts of old friends who might conceivably help him along his route.

After a few days, however, he began getting restive to be on his way. He asked the oracle's sister to tell her brother that he did not want to impose on his hospitality or compromise him with the Chinese authorities, and that he thought it was time to leave. 'I explained to her that I needed some money and detailed directions to take me as far as the Indian frontier.' He was given both, as well as stout Tibetan travelling clothes, blankets, eating bowls and a special map, exquisitely drawn by Tampa Sekang and his sister, to guide them through the first dangerous miles of their journey.

They left early one morning, around three o'clock, before it was light, in order to reduce the risk of running into a Chinese patrol. The oracle had advised Lobsang, if he was challenged by guerrillas, to say that he was from the Amdo province, between Tibet and China proper. In the eyes of the Khambas, to be an Amdo was at least one degree better than to be a proper Chinese.

There was one immediate danger to be avoided. They had to pass between two large collective farms which the Chinese army had established in the Lhasa district. One was called the 'July the First Farm', and the other the 'August the First Farm', to commemorate respectively the founding of the Chinese Communist Party and of the Liberation Army. Both lay near the main highway. Lobsang was told to push forward along a trail which ran between the two farms and then to continue for three or four more hours until he came to a steel bridge, which he was to avoid at all costs. Instead, he was to take a track which branched along the near side of the river. At that time hardly anyone used it because of the guerrillas who roamed the area. This track wound over the hill and then back to the river at a point where there was an old-fashioned Tibetan ferry. Here they could cross the river in yak-skin coracles.

In spite of these directions they either miscalculated the time or mistook the landmarks and continued to climb much too far, without catching sight of either the river or the ferry. Towards evening they found themselves in deep snow. The going grew more and more difficult. It was bitterly cold and they were ravenous, exhausted, lost and dispirited. It was out of the question to spend the night at the altitude they had reached. The only thing to do was to retrace their steps in the hope that they would find their way back to the river and the ferry.

Chu was in a pathetic state, shivering with cold and complaining of hunger. All night long they stumbled down the mountainside. At one point they passed a yak, alone and unattended. It was a calf which had strayed from the rest of the herd and it was lowing pitifully for its mother. Chu became obsessed with the idea of killing it and getting some meat to eat. 'I don't know if you've ever tried to catch a yak at night, in deep snow, on a steep hillside. We had in any case nothing to kill or skin it with. After wasting a lot of time and energy, we managed to hobble it by tying its head to one foreleg and then we attempted to drive it down to the nearest village, where we could find someone to butcher it for us in return for half the meat.'

By daybreak they were back where they started, at the foot of the mountain. They were approaching a village when Lobsang heard footsteps behind him. 'Before I could turn to look, I was struck a violent blow on the back of the head, which knocked me senseless.' What had happened was that one of the Khambas to whom the yaks belonged must have seen them with the calf and been following them at a distance. When Lobsang recovered his senses, the first thing he saw was Chu weeping. When he asked him what had happened and why he was crying, Chu could only reply that he had thought he was dead. Lobsang then noticed that the Khamba was still standing near them, and asked him why he had hit him. 'Because you stole my beast,' replied the Khamba. Anxious to avoid complications, Lobsang tried to placate him by saying that if the animal were really his, he would naturally return it, but that he couldn't see why, when he was driving it back to safety, there was any reason to have attacked him. 'But that's typical of Khambas. They hit you over the head first, and ask questions afterwards.'

This Khamba, at any rate, refused to be appeased. He may have been under orders to treat all Chinese with suspicion, whatever their story. The guerrillas went in constant fear of agents or informers who might give away their whereabouts or the strength of their bands to the Communists.

Fortunately for Lobsang and Chu the magistrate at Chushul Dzong who heard the yak-herd's complaint had a more sophisticated approach to his judicial duties. He was the dzong-keeper's assistant, a quiet, elderly man who, in these turbulent times, probably had his own reasons for disliking Khambas in general and Khamba guerrillas in particular. By a stroke of luck, he himself had seen Lobsang and Chu from a distance the day before, climbing the hill and without a yak. After hearing the Khamba's deposition, he told him fairly curtly that, as far as he could see, all that had happened was that his lost yak had been found and restored to him; that, in his experience, the Chinese were not cattle-thieves and that the Khamba himself had committed an unprovoked assault. 'If this is indeed your animal, as I assume, then take it and consider yourself lucky.'

After dismissing the case, the magistrate asked Lobsang, very amiably, what had brought the two wanderers, being Chinese, into his district. He had heard all the Chinese non-Communists in Lhasa had been arrested in February 1953 and deported to Chinghai. Lobsang told him his story, adding that he might have seen the reports of the gun-battle outside the jail or the news of his own arrest which had appeared in the newspaper in Lhasa.

'Ah,' replied the magistrate, 'in that case we must be very careful.' He gave them food and also offered them some small denomination Tibetan paper money. When Lobsang declined it, saying that he already had money, the magistrate inquired how he had obtained it if he had only just escaped from prison. Lobsang judged that he was friendly and discreet enough to be taken into his confidence and explained how it had been given him by the oracle Tampa Sekang. The magistrate was duly impressed but more than ever insistent on the need for absolute secrecy. 'So Tampa Sekang helped you, did he? You must on no account mention that to anyone else.'

He then produced some provisions, including a special kind of hard sausage, for their next march, and gave them detailed directions. They were to cross the river by the same ferry they had missed and then make for the Nagartse Dzong, a few miles from the Great Yamdrok Lake. This time they found the ferry without difficulty, and crossed the Tsang Po river, which is the Tibetan name for the upper reaches of the Brahmaputra just west of the point where the Gya Chu, the tributary on which Lhasa is situated, flows into it from the north-east. The yak-skin coracles in which they made the crossing are still in common use in Tibet. It was by using them that the Dalai Lama and his party escaped from Lhasa in March, 1959, without being detected by the Chinese army.

Both Lobsang and Chu were very tired after the trials of the last two days and, on the other side of the ferry, they found themselves faced with a steep climb along a narrow winding track, hardly wide enough for a string of horses or cattle in single file. After three or four hours of this slog, they came to a small hamlet, about halfway up the mountain and just off the track. There was a ramshackle tavern where the local people seemed surprisingly friendly. Lobsang and Chu allowed themselves to be plied with drinks and accepted an invitation to spend the night in something between a cave and a cattle-stall, into which the innkeeper locked them from the outside. At this altitude, it was freezing hard, and they tried unsuccessfully to kindle a fire with scraps of rubbish they found on the floor. It was so cold that Lobsang remembers fighting with a Khamba who was also sleeping in the out-house over the only available blanket. They slept badly and got up at first light to ask the way to the Nagartse Dzong. A prosperously-dressed Tibetan who had been drinking with them the night before said that, as he was also going in that direction, he would put them on their way if they would wait and start with him.

'When we eventually set off, I noticed some cows grazing on the other side of the valley, straight opposite us. They were black and white, bred from Friesians imported from the Netherlands. I remember it striking me as odd that they were out at pasture at this hour, when one would have expected them to have been indoors being milked. The explanation was that this black and white herd was used as a simple but ingenious way of signalling to the guerrillas. By putting out more or fewer black and white beasts to graze, code messages could be passed. The tavern where we had spent the night and the hamlet, which commanded the whole countryside, were used in this way by the Khambas as an observation post to give them warning of anyone suspicious using the track. We had just walked down to the level of the track when I saw twenty or thirty horsemen standing motionless a little above us round the slope of the hill. They had rifles slung across their backs and swords stuck through their belts. As soon as they saw us, they began brandishing their swords and letting out bloodcurdling yells, rather like redskins in an old-fashioned American Western.'

As they rushed downhill, they must have presented a terrifying spectacle. Poor Chu was so scared that he covered his head with his hands and started wailing. Lobsang told him to shut up and keep walking and look as natural and unconcerned as he could. But Chu froze in his tracks and was impossible to budge. As the Khambas reached them, some of them began belabouring Chu with their heavy horsewhips. Lobsang tried to call them off, shouting in Tibetan that they were harmless merchants. They started to interrogate him roughly and he explained that they had just escaped from jail in Lhasa. The guerrillas were quite unimpressed. They tied their wrists tightly with ropes and attached them on a short rein to their horses. Then they wheeled round and set off at a brisk pace. This, says Lobsang, was a really hideous ordeal. 'We were half dragged, half stumbling over the rough ground. Our bonds were very painful and every time the horse I was tied to jerked its neck, I felt that my joints were being pulled out of their sockets. It was probably only a few kilometres to the Nagartse Dzong, but it felt like an eternity. When the horses broke into a trot, we were made to run by sharp taps with a whip.'

At Nagartse, both the dzong-keeper, a lama, and his deputy, a nobleman, were in residence. They questioned the prisoners, trying to establish whether, as the guerrillas were already convinced, they were spying for the Chinese army. Using the same tactics which had served so well at Chushul, Lobsang reminded them of the arrest of the workshop proprietor in Lhasa and of his attempted rescue by the workshop staff. 'I seem to remember,' said the dzong-keeper, 'aren't you the man who used to own the trucks and lorries?' Lobsang began to sense that he was conducting the interrogation more for the benefit of the Khamba guerrillas than to satisfy himself further about his prisoners' *bona fides.* He realised that the dzong officials themselves were in a delicate position. If they dismissed the guerrillas' suspicions too lightly, they might antagonise them and even provoke them into taking the law into their own hands. They had to convince them, step by step, that there was some foundation for Lobsang's story, and that he was not the dangerous character they believed. Blessing his luck to have found such intelligent judges, Lobsang almost began to feel that the law was on his side. After further questions, framed so as to establish that he had been a genuine trader and that he had fallen foul of the Chinese army, the dzong-keeper said to the leader of the Khambas. 'You can leave him to me. I will deal with him.'

In full view of the Khambas, who were obviously not satisfied with this turn of the proceedings, they were led to the dungeon of the dzong. 'It was', says Lobsang, 'a nice roomy dungeon and, once the doors were closed, we were made to feel quite at home. During our stay we only spent our nights there. Most of the day we were sunbathing in a sheltered back courtyard. As soon as we were let out of the dungeon, we were given a slap-up breakfast – top quality tea and delicious toasted rice cakes of a kind which in Tibet are only given to honoured guests. Actually, even the nights in the dungeon were surprisingly agreeable. The lama dzong-keeper, an old man of over sixty, had recently married a girl of just over twenty. He was very proud of their baby. She was a delightful girl. When she heard our story, she went out of her way to look after us and make us comfortable after the hardships we had been through. She even came to the dungeon at night, saying she had brought us some food in case we were hungry. A very kind girl – I have a charming memory of her. Apart from the oracle's sister, she provided the first female company I had enjoyed since my arrest nearly a year and a half earlier.'

This gentle captivity continued for three days. Every day the guerrillas or their agents came to the dzong to collect provisions. The leader of the guerrillas in the area, the dzong-keeper explained, was a certain Amdo Leshey, who had established his headquarters at Dhor Dzong, two days' journey to the east of Nagartse. His was one of two guerrilla groups composed of Amdos, as distinct from

Khambas. The other was commanded by Amdo Thimpa. From the courtyard where they were allowed to take the sun, Lobsang noticed another visitor who awakened his curiosity by his air of authority and distinction. He was an elderly Tibetan who wore a long robe in the style of a senior Chinese Mandarin of the old school. In his ear hung the unmistakable insignia of rank – a very long, heavy ear-ring set with a huge, rough-cut turquoise. On inquiry, the dzong-keeper's wife told Lobsang that he came from a nearby monastery and that he was the Dorji Paghmo's agent.

Lobsang could scarcely contain his excitement. He asked to be introduced to the venerable gentleman and inquired whether the Dorji Paghmo was at present in residence. It seemed that she was, but when he asked if he would carry a note to her, the agent replied, courteously but firmly, that he would have to take the matter up with the keeper of the dzong. In spite of his impatience, Lobsang felt that it would be tactless not to fall in with the old man's wishes. He was, after all, an important personage. He looked after all the Dorji Paghmo's estates and properties and supervised her purchases and the daily management of her worldly affairs. It was this that brought him to the Dzong to inquire whether there were any matters of importance which needed his attention.

At the first opportunity, Lobsang sought out the keeper of the dzong and told him of his wish to send a message to the Dorji Paghmo. At first he was astonished that his prisoner should know such an exalted lady. In her own district, the Dorji Paghmo was naturally held in particular awe. But when Lobsang explained that he had conducted the lamas on their visit to China and had helped the Dorji Paghmo throughout the tour, he seemed suitably impressed. So much so that he volunteered to write the letter himself, in order to make sure that it was couched in language proper to such a petition. He informed the Dorji Paghmo that two Chinese had been handed into his custody by the guerrillas and that one of them claimed to know her personally from the time of her visit to China with the Buddhist Society. He felt it his duty to report to her and humbly awaited her instructions in the matter. The letter was sent at once by a dispatch rider. To Lobsang's astonishment and joy, he was back with an answer within a few hours. This meant that the Dorji Paghmo's monastery at Samting was much nearer than he had realised.

Her reply was a model of discretion. She informed the keeper of the dzong that she was indeed acquainted with the Chinese in question; that he had been of service to her as secretary of the Buddhist Society and that she would be pleased to have an opportunity to express her gratitude in person. In order, perhaps, to ease the dzong official's position with the guerrillas, she also added that, to the best of her knowledge, the Chinese gentleman had no political ties. He had been known to her, apart from his connection with the Buddhist Society, as an honest and reputable trader. It was therefore to be presumed that his movements were harmless.

The whole tone of this exchange of letters between the dzong-keeper and the Dorji Paghmo throws a revealing light on the equivocal position in which many Tibetans of high rank or in responsible positions found themselves as a result of the Khamba uprising and of the contradictory policies pursued by the Dalai Lama and his government. They had to steer a middle course between the official policy of co-operation with the Chinese plan for the new Tibet and the rising tide of Tibetan nationalism. Their words and actions had to be calculated so as to antagonise neither the Chinese authorities nor the guerrillas. It was often a nice calculation, requiring a shrewd, long-term assessment of which side was likely to prevail and an even shrewder short-term flair for playing along with both camps in order to be able to pursue their own traditional way of Tibetan life with as little day-to-day interference as possible.

The Dorji Paghmo, for a girl still in her twenties, seems to have been an accomplished practitioner in this difficult art of playing both ends against the middle. Her religious importance and the veneration in which she was held by devout Buddhists were both an advantage and a handicap. In her own district they gave her an absolute authority which very few dared challenge openly. The Khamba guerrillas, who were mostly devout and superstitious, flocked to her monastery to seek her blessing in their struggle, much as medieval crusaders might have sought a papal blessing for their crusades. This practice had lately become such a nuisance that, at the time of Lobsang's arrival, she was officially incommunicado, on the pretext that she was engaged in a period of solitary meditation – a cast-iron excuse for fobbing off importunate visitors. In order not to disturb her, the Nagartse dzong-keeper, anxious to observe strict protocol and not to exceed his authority, decided that the first step was to send Lobsang to the monastery to see whether arrangements for an audience could be made on the spot. He sent him next day on horseback, escorted by a single Khamba.

The Samting Kumba, as the monastery is styled, is surrounded on three sides by water, and backed on the fourth side by a mountain. The water is a branch of the great Yamdrok Lake, which has two separate halves, linked by an underground conduit. No rivers flow into the lake, whose water-level remains constant throughout the year, maintained by springs and possibly also other subterranean channels. Lobsang speaks of the monastery as the most beautifully situated building he has ever seen – a kind of earthly paradise. But during this visit he was too preoccupied with his reception by the monastery officials to take in his surroundings properly. He and his escort dismounted in front of the imposing entrance of the great white-washed fortress and climbed the steep main staircase which led to the ceremonial audience-hall on the first floor. As he went up the steps, which are on the outside of the building, he glanced upwards and fancied he caught sight of a half-hidden face peeping from behind a curtain in a window on the top floor. Before he could make out whether it was really the Dorji Paghmo or only his imagination, it disappeared, and he went in through the great metal-studded doors, to be received by the head lama of Samting.

Any doubts about the constancy of his lover's affections were set at rest by the sight that greeted him. A reception committee of all the highest lamas was seated in a banqueting hall, where a table was set with dishes of every sort and special sweetmeats reserved only for the grandest occasions. The head lama of Samting, in his ceremonial robes, was seated in the middle, flanked by his colleagues in descending order of monastic hierarchy. Lobsang was invited to sit in the place of honour next to the head lama. With a diffidence which he seldom displays, he declined this privilege in favour of the Dorji Paghmo's brother-in-law, who was staying in the dzong with his wife, and also of his Khamba escort, who was placed in the second seat of honour. This modest gesture may also have been prompted by a desire to see how the conversation would turn before finding himself tête-à-tête with the head lama. Throughout the banquet, talk was confined to polite commonplaces, with the head lama occasionally asking Lobsang a probing question which he was able to parry without too much difficulty.

At the end of the banquet, the Dorji Paghmo's brother-in-law suggested, in order to get the Khamba escort out of earshot, that he might care to make a tour of the monastery's holy places, where, as a good Buddhist, he could perform his devotions. As soon as the Khamba disappeared, he drew Lobsang aside and asked him point-blank whether he was working for the Communist authorities. Lobsang was caught quite unprepared. Should he try to ingratiate himself by letting the brother-in-law think that he was a Communist sympathiser, which was what he half seemed to expect? Or would that make him suspicious that he had been sent by the Communists to check up on the real loyalties at Samting? On the other hand, if he denied all connections with the Communists, might it not be taken as evidence that he was too friendly to the Khamba guerrillas who, if not actually hostile, were clearly in some respects rivals for authority to the Dorji Paghmo and her entourage? While he was still hesitating, his Khamba escort providentially reappeared, and created a diversion by producing a charm-box of the kind often carried by Tibetans for the head lama to bless. Lobsang whispered to the brother-in-law that he would tell him everything later, when they were alone and could talk freely.

He and his escort took leave of their hosts soon afterwards and rode back to Nagartse Dzong. The keeper appeared delighted that the reception at the monastery had gone off so well, and was full of attentions. He had arranged for Lobsang to be moved up from the dungeon into a guest-room in his own apartments. However, to cover himself completely, he explained that he felt it necessary to get the approval of the Khamba command to transfer the two Chinese they had brought to him out of his own safe-keeping. This took a day or two, but, at last, Lobsang and Chu were seen off, with every mark of honour, by the dzong-keeper and his kind-hearted young wife, and were dispatched once more to Samting, the monastery of Soaring Meditation.

15

THE LADY OF THE LAKE

The aptly named Monastery of Soaring Meditation, stands high up on the hillside. To the south, in the distance, are the great peaks that separate Tibet from India. From the flat roof of the monastery prayer-flags in the breeze send out their message of eternal supplication. Below, the hills stretch their green velvet arms down into the lake, creating a series of little bays.

This time there was no monastic reception committee. Because she was still officially in solitary contemplation, the Dorji Paghmo was not there to welcome Lobsang herself. Her sister and her husband received him and took him immediately to their own apartments. These were situated in the same building as the Dorji Paghmo's private suite and immediately below it. The two apartments had direct private communication by a small secret staircase. The whole house, of three stories, was isolated from the rest of the monastery buildings and from the great Shrine Hall where the lamas performed their devotions by a high surrounding wall.

'It was very convenient and might almost have been designed for a clandestine affair. I was to stay in the sister's and brother-in-law's flat. There was a central living-room, with a large bedroom on either side of it. They shared one and Chu and I the other. I was relieved to find that the sister and her husband seemed to know all about my relationship with the Dorji Paghmo. They were very tactful and understanding. The sister was a well-educated and broad-minded girl – partly, perhaps, because of her interest in the various Communist-sponsored cultural committees. She was in any case not at all a typical conventionally-minded upper class Tibetan. She was older than her sister and extremely beautiful. Much prettier than the Dorji Paghmo, who had a rather lean and Mongolian look, and smaller in stature. What I found appealing in the Dorji Paghmo was not so much her looks as her openness, honesty and absolute sincerity. Now, for instance, when she finally appeared, she dropped any show of formality and just flung herself into my arms like any girl reunited with her lover.'

Lobsang has an extraordinary ability to adapt himself to sudden changes of fortune and style of living. To be dragged at a Khamba's saddle-bow and flung into a cow-stall or dungeon one day and be cosseted by a Lady Living Buddha in her secret love-nest the next seems to come quite naturally to him. He was not in the least embarrassed or put out of countenance by the role into which he was now cast. Things were beginning to run his way. That was all. Of course, there were still a few little problems to be sorted out, but they could wait until tomorrow. Meanwhile, he was king of an enchanted castle, and settled in to his new surroundings easily enough.

Lobsang is a good deal more forthcoming about this second encounter with the Dorji Paghmo than about their hide-and-seek relationship on their Chinese tour. He realised, with some surprise and a certain amount of apprehension, that she was really in love with him. Their long parting seems to have deepened their feelings for each other. They slept in her room and ate at the same table every day. During almost the whole of Lobsang's stay at Samting they were more or less confined to the Dorji Paghmo's quarters. Quite apart from the danger of the news of Lobsang's whereabouts leaking back to the Chinese authorities, his presence in the Dorji Paghmo's apartment, which was forbidden even to the lamas, would have been a major scandal to the Buddhist community if it had become general knowledge. This, combined with her period of meditation, made it impossible for them to enjoy all the possibilities of exploring their idyllic surroundings. Lobsang discovered that, over every crest and round every hillock, there was a new prospect of breathtaking beauty. The beaches of the lake were made of a kind of crystal salt deposit – 'not quite so tasty as ordinary salt, but still quite good,' comments Lobsang with more gastronomic than geological interest – which made them glitter like diamonds with an almost magical quality. On moonlit nights, the whole lake sparkled and it seemed impossible to believe that anything could shatter the peace of this little private world.

Lobsang lost count of time. He calculated that he must have spent more than a month at Samting, but the days and weeks slid by, with only occasionally recurring misgivings about the wisdom of the whole affair and his fairness to the Dorji Paghmo in allowing it to continue. He was struck by her mixture of sophistication, shrewdness and downright innocence. At the beginning of their friendship in China, he had questioned her about her experience with men, and she had astonished and disconcerted him by insisting that he was her first lover. She had also sometimes embarrassed him by her apparent total unawareness that sex was in any way taboo as such. He realised that in her monastery, where homosexual practices among the lamas were openly indulged in, she may have grown up to take sexual experience as a fact of life. He could even accept that her contacts with the Communists and her visits to China might have given her ideas about the emancipation of women. But it was the streak of naïveté in her whole attitude to sex that he found at once disarming and incredible.

The Dorji Paghmo was much less worried than Lobsang about the immediate future, both in terms of their own relationship and of its political and religious significance and repercussions. One day, as Lobsang was about to leave his own bedroom, he overheard a disquieting conversation next door in the living-room between the Dorji Paghmo's brother-in-law and the head lama of Samting. The lama was saying that he was afraid that if the Khamba guerrillas got to know that the two Chinese were living in the Dorji Paghmo's forbidden sanctuary, they would use it as a pretext for some hostile action against the monastery, or for stepping up their already exorbitant demands for supplies. The brother-in-law tried to dismiss his fears by pronouncing the single word '*Rimpoche*', as much as to say 'She is an incarnate Buddha and can do no wrong.' The lama muttered, 'Of course,' but Lobsang could tell that he was very worried and had serious misgivings himself about where this train of thinking might lead. The fact that the Dorji Paghmo herself fully understood his predicament and was prepared to help him to the limit would not prevent the lamas from planning to eliminate the threat that he represented to their community if an opportunity arose. If they had come to the conclusion that he was a Communist agent, they might try to turn him over to the Khambas, who could be counted upon to give him short shrift. If, on the other hand, they concluded that his sympathies lay with the guerrillas, there was always the danger that they might fall back on the time-honoured practice of liquidating him themselves.

When Lobsang told the Dorji Paghmo what he had overheard, she refused to take it too seriously. She said she had talked to the head lama and made it clear to him that it would be quite improper and unethical for her to fail an old friend in his hour of need. She had confessed to Lobsang, with her usual frankness, that when she received the news of his arrival at Nagartse Dzong, her first reaction had been to wonder whether he had been sent by the Communists to spy on the Khamba guerrillas. That she nevertheless agreed to his coming to Samting may be explained simply as evidence of her desire to see her lover again, but it also suggests a not very sympathetic attitude towards the Khamba insurrection.

Her brother-in-law's loyalties are even more open to contradictory explanations. His apparent readiness at his first meeting with Lobsang to collaborate with him in supplying information to the Communists, unless it was simply a piece of cautious reconnaissance, also seemed to indicate an anti-Khamba bias. On the other hand, his father was a former official in charge of the Dhor Dzong, which had been a notorious guerrilla hideout and headquarters for some time. Lobsang says that, while they were sharing the flat, he did not talk as if he was afraid either of the Khambas or the Communists. The truth may be that, like so many upper class Tibetans, both he and the Dorji Paghmo were keeping their options open until it became clearer what the outcome of the Khamba rebellion would be. Lobsang could understand and even sympathise with this equivocal behaviour, but sometimes found it tiresome as it affected him personally. 'Everyone was always thinking that everyone else was either a spy or an informer. I seem to have been fated to be taken for a spy. It has happened to me so many times. Generally, I think, because people allow themselves to jump to conclusions, through stupidity or laziness, without bothering to go into the real facts or probabilities of any given situation.'

Meanwhile, in spite of the gathering storm signals, life at Samting continued to be very enjoyable. For one thing, of all the places Lobsang visited in Tibet, it had the most agreeable climate. 'It was just warm enough to be pleasant, and there was always a little breeze, without any humidity, which made you feel very healthy and exhilarated. This prevailing breeze has a special quality. For instance, if you hang meat out of doors in a draughty place, it dries completely in three days. The local lamb, grazed on the lush pastures of the surrounding hills and dried in this way, is particularly delicious.'

Asked how poor Chu kept himself occupied at Samting, Lobsang replies with a wink, 'I think he amused himself with the Dorji Paghmo's nun-in-waiting, Ani-la, the same one who was with us in China. She was much older than he was, thirty at least, but she was the only other woman at Samting Kumba. Not a bad old bird really.' For the rest, Chu, as usual, seems to have been taken for granted as an appendage whose actions and reactions are hardly considered worth recalling.

Eventually, the Dorji Paghmo received a summons from Lhasa to attend an important session of the Preparatory Committee for the Autonomous Region. As she could obviously not ignore this summons, Lobsang used the occasion to broach the subject of his departure. He explained that, from every point of view, it was advisable for them to separate and meet again as soon as it was feasible, suggesting that India might be a suitable place. At first, the Dorji Paghmo reacted like any girl of her age in love. She said that she would never leave him and even that she would try to arrange things so as to be able to marry him. Lobsang did not find it easy to offer her fatherly advice. 'I tried to convince her that our affair had been a completely private thing, and that we had not the right to do anything that would harm the interests of her religious followers or her own monastery. I even argued that what

I had overheard the head lama say might have some truth in it.'

For three or four nights, they went over and over the arguments of sentiment, security and the responsibilities attaching to the Dorji Paghmo's office. She wanted Lobsang to stay at Samting at least until her return from Lhasa. He was by now determined to leave the monastery before her departure. Eventually, they hit on a compromise. He would try to get out of Tibet, and if he succeeded, she would follow him as soon as possible. Considering the consequences if he had been recaptured by the Chinese army, this arrangement was not as unchivalrous as it sounds. On the Dorji Paghmo's side, too, there were considerations which made flight to India less improbable than it might have appeared. It was true that she was in such good standing with the Chinese that it was unlikely that anything would happen to her personally. But there was a very real danger that members of her entourage and family might be fatally compromised by their connections with the guerrillas. Her brother-in-law's father was still living at Dhor Dzong, and had family estates in the same neighbourhood.

Lobsang had learnt that the guerrilla leader who was using the Dhor Dzong as his headquarters was a former acquaintance of his named Amdo Leshey. He belonged to the class of rich merchants who acted as agents for important lamas and their monasteries. He was reputed to have spent large sums on recruiting Amdos from the Chinghai border province who were living in Tibet in the area around Dhor Dzong. He had, Lobsang was told, contributed something like half a million silver dollars to the guerrilla cause and had succeeded in raising a sizeable force by letting it be understood that he was acting directly on behalf of the Dalai Lama.

As his plans for departure began to mature, Lobsang decided to get a message to this Amdo Leshey, through the keeper of Nagartse Dzong, to inquire whether it would be in order for him to go to Dhor Dzong. He mentioned that he was making for India, or any other non-Communist country that could be reached from Tibet. The days till the date of the Dorji Paghmo's departure for Lhasa were slipping by alarmingly, but eventually a reply came to say that his request had been favourably considered.

The fort at Phari – the trading post in Southern Tibet where Lobsang stayed just before his arrest in Lhasa

The fortress at Talbe – across the Yamdrok lake from the Dorji Paghmo's monastery at Samting. Below, a corner of the courtyard in the Dorji Paghmo's palace showing the steps to her private apartments

Now that things were actually on the move, Lobsang began to display his usual energy and decision. He felt it was vitally important not to stay a single day at Samting without the direct protection of the Dorji Paghmo's presence. He insisted that Nagartse Dzong provide him with an escort, preferably of Khambas, for the onward journey. He had no wish to be captured again, along with the compromising Chu, by stray guerrillas. Now that she had accepted his plans, the Dorji Paghmo gave him a personal letter to Amdo Leshey, explaining that Lobsang was a close and trusted friend and asking him to give him protection and help. 'All the same, when the messenger arrived, with the permission from Dhor Dzong, she broke down and wept.'

As in his previous tragic partings, Lobsang felt miserable and ashamed at putting his own freedom before the demands of love. 'But,' as he says with compelling logic, 'what to do?'

It seems questionable whether he could ever have been happy for long as the consort of a reigning Living Buddha. Even if she had opted for exile, and, so to speak, renounced her divinity in order to marry the man of her choice, could she have adapted herself to the role of a mere wife, even the wife of a husband of Lobsang's calibre?

As things turned out, she did follow him out of Tibet, after the Dalai Lama's flight from Tibet to India, but, having failed to trace him, she returned to Lhasa. There, as far as Lobsang knows, she has contrived to co-exist with the new regime, living as a respected citizen of the new Tibet and an ornament of Sino-Tibetan co-operation. Presumably, her divine rights as the Diamond Sow have officially lapsed, as the whole fabric of Tibetan theocracy has gradually been dismantled by the Communists. Lobsang would be the last person to hold her politics, or for that matter her religion, against her, however little he may have agreed with them personally. He remembers her as the most improbable and baffling of his loves – a sort of *dea ex machina* who picked him up and put him into a succession of quandaries at which even his comprehensive experience boggled. He remembers her, too, more personally, as a pathetic little girl, herself placed in a totally unnatural situation, who threw herself at his head in an attempt to escape from it, or at least to mitigate its boredom. And what of Samting itself? Have the Communists still left lama caretakers in the enchanted monastery? And, if so, do they still look out over the lake, dreaming of the day when the Diamond Sow will return round the mountain to restore their order to its former glory? Do they ever remember the days just before the Communist takeover when the two Chinese arrived in their midst in such mysterious and inauspicious circumstances?

16

THE END OF AN ERA

While the Dorji Paghmo was still getting ready for her journey to Lhasa, Lobsang got his way and left Samting ahead of her. This time his plans were carefully laid. He had seen enough of the pitfalls of travelling unheralded through Khamba country to take no chances. First he called at Nagartse Dzong, where he was provided with a Khamba escort for the two-day journey by horse to Dhor Dzong.

He had explained in his letter to Amdo Leshey that he was prepared, if he could be useful, to volunteer for service with his guerrillas. At this time there were several Chinese fighting with the rebels. The most interesting of them was a former major in the Communist army who had got himself into trouble in Lhasa over an affair with an important Tibetan official's wife. His knowledge of Chinese strategy for containing the guerrillas and of the Communist army's likely available strength was extremely valuable to the Khambas, whose notions of fighting a modern professional army were sketchy and sometimes unnecessarily reckless. He was also an experienced artillery officer and by his use of some light pieces which the guerrillas had managed to get hold of, had enabled them to score several local successes. Lobsang came across his trail later in India, where he had escaped and settled under the Tibetan name of Losang Tashi. There were also about twenty miscellaneous anti-Communist Chinese, mostly from the border provinces, who had thrown in their lot with the rebels.

It was during this period that Lobsang heard rumours of airdrops of arms to the Khambas in Southern Tibet. From what he was able to piece together then and later, he believes the arms were provided by the Chinese Nationalists, but has never established whether they were actually dropped by planes from Taiwan, or were brought to India for delivery by Indian planes. Whether these rumours were true or not, he considers that the belief that the KMT was actively supporting the Khamba uprising, almost certainly with Indian connivance, was an important factor in deciding the Chinese Communists to abandon kid-glove methods in Tibet and to crush the Khamba uprising before it became a full-scale national resistance movement. Lobsang himself feels strongly that if the Dalai Lama had at this time joined the rebels as the national leader of a guerrilla war in his own country, there might have been at any rate an outside chance of mounting a prolonged struggle for independence. Ordinary Tibetans had had time to see through Peking's promises and discover China's real intentions for Tibet and, in Lobsang's judgment, would have rallied solidly behind the Dalai Lama as a fighting leader.

Owing to his own petition and the letter of introduction he carried from the Dorji Paghmo, Lobsang was received cordially at Dhor Dzong by Amdo Leshey. He reminded him that they had at one time been neighbours in Lhasa and, finding him well-disposed, gave him a full account of his imprisonment, not forgetting to mention the lorry accident and the suspicion of gun-running for the Khambas among the probable reasons for his arrest.

Amdo Leshey was equally frank. If the guerrillas won the war, he promised Lobsang that he would be welcome back in Tibet. But he added that, for the moment, it would be wiser to prepare for the worst. He thanked Lobsang for his offer of services but said he had decided to send him and Chu to a safe place near Tibet's southern border with Bhutan. He was also sending three other Chinese who were being held in custody at Dhor Dzong. Two of these were Moslems from Chinghai who had been working on the Chinghai-Lhasa highway and were regarded as harmless. The third had been stopped by the Khambas on suspicion of working for the Communists. He spoke Tibetan as well as Chinese, and was alleged to have acted as an interpreter for the Chinese army. The Khambas had flogged him mercilessly before putting him in fetters and chains. He had received five hundred lashes with a grim instrument made out of a yak's penis stretched over a wooden stick. Lobsang was told that for his own safety, he and Chu would be housed in the Dzong prison. Amdo Leshey also warned him not to tell anyone that they knew him, as it would be inadvisable for him to admit to having Chinese friends.

As at Nagartse Dzong, Lobsang and Chu therefore slept in the dungeon at Dhor Dzong, with the difference that this time they had to share it with other prisoners. They found the unfortunate interpreter, still in chains, trying to sleep with his bare bottom sticking up in the air. It had been cut almost to the bone, and was still a mass of festering wounds. Lobsang was amazed at his comparative cheerfulness and had several long conversations with him in very passable Mandarin. Three days later, all the prisoners were mounted and, with two Khamba escorts, dispatched on their way to Lhakang Dzong. This dzong lies just over fifty miles as the crow flies due south of Dhor Dzong. The route, over bleak Himalayan hill country, with snow peaks and deep river valleys, crossed several high passes and was much longer than it looked on the map. How a man with a lacerated behind survived this journey on horseback is hard to imagine. It also says a good deal for the rugged Tibetan horses that it was reckoned as only two stages, with an overnight rest and a change of horses at a small dzong on the way.

Lhakang is only a few miles from the frontier of Bhutan, across which the Tibetans used to conduct a small but long-established local trade. The prisoners were handed over to the officer on duty at the dzong, who was the dzong-keeper's brother-in-law. Once again, Lobsang was made to give a detailed account of his identity and case history. He had learnt from experience that it paid to do a certain amount of judicious name-dropping, and he took care to pepper his recital with reference to friends and acquaintances.

Travelling across wide country always seems to have an exhilarating effect on Lobsang and, on the way over the high passes he had been reminded of a Chinese poem, dealing with the subject of individual luck, which says 'Even if there is no path over the mountain, there must be a path for me.' His premonition was not disappointed. At the mention of his old friend Losang Yishi, his interrogator almost jumped with pleased surprise. 'You must meet my brother-in-law. He is *Chunsin* Losang Yishi's best and oldest friend. They studied and graduated together at the Sara Monastery and have remained on the most cordial terms ever since. Now that I come to think of it, I have heard about you in connection with the Chunsin's marriage to the sister of the oracle Tampa Sekang.'

So Lobsang was hurried off to be introduced to the keeper of the dzong, who immediately plunged into a maze of reminiscences and mutual acquaintances. After considering Lobsàng's situation, he decided that it would be better for everyone if he did not stay at the dzong with the other Chinese. If he had entertained him as he would have liked, it would mean complications with the Khambas, who came regularly to Lhakang to collect supplies. Instead, he arranged to board him out on one of the wealthiest landowners of the district, about twenty miles from the dzong.

His new host, Kanjung Sara, lived a comfortable, easy-going life as a country gentleman, and shared his big house with a younger son, who used the local style of Kintara, or Young Master of the House. He and an elder brother had formerly both been married to the same wife, a practice not uncommon among well-to-do people in Tibet and other Himalayan countries where polyandry is recognised. The elder brother had subsequently made a fortune in another part of Tibet and taken a second wife, leaving Kintara to look after his father.

The family mansion, for all its charm, was very isolated and Kintara, who was a gregarious fellow, welcomed Lobsang as a heaven-sent distraction in his otherwise rather uneventful life. He made Lobsang's visit the pretext for a round of calls. Almost every day they would ride off together, often considerable distances, to find new company and entertainment. One day, finding nothing to do in the house, Kintara said how much he would have liked to have some music, but regretted that his gramophone was broken. Needless to say, Lobsang offered to put it right. By welding together the two pieces of a broken spring, he soon had the old hand-wound machine in working order. Kintara was delighted and the news of Lobsang's skill spread like wild-fire through the countryside. Requests for repairs to gramophones poured in so quickly that Lobsang soon found himself a new circle of friends. In the country houses and villages where he resuscitated these antiquated phonographs, he received all sorts of marks of esteem and gratitude. The local girls were charming, and some of them insisted on making and presenting him with new Tibetan clothes. He often called in at Lhakang Dzong to thank the dzong-keeper for sending him to such a comfortable billet and to pass the time of day in his amusing company. One day, discussing current developments in Tibet, the dzong-keeper remarked jokingly 'Well, if things come to the worst, you are all set for your escape. Come to think of it, if things really get bad enough, I might do worse than to come along with you.'

Lobsang's stay was now running into its third month. He had fallen so easily into the cosy life of a country house guest that the sense of urgency about his escape was half dissipated. Lhasa and the Chinese occupation authorities seemed a world away, and even the Khambas did not bother to come as far as Kintara's house.

It was there, on the evening of 18th March, 1959, that, listening to the radio, he tuned into Peking and heard the news that the Dalai Lama had left his summer palace, the Norbulinka, and escaped with a bodyguard of soldiers and the members of his family. The Peking Radio announcer read this item, half-way through the news bulletin, in a flat, undramatic voice, as if to belittle its importance. His only comment was to add that if the Chinese authorities wished to put their hands on the fugitive it would be as easy as catching a day-old chicken, but that it preferred to let him go. It was presumed that he was making for India by some secretly prearranged plan.

'At first I could not believe the news and old Kanjung Sara and Kintara were even more incredulous. It seemed to us all such a misguided move that we racked our brains to guess what motive Peking could have for putting out such a story to the world. But, if it did turn out to be true, then we agreed that anything might now happen inside Tibet itself.'

The Dalai Lama has given his own account of why he decided to flee although loyal Tibetans, believing that the Chinese army intended to kill him or make him a prisoner, flocked into Lhasa to demonstrate and to protect him. However, Lobsang considers that his decision to leave secretly, without any warning to these demonstrators, was unpardonable. As soon as the Chinese discovered that the Dalai Lama had gone, they vented their anger on the thousands of Tibetans who had been in the streets and whose only escape lay up a road commanded by Chinese riflemen and machine-gunners. They were able to pick off everyone who was carrying arms or looked like a person of importance. Most unarmed lower-class Tibetans were, according to Lobsang, allowed up the road unscathed. It was here that his friend Losang Yishi was killed trying to film the massacre with his cine-camera, which may conceivably have been mistaken for an automatic weapon by Chinese marksmen.

When they heard news of the Dalai Lama's flight Lobsang, Kintara and Chu set off at once for Lhakang Dzong to try to verify the news, but found that no one there had even heard it. They were advised to stay near the dzong until hard information became available. For three days they waited in suspense, but Lobsang noticed that the usual caravan of packhorses which left the dzong regularly with supplies for the Khambas had returned, fully loaded, just as it had set out. 'When I tried to question the caravan team, they refused to explain what had happened, but I told the dzong-keeper of my suspicions.' Under his close interrogation, the caravan drivers admitted that, when they had arrived at the Dhor Dzong, the whole guerilla garrison had disappeared and their headquarters were apparently abandoned. They had been told that the guerrillas had been attacked by the Chinese air force and had tried to escape on horseback. When the planes had dived over them, instead of dismounting and taking cover, they had galloped on in large groups, presenting the air gunners with an easy target. The planes had returned several times, mowing the Khambas down like cattle. Later, the Chinese army, whose intelligence about the Khambas' dispositions must have been detailed and accurate, shelled the dzong itself with their artillery.

The End of an Era

The Lhakang Dzong-keeper and Lobsang agreed that there was now no time to lose. The magistrate decided that his Chinese charges should be sent at once to the Bhutan border. The prisoner who had been flogged, who was still in chains, had to be left behind as unfit for travel.

The dzong-keeper himself accompanied them to a small village on the Tibetan side of the frontier, where the village headman appeared and tried to stop the party from going any farther. If the local Bhutanese thought that there were already Chinese in the area, he objected, they might stop trading and cut off the supply of rice on which the people on his side of the border depended. The dzong-keeper was furious at what he regarded as the headman's insolence. He shouted at him, '*Kunwe, Kunwe*', to establish his identity and authority as a high government official, as much as to say that he had better obey him. He told Lobsang and the other Chinese to go ahead into Bhutan and had each of them issued with a knife in case they had further trouble in dealing with the border villagers.

They followed a road leading along a river towards the frontier until they heard voices from behind a hedge of bushes which ran along the roadside. Lobsang shouted in Tibetan and some villagers appeared who barred their way and repeated their headman's arguments and objections. Lobsang was in no mood to trifle and told his three companions in Chinese to fight their way through. They brandished the sticks they were walking with and chased the villagers off, but almost immediately a shower of stones came whistling from the other side of the bushes. They were obliged to take cover behind the large boulders on the edge of the river on the opposite side of the road and, to their surprise and relief, their assailants withdrew. They waited a full hour to make sure that there was not going to be another attack. Then Lobsang decided to abandon the road and take to the hills, calculating that in any case they would stand a better chance of getting into Bhutan if they bypassed the road check-point. The frontier ran along the top of the range of the High Himalayas, and soon they were climbing through deep snow. In places they sank up to their necks and had to roll themselves into balls and help each other down stretches where the snow was soft and deep.

It was altogether an uncomfortable and undignified passage. They negotiated two passes and then, when Lobsang judged that they must be in Bhutanese territory, made their way cautiously down into the valley.

Once again Lobsang had kept ahead of the advance of the expanding empire of the People's Republic of China by the skin of his teeth. But once again the final curtain had come with unexpected suddenness. Five years earlier, when he had hitch-hiked his way to Lhasa through the mountains of Kham, the writing had been on the wall, but Tibet had still been a recognisable nation, with its religion and its theocratic institutions intact.

Now, as he struggled out through the snow-peaks, he knew that, with the departure of the Dalai Lama, the lynch-pin which held the old Tibet together had been removed. He had seen enough of Tibet and Tibetans of all classes to convince him that this was the end, not simply of an era and a way of life, but of Tibet as a sovereign nation.

PART *III*

Bhutan

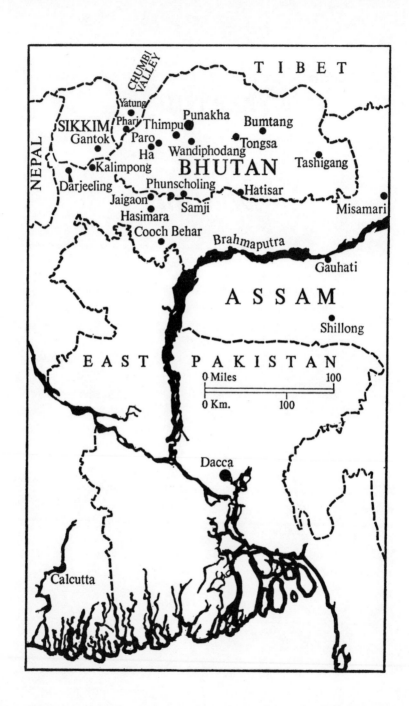

17

RADIO BUMTANG

The people in the first houses they came to turned out to be Bhutanese, but showed no sign of hostility. They gave them some dried fruit and put them up for the night. By next morning, however, news of their presence had reached the authorities and half a dozen soldiers turned up to take them into custody. They explained that their orders were to allow Tibetans and Khambas entry into the country, after disarming them, but to send all Chinese back across the border. In the turmoil in Tibet which followed the flight of the Dalai Lama, Bhutan was understandably nervous of getting involved in any international complications. The country at this time was virtually defenceless, even by Tibetan standards, and the Bhutan government was determined not to find itself saddled with an influx of Tibetan refugees who might try to use Bhutan as a base for guerrilla operations across the border or, worse still, as the seat of a political movement in exile. It was also on the look-out for Chinese agents who might try to cross the frontier, on one pretext or another, either to infiltrate the Tibetan refugee community or to gather information about the state of Bhutan's defences.

Lobsang told the soldiers that, whatever the orders were, he and his party were not going back. 'I told them that if they would not allow us in, they had better shoot us. We would prefer that to what would happen to us if we were handed back to the Communists.' Faced with such an uncompromising attitude, the good-natured Bhutanese soldiers decided to take the party to the nearest authority and hold them until instructions could be got from Bumtang, the main administrative centre of the area.

Communications in 1959 in Bhutan were still very primitive. The country was almost without roads of any kind, and only the main frontier posts and one or two of the dzongs which served as major centres of administration were equipped with small radio transmitters and receivers. It is also misleading to speak of Bhutanese towns or villages, as we understand the words. Even more than Tibet, Bhutan had remained isolated from the modern world. The country was administered from a few big dzongs, each commanding one of the major river valleys which run down from the snow peaks of the northern frontier to the tea-gardens of India and the valley of the Brahmaputra, at most points a distance of roughly a hundred miles. The tremendous mountain barrier in the north had kept the country free from invasion from Tibet and, in the south, it was almost as securely protected by a broad belt of some of the densest jungle in the world.

After a few days orders came from Bumtang to send the prisoners there. Jigme Dorji, the eldest brother of the Queen of Bhutan, who held the highest executive office next to the king, happened to be in Bumtang, dealing with the state of emergency created by the sudden invasion of refugees from Tibet. He had acted for years as the King's principal agent and adviser on external relations, spending much time in India. Between them, they were responsible for all the important policy decisions.

Lobsang and his party, on the presumption that they might be Communist spies, were to be blindfolded throughout the journey. Their guards, however, took this instruction with a pinch of salt and told them that they need only pull the band over their eyes if they met anyone on the way. On arrival at Bumtang, they were immediately taken before an official referred to by everyone as Ha Trungpa, or Lord of Ha. He was clearly a very important official but, after the elaborate airs and circumlocutions of Tibetan authorities and notables, his directness and simplicity of manner at once took Lobsang agreeably by surprise. He saw that the prisoners were exhausted and, before attempting to interrogate them, assigned them a tent and gave instructions to a cook to see that they were given a decent meal. This consisted of a leg of pork, highly seasoned with chilis, and a great dish of the pink mountain rice which is native to Bhutan. After their first Bhutanese meal, they were left to sleep off the effects of the physical and nervous strain of the past few days.

Although Lobsang did not realise it at the time, the Ha Trungpa and Jigme Dorji were one and the same person. Next morning, Jigme listened to Lobsang's story. He asked him intelligent and searching questions, but in such a straightforward and good-humoured way that Lobsang felt immediately at ease. Jigme's wife was the daughter of a Tibetan nobleman who was chief minister in the Dalai Lama's government. He knew Lhasa well and Lobsang was quickly able to convince him that he knew his wife's family and many of Jigme's other Tibetan friends and acquaintances. When he told him how he had set up his workshop, Jigme inquired 'Are you a proper engineer? Well, let's see if you can mend my radio transmitter. The damned thing's been out of order for days and my signals officer tells me that it's impossible to repair it and that we shall have to send to India to get it done.'

Lobsang, as a matter of fact, had never been called upon to try his hand with any kind of radio transmitter. Under the critical eyes of Jigme and the radio-operators, he gingerly began to dismantle the set. 'As I removed it, I put each part very carefully in sequence. To my relief, there didn't appear to be anything particularly complicated or mysterious about their respective functions. But I simply couldn't discover anything wrong. As I slowly took the thing to pieces, everyone was watching and waiting for me to make my diagnosis. I was sweating with anxiety. When I had almost stripped the transmitter, there was nothing left to do but admit defeat.' With infinite care, and a sinking heart, Lobsang reassembled the set, and told Jigme that he couldn't find any fault. 'I said I couldn't understand why it should not work, and without much hope, I asked the operator to have one more try. Immediately, the signal came through loud and clear, and in no time we were in contact with Thimpu, in Western Bhutan, where the King of Bhutan was in residence.' Jigme was delighted and half-teased, half-scolded the signals operator. 'So you said we would have to go to India to get it put right. And now along this Chinese comes and fixes it first shot. What sort of engineer do you call yourself?' He lost no time in getting put through to the

King and, after they had discussed the general situation on the Tibetan border, he told him that his transmitter had been repaired by a Chinese who had walked in from Tibet and refused to be sent back. 'I haven't been able to check his story, but it sounds fairly plausible to me and should be possible to verify. He seems a pretty competent engineer and may be useful. So, if you agree, I propose to let him stay.' The King approved and, from that moment, Lobsang's friendship and lifelong sense of gratitude and obligation to Jigme began.

The confusion over his identity, which was later to have curious consequences for Lobsang, was easily explained. The Ha valley in the west of Bhutan is the family seat of the Dorjis. It marches with Tibet, overlooking the Chumbi valley – the triangular spit of Tibetan territory which separates Bhutan to the east from Sikkim in the west. So the people in Bumtang, in the centre of the country, referred to Jigme by his local title.

Already Jigme and Lobsang were on friendly and informal terms. Both were men of action, impatient of subterfuge and liking to go straight to the point. They both had quick tempers and found it impossible to dissemble their feelings.

In spite of the worries of the situation he had on his hands, Jigme found time to discuss Lobsang's own problems with attention and sympathy. Lobsang had had enough of the Communists, and although he had never had much admiration or sympathy for the KMT or Chiang Kai-Shek, he felt that the Nationalists in exile might have something better to offer him than his frustrating attempts to lead his own life on the fringes of Chairman Mao's China. So he had decided that the best course left to him was to make for Taiwan, now the seat of the Chinese Nationalist government in exile. Above all he was tired of being dependent on other people's patronage. Grateful as he was to Jigme for his reception, he did not want to be beholden to him or become an embarrassment in the delicate situation in which Bhutan was placed.

Acting on impulse, a few days later, he left very early one morning and headed south with Chu, joining up with some Khambas who were eager to rejoin the Dalai Lama and his followers, who had now been reported safely in India. They had gone about a day's journey south towards the frontier when they were overtaken by a messenger on horseback, sent by Jigme to ask Lobsang to return. Back in Bumtang, Jigme scolded him gently for leaving without saying good-bye. He also warned him that he might run into difficulties at the Indian frontier. It was still three years before China's open split with India and her attack in the North-East-Frontier Agency, but relations between Peking and New Delhi were already becoming seriously strained.

Lobsang is in no doubt that the Indian government knew in advance that the Dalai Lama was going to leave his country and had even made preparations for accommodating Tibetan refugees on a fairly large scale. Ever since the Dalai Lama's visit to India in 1956, Chinese intelligence had been receiving reports suggesting that India, as well as the Chinese Nationalists, was encouraging him in a policy of resistance to Chinese demands for co-operation. Jigme therefore had reason to believe that the Indians would look very closely at any Chinese arriving from Tibet. He told Lobsang that if he encountered any difficulty, he was to ask the Bhutanese official in charge of the frontier checkpoint at Hatisar to contact him by radio and he would do what he could to help him.

Lobsang remained two days in Bumtang. He had more opportunity to appreciate Jigme's friendliness and good company. They discussed many things as man to man and Lobsang was touched to find that Jigme was prepared to accept him at his face value. He appeared to have decided that he was a man he liked and could trust. He no longer bothered to ask too many searching questions about his past or his political sympathies. He did however inquire why Lobsang had taken so long to reach Bhutan from Samting. When he told him of his friendship with the Dorji Paghmo, Jigme was able to inform him that she had recently left Tibet herself and had travelled through the North-East-Frontier Agency on her way to join the Dalai Lama in India. He said that some Tibetans regarded her as a Communist agent and added jokingly 'Perhaps you're one too?' Jigme also told him that the Dorji Paghmo's sister's father-in-law, the former magistrate of Dhor Dzong, had made for Bhutan with a caravan of 600 yaks, loaded with valuables belonging to the Dorji Paghmo and him-self. He had been beaten to death by Khamba guerrillas, also in flight, on the pretext that his son had accompanied the Dorji Paghmo and her sister on their first journey to China and were therefore Chinese agents. They stole the yaks and drove them through Bhutan to India. The poor old man's wife and two of her children escaped into Bhutan, where they were looked after by the Bhutanese government.

Before he left, Jigme insisted on Lobsang accepting some money – a big silk handkerchief full of silver coins. He told him not to think of it as payment for mending the transmitter, but simply as a token of friendship and to help him on the next stage of his journey.

18

LOBSANG'S MAGIC FLY-BUTTON

At the Hatisar checkpoint the Indian police announced without further ado that they would arrest all the Chinese in the little party which had accumulated during the six-day journey from Bumtang. They were seven in all, including Chu and the two Amdo boys from the Dhor Dzong.

Lobsang asked to be allowed to contact the Ha Trungpa by radio, but the Bhutanese official at the checkpoint, a mere deputy district officer, was a timorous old bureaucrat. He asked Lobsang if he had written authority to use the radio and when he found he had not, said he was too junior an official to make the communication on his own responsibility. The Indians were, in any case, determined to detain the Chinese and they were all driven over the border to Kokorajah, twenty miles inside Indian territory in the state of Assam. Here there was an improvised reception centre where all the Tibetan refugees were housed in one compound and the Chinese kept separately under lock and key.

The next day Lobsang and his three immediate companions were sent by rail to Misamari near Tezpur, where a full-scale refugee camp was already in operation. As Lobsang remarked to the Indian security officers who interrogated him, it was obvious that such a large camp must have been prepared well before the Dalai Lama's flight from Lhasa. When one of them assured him that Indian policy towards China was still one of friendship, Lobsang retorted that, on the contrary, the old fraternal slogan of 'India, China, bhai, bhai' (brothers) was already meaningless. He reminded them that the old quarrel between Tibet and the government of British India, which had resulted in the 13th Dalai Lama ceding territory to India in what is now the North-East-Frontier Agency, had never really been accepted by Peking and that China, now that she had absorbed Tibet, would never accept the present Indo-Tibetan boundary as definitive.

The conditions of detention at Misamari were not rigorous. The detainees, escorted by a policeman, were allowed out every day to collect their refugee rations. The Indian security police, however, were extremely thorough and, as Lobsang's interrogation proceeded, became increasingly curious about his past. Given the situation in Tibet and the state of Sino-Indian relations, this was hardly surprising. What was a Tibetan-speaking Manchurian, who admitted to having been in Sinkiang and apparently also spoke Russian and Japanese, doing wandering into India across a remote frontier post in Bhutan on the improbable pretext that he was on his way to join the Chinese Nationalists in Taiwan? The local security men decided that it was beyond their powers to pronounce on such a case.

Intelligence officers came from Delhi and spent many hours with Lobsang, asking every sort of question of a personal, political and military nature. They produced maps and asked him to pinpoint Chinese armaments factories and military dispositions. Lobsang could not make out whether they were more interested in checking the truth of his story or in picking his brains about China's military preparedness and her intentions towards India.

The truth is, probably, that Indian thinking about China was at this time in a considerable state of flux. At the beginning of Indian independence, Nehru had set great store by his policy of friendship with China. It was all part and parcel of the five principles of peaceful coexistence for Asia which had been worked out at the conference at Bandung. Nehru clung to this policy in the face of mounting evidence that Peking was going to be an awkward partner, particularly when it came to any question of the disputed frontiers along the entire length of the Himalayas. At the same time there were hard-headed realists in the Indian armed services and in the back-rooms of the Ministry of External Affairs in New Delhi, whose opinions did not always coincide with Nehru's public utterances on the subject of the government's official China policy.

As a result of his interrogation, Lobsang was asked to put on paper an appreciation of current relations between India and China. He produced a brutally frank document, which is perhaps still gathering dust in the files of some intelligence department in New Delhi. In it, Lobsang said flatly that India could expect no goodwill or friendly concessions from Peking. He added his own honest opinion, based on the Communist Party reports he had seen in Lhasa during the Dalai Lama's visit to India in 1956, that China had been deeply suspicious and disapproving of India's intentions in Tibet for some time and that sincere relations between the two countries would be impossible as long as India harboured and supported the Dalai Lama and his administration in exile.

All in all, it was not a tactful document. Much later, after China's attack on India in 1962, it was to have interesting repercussions as far as Lobsang himself was concerned. He also remembers, in his conversations with the Indian intelligence officers, predicting that relations between China and the Soviet Union were now so strained that serious trouble between them was inevitable. As an example of the mutual suspicions that were developing, he cited the quarrel over Chinese proposals to develop new oil fields in Chinghai. The Russians had been afraid that this would affect production in one of their own fields – the Number Six plant in the High Pamirs – and Soviet advisers had deliberately given an adverse report on the prospects of the proposed Chinese Tsadam oilfield at Germo which proved to be completely misleading when China actually developed it.

China's deepest grievance, Lobsang insisted, was over the question of Soviet aid during the Korean war. This much-publicised aid had in fact consisted largely of old Japanese war material and plant, captured or dismantled by the Russians in Manchuria, which had been carelessly reconditioned and given a coat of new paint. China's resentment at being fobbed off with such shoddy second-hand goods became even more acute when Moscow claimed that this military aid represented a loan of six hundred million roubles on which China had been made to pay full interest between 1951 and 1957. According to Lobsang's report, this and other instances of Soviet selfishness and bad faith, were among the main reasons which had made China decide in 1957, to expel Soviet technical aid advisers and had in turn, led directly to the open split between Moscow and Peking.

While he was at the Misamari camp, Lobsang was driven out to the nearest airport and asked to do some repair work on aero-engines. He is not sure whether this was in order to check his claim to be a qualified engineer or simply to make use of his skills, but he objected that the Indian authorities had no right to use a political detainee as unpaid labour, and refused to go on with this sort of work.

The Tibetan refugees in the camp were in constant touch with the Dalai Lama's entourage, which was now established in the foothills of the Himalayas at Mussourie. Lobsang himself saw both the Dalai Lama's brothers when they visited the camp, and they promised to put in a good word for him with the Indian authorities, but he doubts whether in fact they bothered to follow this up. He admits that he may have antagonised one of them by making some pretty blunt criticisms of the Dalai Lama's actions and of the advice upon which they had been based.

Life at Misamari was, above all, monotonous and boring. The weather had become extremely hot and the improvised huts were stifling. The Tibetans in particularly suffered acutely, developing painful heat blisters whenever they exposed their bodies to the sun. The Chinese detainees were comparatively free to mix with the miscellaneous staff which had been recruited to man the various services and look after the refugees. Lobsang and Chu became friendly with two nurses who worked in the camp hospital, which was in the same compound as the building where they were housed. One of these came from the Kazi Hills, just south of Shillong, whose people have a language and culture of their own and, like the Nagas and other hill peoples in this area, have pronounced nationalist leanings. She showed a lively and sympathetic interest in Lobsang's dilemma and eventually suggested that it would be easy enough for him to slip out of the camp and find employment in Shillong, the capital of Assam State. She herself normally lived in Shillong and would soon be returning there.

She explained to him how to get to the nearest railway station and they arranged a rendezvous in Shillong at a Chinese restaurant in the main bazaar. The proprietor, she said, would always know how to get in touch with her. She herself left for Shillong two days ahead, promising to make arrangements to harbour Lobsang and find him some paid work as a mechanic.

Compared with his jailbreak from Lhasa, Lobsang's escape from Misamari was almost ludicrously easy. In company with Chu and one of the Amdo boys who had been arrested with him at the frontier, he simply absconded. There was, admittedly, a trifling affair of knocking out a sentry, which Lobsang mentions apologetically. 'There was no noise, nothing. We just hit him and ran. No trouble at all. It was dark and as we ran down a path through some woods, we could just see that it was crawling with snakes, but we finally made our way along the railway line to a station where we caught the first train to Gauhati.' From Gauhati they took a bus south to Shillong. At the Chinese restaurant, which they had no difficulty in finding, the proprietor denied all knowledge of the Kazi nurse and volunteered no helpful suggestions as to where to find her. Everything had gone so smoothly that this was an unexpected reverse.

The three escapees spent the rest of the day exploring the bazaars of Shillong, a charming town, built on a series of hills with a mixed population living the leisurely but fairly animated life of a biggish provincial capital. Lobsang felt sure that the nurse had not purposely misled him and therefore concluded that the Chinese restaurant owner must have his own reason for not being more communicative. As he was their only contact in Shillong, Lobsang decided to go back to dine at his place and have another try to get him to talk. They ordered themselves a good Chinese meal, during the course of which Lobsang hoped the proprietor might relent and at least tell them what had become of the missing nurse.

Just as they were beginning to feel replete and Lobsang was preparing himself for a second onslaught on the taciturn proprietor, an Indian with an unmistakable air of authority came into the restaurant and made straight for their table. 'Have you finished dinner, gentlemen?' he inquired politely, 'because if so, I think that it is time that you came along with me.'

Indian security, Lobsang reflected, might sometimes appear lackadaisical, but the CID seemed to know its job.

The three detainees were taken to a police station and, next morning, driven to Shillong's central jail. To one side of the main prison, which housed common law offenders, was a block reserved for political prisoners. These were classified as Class A prisoners, which meant that they enjoyed better conditions than convicted criminals. If Lobsang hardly regards his escape from Misamari as a real escape, he also talks of Shillong as if it was hardly a real jail. Considering how infuriating and unjust the circumstances of his arrest at the frontier must have seemed to him, he describes Shillong with something bordering on affection. The political wing was not overcrowded. Several prisoners lived together in a large room. 'It was spacious and at the same time sociable. The prison was kept decently clean and, as political prisoners, we were allowed to supplement our rations by ordering anything we liked from outside the jail. Our chief warder was a Madrasi, a former Indian army *subidar*, who talked good English. He was smart and soldierly, and not at all a bad fellow.'

As a connoisseur of prison accommodation and regulations, Lobsang gives the Indian prison system in general, and Shillong jail in particular, something better than a pass mark. He thinks that the legacy of the British judicial system, with its distinction between prisoners who have been tried and convicted and those awaiting trial or detained pending investigation, may have had something to do with this.

For five months – he had already spent about the same time at Misamari – he suffered from boredom and irritation at the Indian government's refusal to charge or release him, but never complained of being physically or psychologically ill-treated. Some of the other political detainees were interesting companions. The son-in-law of one of the leaders of the Naga secessionists, whose uprising in the nearby Naga Hills kept the Indian army busy for years, taught him a good deal about Indian politics and the problems of federal and state government. He also picked up a smattering of several Indian languages from his guards and fellow-prisoners. In this polyglot prison he soon came to terms with the linguistic complications of the sub-continent without either book-learning or much apparent difficulty.

After the hostile vigilance of his guards in Lhasa, the warders at Shillong were a friendly lot. Class A prisoners had an allocation of five rupees a day and could order what they liked from the prison kitchens. 'When we had made up our minds what we wanted for dinner, we used to call out to one of them and place our orders, and they would bring it back, still hot and appetising, to our room.' This room service helped to pass the time much better than his old Lhasa game of cooking and eating an imaginary meal. There were other time-killers too, also obtainable through the good offices of the prison staff. 'We political prisoners could buy cigarettes. The other prisoners were not allowed to smoke by the regulations but most of them managed to smoke *sarja* (hash) which they bought through the soldiers on guard, trading shoes and blankets, sometimes pilfered from new prisoners.'

One day, over the prison compound, Lobsang was surprised to hear the familiar noise of MIG jet-fighters flying low. For a moment he wondered whether they were Chinese planes coming to attack India and when the warder could not explain their identity, he asked him to fetch the officer in charge of the prison. The warder refused and Lobsang was suddenly seized with an inexplicable pent-up fury, triggered off by the sounds and associations of the fighter planes. Wrapping a blanket around his fist, he proceeded to smash the window panes of the big room in which he had his quarters. Chu and the Amdo boys seized wooden bed-legs and joined in, until there was scarcely a whole pane left. A strong contingent of Assam police, armed with *lathis*, was paraded outside before the warders dared open the door and put the rioters in chains and fetters. As a result of this outbreak, the Chief of Assam police visited the jail and heard Lobsang's account of his inexplicable conduct. Lobsang thinks he must have inquired into the circumstances of his detention and asked what charges were pending against him. Two days later a CID officer came to interview him in jail and Lobsang decided that, as he could only conclude that he was suspected of being a Communist agent, he would try at least to prove conclusively that this suspicion was unfounded.

He still had in his possession something which, if it was accepted as evidence, might convince them of their mistake. This was a small plastic button, which had been distributed to selected KMT officers on the instructions of Chiang Kai-Shek before his withdrawal from mainland China to Taiwan. It was a secret identity disc which, they had been told, would be recognised, wherever the new headquarters of the KMT were in due course established, as evidence of its owner's past services. Lobsang, whose allegiance to the KMT had at best been half-hearted, had never seriously considered trying to rejoin the Nationalists until after the Chinese takeover in Tibet.

He had only preserved the button because he had sewn it on to a pair of trousers in the place of one of the fly buttons and had collected these trousers when he was allowed to go to his workshop. He had put them on underneath his outer layer of clothes on the day of escape from Lhasa jail. He felt pretty sure that, with relations with China deteriorating so rapidly, the Indian government must now have well-established if unofficial contacts with the KMT government in exile. So he decided to play his last card – his secret button – on the off-chance that it might still turn out to be the trump that its KMT inventors had originally intended it to be.

Without much faith in its efficacy, he explained to the CID officer that, when opened, it would be found to contain his name and rank and identify him as a member of the 'Anti-Communist-Country-Saving-Army', pledged to continue the struggle against the victorious Communist army. To Lobsang's amazement, the button produced results in an incredibly short space of time. He presumes it was sent to Delhi and that a decision was taken there by the security authorities. Within ten days, and with very little fuss, he was driven to the office of the High Court in Shillong. There was no hearing and no judge. He was formally asked his name and where he had come from and then notified that he was no longer under detention and was free to leave. There was not even any problem over his obligation to look after Chu.

With Lobsang's case settled, the authorities appeared to have no further interest in Chu and he was allowed to leave prison a few days later.

19

❦

AT A LOOSE END IN INDIA

The next few months Lobsang spent roaming rather aimlessly about India, exploring the country to discover whether it could offer him a permanent asylum and a decent livelihood. He was still only thirty-five. That he was once again penniless did not in itself seriously undermine his confidence in his ability to make a new start and put his skills and experience to account.

From Shillong, he made his way gradually to Calcutta. The great straggling capital of West Bengal, with its long mercantile tradition and its extremes of riches and poverty, was well suited in many ways to the launching of a new Lobsang enterprise. It had the biggest Chinese community in India, long-established and often prosperous. It was accustomed to ambitious newcomers who were prepared to make their way by hard work and ingenuity. Lobsang quickly managed to raise a loan of five thousand rupees from a Chinese businessman. For three thousand he leased a likely-looking site for a mechanical workshop. The other two thousand he invested in tools and equipment.

In his enthusiasm to get started, Lobsang had not taken the precaution of checking the credentials of the Bengali who leased him the site. Just as the workshop was beginning to take shape, he received a call from the municipal authorities, who served him with a notice to quit the premises he had newly acquired. Too late, he discovered that the entire building in which he had rented space was due for demolition under an urban development scheme. Needless to say, his lessor had vanished without trace.

Disgusted with Calcutta property racketeers and his own gullibility, Lobsang promptly put the whole width of India between him and the scene of his humiliating disaster. He could not even afford the price of a railway fare, but took a platform ticket and boarded a train to Bombay. There, the ticket-collector called the police, who agreed to allow Lobsang to try to raise the price of his journey in the Chinese quarter of the city. A policeman escorted him and, in the first shop he entered, he managed to charm the proprietor into bailing him out of his temporary embarrassment.

This good-hearted compatriot, a Mr Tsu, ran a baker's shop which specialised in the hard bread of his native province of Shantung. For a month, Lobsang worked in the bakery in return for his lodging. For a time it looked as if there might be some prospect of a serious job in a shipyard owned by a local Chinese. The project fell through because the Indian government had nationalised the yard and Lobsang decided that it would take the owner too long to negotiate the conditions under which the government would allow him to re-open the workshop in which he was to have been employed.

His next move was to New Delhi, where he decided to find out whether the Indian government, now that it was presumably satisfied about his political reliability, could offer any practical advice to someone in his situation. He started his inquiries at the Central Information Department of the Home Ministry. There the officials discussed his case amicably, but were unable to find an exact precedent or to place him in any official category for assistance. India, they told him, as a neutral member of the United Nations, had agreed to receive a number of Chinese prisoners taken by the United Nations Forces during the Korean War. They remembered that one group of these prisoners – two Chinese and five Koreans – had been given a government grant to help them start a battery chicken farm not far from New Delhi. They suggested to Lobsang that if he would care to submit a petition for assistance, accompanied by detailed plans for some equally constructive project, it might be possible to work something out. Lobsang, who hates bureaucracy and delay, did not care much for the idea of putting himself under an obligation to any government.

At about the same time he met a Mr S. T. Wang, the secretary of the Overseas Chinese Club of New Delhi. This gentleman was also the proprietor of a Chinese restaurant called the Golden Dragon. Among his many helpers in moments of need Lobsang has a particularly soft spot for S. T. Wang. He invited him to occupy an empty room at the Overseas Chinese Club and, as Lobsang had found a job servicing and repairing jeeps in a government workshop, his immediate problem of earning his living was more or less satisfactorily solved.

Even so, his Indian reconnaissance had not really been a success. Nothing had happened to make him feel that this was a country where he could settle down contentedly. Two years later, at the end of 1962, after the Chinese army had attacked India, the Chinese communities in most big Indian cities were rounded up and were either expelled or interned. Many of them, influenced by official propaganda during the early days of Sino-Indian friendship, had taken out passports issued by the Chinese Communist regime and were sent back to China whether or not they wanted to go or had any previous roots in the country.

Lobsang's good angel, S. T. Wang, was among the victims of this expulsion order. Through a lucky delay in Calcutta, he was able to get to the Portuguese island of Macao and from there, after a brief stay in mainland China, to Hong Kong. Lobsang met him again there in 1970 and Wang astonished him by telling him that, at the time of their original meeting in Delhi, the Chinese embassy had asked him to look after Lobsang and had even offered to reimburse him for any expenses that this might involve. Lobsang has never discovered how the Chinese Communists had kept track of his movements in India or what their motives were in prompting Wang to come to his rescue.

During the whole of the three months that Lobsang spent in Wang's spare room at the Chinese Club he was quite unaware that his host and Jigme Dorji knew each other. Nor did he know that, ever since his departure from Bhutan, Jigme had been trying to discover his own whereabouts and get in touch with him. He must have received information that Lobsang was in Delhi and had sent a telegram to the Chinese Club as the most likely place where someone might know how to find a Chinese newly arrived in town. This telegram asked him to come at once to Calcutta and was accompanied by a money order for four hundred rupees to pay his fare and expenses. It had been addressed to Lo Yu-Dei, one of the many names that Lobsang used to cover his tracks at various stages of his progress through Manchuria, Sinkiang and Tibet, but not the one he was currently using in New Delhi. Wang, as secretary of the club, had been puzzled by the telegram, and eventually mentioned it in Lobsang's hearing. Lobsang pricked up his ears when he heard the name Lo Yu-Dei, and asked Wang who the sender, Jigme Dorji, was. Even when he was told that he was the Bhutan's Chief Representative in Calcutta, he only gradually realised that Jigme Dorji must be the same person as the Ha Tumba he had met in Bumtang.

This time, Lobsang had no difficulty in accepting Jigme's invitation. There was something almost regal about the summons that appealed to him, but what moved him most was that Jigme should have remembered him after their one brief meeting and taken so much trouble to track him down. He packed his bag, collected the four hundred rupees, and went straight to Calcutta, to the address of a Chinese friend of S. T. Wang, to whom he had been introduced in New Delhi. Jigme was told of his arrival by telephone, and immediately sent his car to fetch him. The Dorjis, besides their estates in Bhutan, owned family property in the Indian hill station of Kalimpong, near Darjeeling, and had permanent headquarters in Calcutta. For three generations, they had been agents for the government of Bhutan and had offices in Calcutta from which all Bhutan's political and trade business with the outside world was transacted.

Jigme himself had been sent to a Jesuit public school in Darjeeling, had travelled widely outside India, and spoke perfect English. He was very much a man of the world. He had inherited a racing stable in Calcutta from his father, and married the daughter of an important Tibetan aristocrat. They entertained regally and, both in his social and public life, Jigme gave the impression of a debonair extrovert, whose special charm lay in his complete naturalness and his sense of fun.

Above all, Jigme was a realist. He never felt any need to conceal or apologise for his country's isolation or backwardness, and was equally at home in the medieval society of Bhutan and the twentieth century world beyond its frontiers. He was intelligent and modest enough to describe himself as a half-educated person because his father's death and his official duties had prevented him from going to a university. He made up for this by a rare intuitive grasp of men and situations. As a private individual, he refused to take himself too seriously but, when he had to speak or act on behalf of his country, he did so with dignity and authority. Casual acquaintances who only met him in London, Paris or Calcutta easily made the mistake of supposing that he was no more than an attractive playboy but, in the service of his country and its interests, he was completely serious and dedicated.

'Well,' he asked Lobsang, as soon as they were alone and comfortably installed, 'where have you been all this time?' and, when Lobsang had filled him in on his adventures since their farewell in Bumtang, Jigme lost no time in getting down to business.

'Now I really need you. Great things are going on in Bhutan. We are building our first road, linking the interior with India and, for the first time in our history, we need modern technicians. With your experience and your knowledge of Tibetan, which is very like Bhutanese, you could be invaluable to us. We must have a good workshop at Phunscholing, on our side of the Indian frontier, where our road project has its headquarters. I want you to come and run it for me. You're just the right man, and besides,' Jigme concluded disarmingly, 'I like you. I think we could get on and work very well together, don't you?'

Even for someone as accustomed to quick changes of fortune, the job now being dangled in front of Lobsang was almost too good to be true. It was a challenge which would stretch his professional knowledge to its limits in a cause which he could understand, respect and identify himself with unconditionally. It would give him a chance to work alongside a man for whom he already felt admiration and sympathy, and who, he felt instinctively, shared many things in his approach to life and people. Finally, as far as he could judge from their conversation, there were no ideological or political strings attached. If he had been given *carte blanche* to write his own ticket, he could scarcely have done better. The invitation was irresistible and he accepted it on the spot.

To enter Bhutan from India – and there was no other way except through Tibet – all travellers had to obtain what is known as an Inner-Line Crossing Permit from the Indian authorities. India has no right actually to forbid entry into Bhutan, which is a sovereign power, but it can make it impossible to get to a point of entry into Bhutan by simply withholding this permit, which authorises a traveller to cross the restricted military zone of Indian territory which runs along the whole length of Bhutan's southern frontier. As long as Bhutan has no air-link with the outside world, India thus exercises an effective veto over foreigners entering the country.

Four days after his arrival in Calcutta, Lobsang was sent by Jigme to apply for his Inner-Line-Crossing Permit. His application was turned down on the grounds that, as India was financing Bhutan's development scheme and providing the necessary technical assistance, there was no need for the Bhutanese to recruit a Chinese engineer for any part of the project. The Indian authorities clung jealously to their right of veto and this was often a source of irritation to the government of Bhutan. Jigme, with his long experience of dealing with Indian bureaucracy, could be patient and tactful when he cared. Now he was in a hurry to get back to Bhutan, and wanted to take Lobsang with him. So he sent for his executive assistant, Lawrence Sitling, and instructed him to issue Lobsang with a Bhutanese passport on the spot. This document, with its black cover embossed with the double dragon and thunderbolts symbolising the Land of the Thunder Dragon, as the Bhutanese call their country, is still in Lobsang's possession. In all his comings and goings, it is the only passport he has ever had.

'We'll have to give you a Bhutanese name,' Jigme told him. 'What shall it be? . . . I know, Lobsang. It means "good knowledge" or "good brain". Yes, then Thondup. That means "success". A very auspicious name. That,' he added with a mischievous smile, 'ought to fix 'em.'

On 1st December 1960, as an accredited official of the government of Bhutan, Lobsang travelled with a captain in the Bhutanese army, Penjo Ongdei, into his country of adoption. Could it be, he asked himself, that his latest change of name would really bring him luck? For the moment at any rate, fortune was smiling again and, until further notice, the importance of being Lobsang was clearly evident.

20

LOBSANG HELPS TO BUILD A ROAD

Lobsang's first impression of Bhutan, during his first brief passage through it as a refugee, had not been too favourable. He had assumed it to be a kind of miniature Tibet and had had neither the time nor the inclination to observe its special characteristics. Now, in the company of Jigme Dorji and with the prospect of playing a constructive part in the country's development, he began to see it with new eyes.

Anyone going up into Bhutan from the Indian side is immediately struck by a sense of space and freedom. The bustle of the plains of the Brahmaputra valley, with its thronging villages and towns, is left behind and in its place is a sparsely populated land, rising steeply through a belt of dense jungle and opening out into the wonderful alpine uplands of central Bhutan. In so much space every person stands out as an individual rather than being just part of an anonymous crowd. The men, with their gaily coloured handwoven robes, in stripes or checks, hitched up to knee-length by a tight waist-belt, look at a distance like kilted Scotsmen and the illusion is heightened by their typical highlander's gait.

The women are no less arresting. Their short hair, cut in a tight bob, contrasts with the long tresses and elaborate hairstyles of practically every other country in Asia. It gives them an emancipated look which is in keeping with their place in Bhutanese society. In a country where every individual counts and has his or her place in the economy, there is no room for self-effacing oriental womenfolk.

Another thing that Lobsang soon noticed with approval was that there were none of the elaborate social barriers which he had found so irksome in Tibet. Society, it is true, was still largely feudal in its structure, with the King as the absolute ruler and the barons, or *Penlops*, each administering his district as the monarch's local representative. There are however few great fortunes or great landlords with accumulated wealth of a hereditary nature. Almost every family in Bhutan owns and cultivates its own land and the country itself is self-sufficient to an extent unknown in any other country in Asia.

When, two years later, Bhutan took its first hesitant step into international affairs by accepting an invitation to attend a meeting of the Colombo Plan for aid to underdeveloped Asian countries as an observer, the astonishing discovery was made that it, alone of the member states, had no problems of over-population, housing or food, no grinding poverty or dispossessed masses, no unemployment and, apparently, no political strife.

Bhutan's first delegate to the Colombo Plan – *Ashi* Tashi Dorji, the elder sister of the Queen and of Jigme Dorji – had no difficulty in her priorities in listing her country's requirements in terms of assistance from the outside world. Modern education and modern medicine were needed to eliminate illiteracy and a small number of endemic diseases, but even here the requirements were very modest compared with those of most of the member states. Above all, Bhutan was in no frantic hurry to make the leap from its traditional way of life into the age of technology and the industrial consumer society. Bhutanese society was too securely established for its rulers to need to impress the people with costly prestige projects and they saw clearly the dangers of trying to do too much too fast and of disrupting the well-tried pattern of Bhutanese civilisation in the process.

The Bhutanese delegation made such an impression of all-round competence on this occasion that Bhutan was invited to become a full member of the Colombo Plan, thus gaining her first foothold in the Councils of World Affairs. Hers was the only Asian delegation led by a woman. In fact Tashi Dorji was assisted by her sister-in-law, Tess, Jigme Dorji's Tibetan wife. By their charm and common sense both these ladies convinced the delegates, and particularly the Australians, Americans and Canadians, that Bhutan was ready to take her place as a full and responsible member of the Colombo Plan.

As Bhutan's closest and most powerful neighbour, India played the leading part in such development schemes as were cautiously embarked upon. India had inherited certain consultative rights in matters of Bhutanese defence and foreign policy from the British Raj and, with her growing concern over developments in Tibet and relations with Communist China, she began to attach increasing importance to Bhutan as a strategic buffer state. Jigme Dorji's frequent presence in Calcutta made him the natural focal point for discussion of development schemes between the governments of Bhutan and India. He remained in personal charge of development plans and of the newly formed Development Wing.

At Phunscholing, on the frontier with India, workshops and engineering installations were to be set up, both by the Bhutanese government and by the Indian technical aid mission to Bhutan. The first experimental plan for setting up a Bhutanese mechanical workshop had run into difficulties. A young Chinese, educated in the Indian hill station of Kalimpong, had been put in charge of it. He had already failed in a garage enterprise of his own in Kalimpong and, according to Lobsang, was simply not qualified or equipped for such a responsible job. The Indian government, which was paying for the development schemes, made it clear that it considered the reduplication of effort a waste of money and in the end it was agreed to amalgamate the two projects.

While the plans were taking shape, there was not much that could actually be done in Bhutan itself. Jigme Dorji commuted between Calcutta, Kalimpong, the frontier and Central Bhutan and Lobsang often accompanied him on his travels. This gave him a chance to get to know the country and its people and institutions. Language presented no difficulty. Written Bhutanese, which few people outside the monasteries could read or write, is identical with Tibetan and, although the spoken language differs quite widely from standard Tibetan and has many local dialects, a working knowledge of it was not difficult for Lobsang to pick up.

The Southern border district, in which the workshop at Phunscholing is situated, has a considerable Nepalese population.

Many of these Nepalis were recruited in the labour force needed for the biggest single development project, started in 1960 – the building of the road from Phunscholing up to Paro and Thimpu, the two main administrative centres in the West of Central Bhutan. The Indians were closely associated with all these development projects and the smattering of Indian languages that Lobsang had picked up during his detention in Misamari and Shillong made it possible to communicate with almost everyone connected with his work.

Lobsang was able to go shooting and fishing with Jigme and other members of the Dorji family and pay frequent visits to places like Kalimpong, Darjeeling and Sikkim. Bhutan, with its great jungles and its extreme variations of altitude and climate, teems with game of every description and brown trout, imported into Bhutan from Kashmir by Jigme's father, grow to enormous sizes in the beautiful rivers. Most Bhutanese, being devout Buddhists, do not take life, but the Royal Family and the Dorjis were keen sportsmen.

It was during these early days that Lobsang made the acquaintance of Jigme's middle brother, Ugyen, an incarnate lama who had spent his early years in a monastery. After attending a western public school in Darjeeling, he had married the King of Bhutan's half-sister, *Ashi* Choki Wangchuk, and joined the Bhutanese army after completing an officers' training course in Poonah. This brother, affectionately and irreverently known as Rimp (an abbreviation for his title of *Rimpoche*, meaning incarnate lama), later separated from his wife, left the army and started a number of private enterprises. At the end of 1961 Lobsang helped him to organise a motor spare parts business in Phunscholing.

For his first four months in Bhutan Lobsang lived in the government guest house at Phunscholing, then spent eight months under canvas. In case this sounds unusual or uncomfortable, it should be explained that, for well-to-do Bhutanese, camping is part of the way of life. Their painted tents can be elaborate affairs with several rooms and all sorts of amenities. The King or the Prime Minister, when travelling in company, often preferred to set up camp rather than use other accommodation. At the wedding of Jigme Dorji's first cousin the Crown Prince of Sikkim, in 1963, the Bhutan Camp, with its blue dragon emblems emblazoned on the tents, was a feature of the festive scene in the Sikkimese capital of Gangtok which all the guests who attended it remember.

In August 1961 Lobsang married his present wife and the mother of the four children who constitute his existing family circle. Her name is Rinzi Om and she was sixteen years old at the time of their marriage. Many Bhutanese girls marry when they are thirteen or fourteen, and Lobsang's wedding to a girl of her age was not considered either unusual or inappropriate. Her family came from Eastern Bhutan, where her father had been *Daben*, or Master of the King's horses, at the old royal capital of Bumtang. He had died when she was quite young and she had become a protégé of Jigme Dorji in an unusual way.

Jigme was at the time very concerned with the problem of illiteracy. The first lay primary school in Bhutan was started by the Dorji family in their home at Ha and he was doing everything to encourage the opening of new schools and to train Bhutanese teachers to staff them. During a trip in Eastern Bhutan, he talked to a group of small children and asked them if they would like to come back with him to Ha to attend his school. The children were told to ask their parents, whose only response was to lock up their children until Jigme's departure.

Rinzi Om, however, had her own ideas. She was only five at the time but, as soon as her mother had left the house, she jumped from a first floor window and ran after Jigme Dorji, who was already leaving for home. Jigme, who had three sons but no daughters of his own, was so touched that he took her with him to Ha. He paid for her education at Ha and later sent her to a convent-school in Kalimpong. At the time of her meeting with Lobsang, she was staying with the Chief Supply Officer for the new road project in Phunscholing. She had completed the first part of a teacher's training course and was waiting to hear if she had won a place to complete her training in a college in Madras.

This was another of Lobsang's lightning courtships. On the day they met he took Rinzi Om to a cinema in Hasimara, on the Indian side of the frontier. Two days later they married, living first in Lobsang's camp and later in family quarters of the Civilian Sub-District Office in Phunscholing. Jigme Dorji, when he next passed through and heard the news, sent for Rinzi Om and scolded her. There had already been several cases of Bhutanese girl teacher-trainees marrying and deserting the jobs for which they were so badly needed. As a result teacher-trainees were obliged to give an undertaking to teach for at least three or four years before retiring into domestic life. Rinzi Om was not, strictly speaking, a government subsidised trainee, since she was Jigme's own charge, but he told her that she should at least have asked his permission before plunging into marriage. What made matters worse was that he had just heard that she had been given a place in the college at Madras. However, he soon relented and Rinzi Om made amends by teaching in the little school which had recently been opened in Phunscholing.

Lobsang, whatever he may sometimes pretend, respects educated women and acknowledges that his wife, though very young, has shown character and devotion throughout all the ups and downs of their married life. Except where the children and their education are concerned, she has shown herself an un-demanding wife, who takes Lobsang's amorous peccadillos philosophically and uncomplainingly. She has shown courage and steadiness in adversity and, like all Lobsang's wives, has intelligence and beauty combined with a devotion which, even if at times he appears to take for granted, he certainly appreciates. He returns it with his own brand of loyalty, which is quite unaffected by his occasional lapses from strict marital fidelity.

At the time of his marriage to Rinzi Om, work on the Bhutan Road Project had settled down into a full-time job. Construction of the new road was in its early stages and all the mechanical equipment was not yet available. The result was that Lobsang's mechanical division spent a good deal of its time doing heavy manual work. The terrain, particularly through the lower jungle reaches, was appallingly difficult. During the monsoon Southern Bhutan has one of the heaviest rainfalls in the world and road-making was complicated by frequent landslides.

Everyone who has travelled up or down this astonishing road

in its heroic early years has memories of hours or days spent immobilised in his jeep or truck, waiting for the roadblocks caused by the landslides to be cleared away by emergency gangs. In really bad cases, passengers had to be 'transhipped', baggage and all, round the block to another vehicle on the far side. Lobsang's experience had taught him many useful tricks of improvisation in this sort of emergency situation. He was physically very strong and fit and he stuck religiously to his principle of setting his labour force an example by showing them himself how to deal with every difficulty as it arose. Some of the Indian engineers had not been brought up in this tradition of doing the dirty work themselves, but the Indian mechanics and the unskilled labourers who made up his road-gangs appreciated his methods and repaid his example by giving loyal and unstinted service.

'All the Indian mechanics used to call me *dada* – the Bengali for Big Brother. Funny; the same name as my Chinese workshop boys gave me in Tibet, only perhaps more familiar. I took it as a great compliment, and we got along very well together. Often the work was really hard and I had to be a bit of a slave-driver when conditions made it essential to get things done in a hurry. I know I was sometimes impatient and hot-tempered, but I was very keen to do a good job and they never seemed to resent it because I never asked them to do anything that I wasn't prepared to do myself.'

During the monsoon, Lobsang would stay up on the site for long spells, returning to Phunscholing for three or four days' rest only when the particular piece of work he was doing was satisfactorily completed. Jigme Dorji, who visited Bhutan about once a month, sometimes discovered him, sweating and mudstained, doing heavy manual work with his assistants looking on. Jigme teased him good-naturedly, telling him he was doing all the work himself instead of training others to do it. Lobsang's status was in truth something of an anomaly. Officially he was an engineer working for the Bhutan Engineering Service. He was paid by the Indian aid mission but, as a Bhutanese national, got none of the allowances paid to the Indian engineers. He had been transferred to the Engineering Service personally by Jigme and had never been given any written terms of reference. As a result his authority depended solely on whatever relationship he could establish with his Indian colleagues. He had never bothered to point out to Jigme the drawbacks of all this.

The two men shared the same enthusiasm for the project and the same impatience and determination to drive it through in record time. While he was busy with his work on the road Lobsang received proof of how staunch Jigme's trust and confidence could be. 'It was during the monsoon and we were working on a very difficult winding section of the road. Just as we had finished one stretch, a landslide came down and made it impassable. We were hurrying to bulldoze it clear as we were expecting a very important party up the road any day. One of my assistants, a Nepalese, was living on the site in a tent with his wife and son. He had an accident with a primus stove, causing an explosion and setting the tent on fire. In trying to protect his family, he burnt his hand very badly. I had been informed that there was an Indian doctor named Vatyacharchi on his way up the road, so I went down and found him with a half-ton truck and several assistants. I told him of the accident and explained that the nearest first aid post was over ten miles away and I had no transport to take the patient. He declined to do anything, on the pretext that he had no drugs or equipment.' Lobsang saw that the lorry was loaded with medical supplies that belonged to the doctor, but the latter insisted that they could not be used because they were being delivered to an Indian army medical centre. 'I argued that it was his duty as a doctor to treat an emergency case at any time or place, even if he was a Nepalese.'

The doctor then said the supplies on the lorry could not be touched because they were consigned to the King of Bhutan in person. Lobsang was enraged by this legalistic quibbling and by the doctor's arrogance and obstinacy. He simply ordered his men to unpack the medical supplies. He told the doctor that, in any case, the road was so blocked that it was impossible for him to continue his journey until it was cleared and asked him, in view of this unavoidable delay, whether he would not reconsider his decision and give first aid to the burnt assistant. While his men were preparing to unload the truck, the doctor said something to one of his companions in Bengali. Lobsang did not catch what he was saying, but the driver whispered to him, 'Don't try to remove the boxes, or they will shoot you.' At this point, Lobsang really lost his temper. 'I was standing on a slight rise and jumped down and went straight for that damned doctor. My men and the drivers came to my assistance and between us, I admit, we gave him quite a rough time.'

The doctor sent a report, containing a strongly worded complaint against Lobsang, addressed to the Prime Minister of India, with copies to Jigme Dorji as Prime Minister of Bhutan, and to the King. A few days later Jigme was in Phunscholing and Lobsang found him in the guest house discussing the case with the doctor and the Chief Indian engineer of the Bhutan Engineer Service working on the road project. When Jigme had heard Lobsang's version, he addressed the doctor in a cold fury.

'First, as a doctor, you refused help to a man when he needed it desperately. Secondly, although you were sent to serve the people of Bhutan, you apparently only think in Indian terms. If you had a complaint to make on Bhutanese territory, it was your business to report it to the authorities of Bhutan. But you intended to by-pass them and take your grievances to the Prime Minister of India. India, it is true, is giving economic aid to my country, but that does not mean that Bhutan belongs to India or has become her dependency. You do not seem to appreciate this, so I do not think you are the right kind of man to work with our people. You were assigned to a small place to attend humble people, but only New Delhi and Prime Ministers seem to be on your working level. Many of the men working on the road are your own countrymen. Perhaps you could not condescend to treat even them, so how can I trust you to take care of my own people? You will leave the country within twenty-four hours.'

Lobsang attaches great importance to this incident, not only because it demonstrated Jigme s loyalty to the people under him, but because he had shown such qualities of heart and compassion and had taken such a firm stand on the issue of Bhutan's national identity and independence.

It was after this incident that Jigme and Lobsang had their first thorough discussion of the basic problems created by Bhutan's various development schemes. Jigme was very worried because the King's own ten-year plan for rebuilding the great dzong in Thimpu, which was to be the seat of central government, was draining three or four thousand labourers from the road project, which already placed an almost impossible strain on Bhutan's own slender manpower resources. He asked Lobsang if he had any ideas on the subject and Lobsang pointed out that anything that could save manpower at the dzong would be in the national interest. He suggested transferring all available trucks, tractors and bulldozers to Thimpu to move the huge trees and stones needed for the reconstruction of the dzong. The saving in labour and man-hours would shorten the whole rebuilding scheme by years and so free an army of labourers who could be used on the roads and for other urgent tasks.

Jigme decided to second Lobsang to Thimpu and to authorise him to use all the plant and equipment he needed from the Bhutan government service. The only obstacle to this scheme was that the road was not yet sufficiently advanced to take the heavy equipment up from the frontier to Thimpu. Only jeeps and small one-and-a-half-ton pick-up trucks could go through the whole way to Thimpu, so Jigme ordered Lobsang to dismantle the heavy plant and get the chassis and component parts humped by hand over the stretches of road which were not able to bear their full weight.

When he returned from his next trip to India, he inquired at the frontier whether the parts had gone up yet and was flabbergasted to be told that Lobsang had already driven all the heavy equipment through to Thimpu in one piece. Lobsang had in fact calculated very minutely the stresses and strains of all the bridges which the senior Indian engineer had declared to be unusable for such purposes, and had come to the conclusion that, with very careful handling and the use of strong wire hawsers as an additional security measure, the job could just about be done.

He had had some heated discussions with the senior Indian engineer, which he had only clinched by saying that he was ready to take full responsibility, and if necessary to go to prison if anything went wrong. In five days, by simply creeping up the road and enlarging or reinforcing it as he came to the stretches which had been pronounced impassable, he had got all the essential heavy equipment through and was already installed in Thimpu, ready to start on his new assignment.

21

A CONFLICT OF LOYALTIES

After his transfer to Thimpu, Lobsang's acquaintance with the King, Jigme Dorji Wangchuk, ripened into respectful friendship. He soon realised the King's problem in providing the labour force needed to build the road at its northern end, up in the interior of the country, where Nepalese were not allowed. Each Bhutanese family was required to provide its quota of workers for the road and, understandably, this semi-feudal recruitment was not popular among a people who were often hard put to it to find enough hands to cultivate their own land. The King employed contractors – or *La-pons*, as they are called in Bhutanese – each responsible for one thousand labourers and a given stretch of road. For all work completed under the contracted time the *La-pon* received a ten per cent bonus. The Indian government subsidy for the road made it possible not only for the King to offer this kind of inducement, but to save money himself if the work was finished on schedule. This he was always anxious to do, if only to help finance his own pet project, the rebuilding of the Thimpu Dzong.

It had become a sort of royal tradition for each King to build himself a new palace and transfer his principal seat of government to the area where he had built it. The King's father had chosen Tongsa, in Eastern Bhutan, transferring his seat there from Bumtang, and the King took a personal pride in following his father's example. His plan for Thimpu was even more ambitious and a great deal more costly. Besides building the new palace in which he now resided, he had decided to pull down and rebuild the dzong to accommodate Bhutan's fledgling parliament, a nominated advisory council which it was intended progressively to turn into a more representative and democratically elected assembly.

It was a gigantic building operation, comparable in scale and skill only to the demolition and rebuilding of a great medieval European cathedral. The whole of the river valley which the dzong commands was transformed into a vast encampment of the country's best artisans – carpenters, woodcarvers, blacksmiths, metal workers and decorators – all prefabricating the component parts for assembly on the site as soon as it had been cleared of the old dzong buildings.

There was also an army of demolition workers, engaged in laboriously pulling down these massive buildings and the outer fortifications which surrounded them. Some idea of what was involved can be got when it is realised that, to transport a tree of the size needed to make a single major beam, ninety men were needed. The quarrying and moving of foundation stones by hand set the same sort of problem of manpower and man-hours.

In charge of the whole dzong project was a venerable hereditary master-builder named Usui. He was a dignified bearded figure who invariably wore a sword of office and had complete confidence in the traditional methods which had been handed down to him and had hitherto served Bhutan so well. Their only drawback was that they admitted of no short cuts and the King, a young man in his thirties, was in a great hurry. The recruitment of the necessary labour force, on top of what was needed for the road project, placed a heavy strain both on the country's manpower and on the royal exchequer. The road project was subsidised by the Indian Government. The dzong project had to be paid for out of the resources of the royal purse.

During the winter building at Thimpu had to be suspended for three months because of the weather. Normally the labour force would have been paid off and returned home. But the King, with an eye to the main chance, proposed to Lobsang to take charge of the dzong labour force and use it to push ahead with a branch of the road running from Thimpu to Wandiphodang, which was Bhutan's main army training centre. He complained that the Indians had been very slow on this branch of the road although he attached great importance, from the Bhutanese internal point of view, to completing the link as soon as possible. Lobsang was put in charge of a total force of something like 6,000 labourers, with six La-pons working under him, for the three winter months of 1962. The King promised him a share of what savings he could effect and Lobsang, by using the dzong's mechanised plant, was able to make sensational progress and was congratulated by the King.

The period during which he was seconded to Thimpu made Lobsang gradually aware of the unavoidable conflict of interest between this royal enterprise and the Indian-financed road project. It also led him to a fuller understanding of the background to the relationship between the King's family, the Wangchuks, and the Dorjis. The events in which Lobsang was involved during the next four years were linked, at almost every stage, with this relationship, which was complicated and sometimes dramatic.

The hereditary monarchy of Bhutan dates from the time of the King's grandfather Ugyen Wanchuk. Previously Bhutan had had a dual system, with a spiritual or *Dharm* King, ruling side by side with a temporal monarch, or *Deb* King. The *Dharm* King, or Shabdung Lama, like the Dalai Lama, was a reincarnation and was discovered, upon the death of his predecessor, by much the same methods of identification as the Dalai Lama. The *Deb* King's office was also not hereditary. In practice, he was usually the strongest of the barons, or *Penlops*, who asserted his authority over his rival *Penlops*, often by force of arms. This system resulted in a succession of baronial wars which helped to keep Bhutan both isolated and economically backward.

Uygen Wangchuk not only succeeded as *Deb* King while he was still a young man, but managed to secure the consent of the governments of both British India and Tibet to the establishment of a hereditary temporal monarchy of Bhutan, with himself as its first King. In this he was assisted by another Ugyen – Ugyen Dorji, the grandfather of Jigme Dorji. He was a prosperous merchant, established in Kalimpong, who spoke excellent English as well as Nepali. He earned golden opinions from the government of British India by acting as successful intermediary in the settlement of a territorial dispute with Tibet. In recognition of his services he was given the honorary Indian title of Rajah Dorji.

The King of Bhutan was equally indebted to him for the results of his diplomacy.

Under the settlement reached through his good offices, Tibet ceded to India some disputed territory, in what is today the North-East Frontier Agency. In return Tibet received arms and equipment which enabled it to create an army of its own, and so made it more independent of China. Bhutan, which was even more isolated than Tibet, was assumed to need no protection and was not asked to receive a British garrison, which both the other Himalayan monarchies, Sikkim and Nepal, had been obliged to accept.

Ugyen Wangchuk, although he was nominally still only Tongsa *Penlop*, was already the real ruler of Bhutan, and he conferred on Ugyen Dorji the title of *Deb Zimpon*. This was roughly equivalent to the functions of Ambassador-at-large. Considering that Bhutan had no foreign service and no formal diplomatic representation abroad, this made him a very influential person indeed. Ugyen Dorji, in addition to his family home in the Ha valley, up against the Tibetan frontier in Western Bhutan, also administered areas farther to the South-West.

A large part of these areas in Southern Bhutan consisted of magnificent virgin forest, and the fine timber was in great demand in India. Fine timber is, in fact, found all over Bhutan, but there were no roads at the time, making transportation virtually impossible. It was Jigme Dorji's idea that a network of good roads throughout Bhutan would solve this problem. He also felt that these roads would enable not only industries dependent on timber to be developed, but would essentially open the way for the exploitation of Bhutan's potentially rich mineral resources.

Ugyen Dorji's son, Tobgye, who continued to use the styles of Rajah Dorji, was also made *Deb Zimpon*. The title was conferred upon him in 1929 in Punakha by Ugyen Wangchuk's son, who by then was the King. At the same time Tobgye's eldest son, Jigme Dorji, received the title of Ha *Trungpa*, by which Lobsang had first known him. At that time the King's eldest son, also named Jigme, the grandson of Uygen Wangchuk, was one year old. His father placed him in the special care of Tobgye Dorji.

When he went to school in Kalimpong, it was Tobgye and his family, who owned considerable properties there, who looked after him. In this way the link between the Wangchuks and the Dorjis was maintained and consolidated so that Jigme Dorji's relationship with Jigme Wangchuk was almost that of an elder brother. Later the two boys went to Britain and stayed in Scotland together at the home of an old friend of Tobgye Dorji. The bond between the two families was further sealed by the King's son adding the name Dorji to his own and thus becoming Jigme Dorji Wangchuk.

The use of patronymics in the Western style dates, in Bhutan, from the establishment of the hereditary monarchy and the foundation of the Wangchuk dynasty. The Wangchuks and the Dorjis were originally the only two families to use regular surnames, but today, with the spread of secular education and administrative bureaucracy, the practice is becoming general.

At first there was no suggestion of rivalry or friction between the Dorjis and the Wangchuks. Gradually, however, owing to the Dorjis' greater wealth and to the extensive privileges they enjoyed in Southern Bhutan, which included the right to levy taxes and appoint local magistrates and officials without consulting the King, there developed a situation where Southern Bhutan almost enjoyed an identity and loyalty of its own. The members of the Dorji family have, as a matter of fact, always been scrupulously correct in acknowledging an absolute loyalty to the throne. They have always rejected any suggestion of dividing the country or undermining its unity and, when Jigme Dorji Wangchuk succeeded his father in 1952, none was more of a stickler in his loyalty to the King than Jigme Dorji himself.

The fact remains that frictions, however unimportant they may have appeared at the time, did begin to creep in. But when the youngest Dorji sister, *Ashi* Kesang, married Jigme Dorji Wangchuk in 1950, the unity of Bhutan seemed assured by this union between the two most powerful families in the country.

Jigme Dorji unquestionably continued to regard himself as the King's loyal agent and executive. As minister in charge of the development plan, as well as of day to day relations with the Indian government over its implementation – and later as Prime Minister – he was sometimes placed in an awkward position by the King's determination to press ahead with his own plans for the Thimpu Dzong at all costs. The plain fact was that Bhutan could ill afford the strain placed on its economy and manpower by the double task of building the road and rebuilding the Thimpu Dzong. Nor could the King easily finance the Thimpu project out of his own pocket. He was therefore tempted to use some of the revenues which came from the Indian subsidies for development schemes and the expansion of the Bhutanese army in order to complete the work at Thimpu.

Probably none of the interested parties thought of things in such crude terms. Jigme Dorji was no doubt ready to stretch a point here and there to please his king and, incidentally, his brother-in-law. Yet, cumulatively, the job of making both ends meet did create personal irritations and a conflict of principle. Lobsang, through his regular contacts with both the King and Jigme, was naturally conscious of these frictions as they began to grow more acute.

During his attachment at Thimpu, he got to know the King extremely well. Without ever feeling in his company quite the same lack of constraint that existed between him and Jigme Dorji, he found him an enthusiastic and generous man to work for. He was a strong character, who lived life to the full and a fine and fearless hunter. Working for him presented a constant challenge, but Lobsang soon noticed that the King was as devious in his dealings as Jigme was frank and open.

One incident which brought this home to him occurred on a day when the King presented him without warning with a handsome knife. Taken by surprise and not realising at first that it was intended as a gift, Lobsang took it with one hand, as he would a tool that was given him to use, instead of receiving it with both hands in a gesture of ceremonial acceptance. He saw at once that the King was annoyed, and soon took his leave. As he was going, he thought he heard the King call his name. He answered, only to realise that he had been calling someone else, and excused himself. The King, rather sarcastically, replied 'How many names have you?' It was a small thing, but it rankled all the same, and made him feel uncomfortable.

Luckily, Lobsang found a firm friend in the old master-builder Usui. The medieval craftsman and the Tokyo-trained engineer recognised in each other the authentic product of their respective schools. Lobsang respected the old boy's detailed knowledge of the traditional art of dzong-building, with its insistence on superb quality of craftsmanship, and was touched by his readiness to accept him as a collaborator and not as an intruder encroaching on his established authority. Usui was big enough, and loyal enough to the King, to see how Lobsang's modern techniques could save time and manpower without lowering the standards of the monument to Bhutanese traditional architecture which it was his task to erect. He accepted in good part an order from the King to build a four-roomed house for Lobsang's use and the two oddly assorted partners never seem to have found any difficulty in working happily in double harness. The King, delighted with the progress they were making, promised Lobsang to award him a Red Scarf, reserved for senior lay officials, if the dzong was completed within three years, instead of ten as originally planned.

It was while Lobsang was working at Thimpu in April 1963 that something happened to the King which had important consequences for the whole remainder of his reign. Lobsang, who was in the dzong, noticed that none of the usual officials were about. On inquiry, he was told that they were all at an archery match at the army camp just outside Thimpu.

Archery is the national sport of Bhutan, and any excuse is good for organising a match. Two teams, at opposite ends of a tree-bordered alley, shoot at a narrow upright target from one hundred paces. Like village cricket in England, archery in Bhutan is a sport where people of all classes and ranks join in what is as much a social gathering as a test of skill. Each team is cheered on by a chorus of half a dozen girls, who dance a sedate measure, holding hands in a circle, and sing encouraging words when their own team is shooting from their end of the alley. When the teams change ends after each flight of arrows, the chorus improvises the broadest ribaldries, often based on personal knowledge of the competitors, in an attempt to make the opposing team laugh and spoil its aim.

The King was one of the best archers in the country and took a keen interest in the sport. It was a steamy day and had rained slightly during the archery match. He was hot and perspiring and in this state he stayed talking and drinking in a refreshment tent by the side of the alley. An attractive Tibetan girl named Yangki, who was known to be a favourite of the King, was also present, and the King himself was in high spirits, joking and drinking with the archers and the rest of the company and apparently without a care in the world.

After dinner at the army camp, he returned to the palace at Thimpu, still in this carefree mood. There, soon after nine o'clock, he had a sudden and very serious heart attack. The only doctor immediately available was Dr Craig, a Scottish physician who had lived for many years in Kalimpong. As the King had had a minor attack a year previously, Jigme Dorji had arranged for this doctor to be in permanent attendance on the King in Thimpu. He had been at the archery contest with him but had no sophisticated equipment and no morphia with which to administer pain-killing injections, and at this time Bhutan still had no regular medical services.

The Queen was in Sikkim for the wedding of her first cousin, Thondup Namgyal, the Crown Prince, to his second wife, the American Hope Cook. Jigme Dorji was in Kalimpong on his way to the Sikkim wedding in Gangtok. The news of the King's attack, and of the doubts as to his survival, was radioed immediately to Gangtok and both Queen Kesang and Jigme Dorji were helicoptered direct to Thimpu, bringing Indian specialists and the necessary drugs with them. Meanwhile, in the palace there were anxious consultations, in some of which Lobsang took part, about the possibility of fetching a doctor from the Indian state of Cooch Behar.

In any absolute monarchy, the death or serious illness of the monarch is bound to create urgent administrative problems. The King was in constant pain but was able to speak and, on Jigme Dorji's arrival, told him, in very brotherly and affectionate terms, to carry on and not to feel himself obliged to seek his authority for decisions that needed taking at once. He said to him that they both understood well enough what had to be done in Bhutan and that he had entire confidence in Jigme as his representative.

22

❦

A SHOT IN THE NIGHT

The whole direction of the affairs of state now fell on Jigme. For the first couple of weeks after the King's attack he stayed on duty round the clock at the palace and, in any case, was too worried to be able to sleep at nights. Sometimes, to pass the time in the early hours, he would call in the Deputy Chief Secretary, Sangay Paljor, Lobsang, one of the King's equerries and a painter called Kamdo to play cards and talk.

For the King's men – the members of his personal household and those whom he had promoted to posts which were sometimes beyond their training or capacities – this was an anxious time. Not all of them were on good terms with the Prime Minister, who was notoriously an outspoken critic of inefficiency and incompetence among government officials. Misgivings about their own future were often mixed with their concern for the King himself.

During these early days a succession of doctors and specialists were flown in to Thimpu by helicopter. A week after the King's attack a London heart specialist arrived and recommended treatment in London as soon as the King was fit to travel. The general opinion of these and later consultants was that only the King's extraordinary constitution had enabled him to survive. Most of them, privately, gave him at best a few years to live. The question in everybody's mind was how many more attacks he could be expected to resist. He showed astonishing recuperative powers, but his progress was punctuated by bouts of depression and lethargy which were only to be expected in his condition.

Lobsang thinks that Dr Craig regarded the constant going and coming of new specialists as a reflection on his own professional competence. Jigme Dorji had spoken to him rather critically for not having detected warning symptoms of such a serious attack.

All this caused Dr Craig to remark, as any general practitioner might have under the circumstances, 'They'll kill him with all those doctors and medicines.' Among some of the members of the King's household this remark was interpreted in a far more sinister sense than Dr Craig had ever intended. They clung to the isolationist attitudes upon which their way of life was founded and which, as they saw it, had successfully withstood the test of hundreds of years. The King's mother belonged to this school of thought and Lobsang believes that, during this period of the King's illness, some of them may have passed on to the King gossip and hints that the Dorji family were scheming to take more power into their own hands.

As a matter of fact Jigme Dorji had been devoting a great deal of thought to how to safeguard the country's stability by ensuring continuity of responsible government. If anything happened to the King or himself – or even to both of them – there would be no ready-made machinery of government. Jigme himself had only one lung. He had had the other removed in Switzerland and used often to refer to himself jokingly as 'the one-lung man'. The King's son and heir was at this time only seven and by Bhutanese custom would be considered a minor until he was eighteen.

Jigme therefore thought it prudent and even urgent to make some provision for any possible new emergency. About six weeks after the King's attack, Jigme submitted to him a plan to appoint a State Council which, if anything happened, would be ready to function collectively as an executive cabinet and take over the government of the country.

Two or three days later the Indian newspapers published a report of a plan for a cabinet in Bhutan with a list of how the portfolios were to be distributed. This report included the name of Lhendup Dorji, the Queen's youngest brother, as minister for transport and communications. In fact Tashi Dorji, her elder sister, was the only member of the Dorji family submitted in Jigme's list. She was suggested as minister for education and health – both fields in which she had had experience in connection with the Colombo Plan. The reports in the Indian press spoke of a State Council being convened by Jigme Dorji to select the heads of government departments in an attempt to form the first cabinet in the history of Bhutan.

The question was, who had leaked the news of this highly confidential meeting on a question of such importance to the State? The King insisted that there should be an inquiry. There had only been two private secretaries present at the discussion. As there seemed no other possible source by which the news could have got beyond the room in which the conference had been held, Jigme decided that one of them should be dismissed. The King also insisted that the whole idea of a State Council should be put into cold storage for the time being, on the ground that, since the Indian government apparently had spies in the palace, it might be dangerous to pursue the meetings until the security aspects of the case had been cleared up.

In actual fact, according to Lobsang, the King himself had made the news available to the Press in Calcutta. Jigme Dorji was completely unaware of this. Lobsang gives this as an instance of how unpredictable the King could be in his actions, particularly after his heart attack, which left him in a state in which he became moody and easily suspicious of the motives and intentions of even those nearest to him. On the surface he and Jigme continued to be the best of friends, working together on terms of absolute trust. On Jigme's side their relationship was based on complete sincerity and loyalty, both to the King's person and to the interests of the country. But Lobsang believes that, even at this time, the King had begun to be suspicious of Jigme. As he lay in bed during his convalescence, there were many visitors and relatives who were ready to play on this feeling by reporting to him complaints about Jigme's management of affairs in ways that suggested that the Dorji family was manoeuvring for power.

It was in this state of mind that, in September 1963, the King, accompanied by the Queen, flew to London for treatment and advice and, from there, went on to Switzerland for a long period of convalescence. Jigme Dorji was left in Bhutan as Regent in the King's absence and as Prime Minister. His sister Tashi was still in charge of the Colombo Plan work which often took her abroad, and her youngest brother, Lhendup, was Secretary-General of the Development Wing.

This meant that Jigme Dorji had virtually sole responsibility for all major decisions of domestic and external policy, in addition to supervising everything to do with development plans. By comparison with the old division of labour between him and the King before his heart attack, this placed a very heavy strain on Jigme. It also brought him face to face with the realisation that, beneath the surface, there were tensions inside the country of which he had not been aware and which often needed careful handling. Most of them, directly or indirectly, were connected with either the development schemes or the expansion of the role of the Bhutanese army in the power structure of the country.

After the fighting between China and India in November 1962, Bhutan was the only one of India's neighbours to side openly with her. Considering that she was totally defenceless, this was a brave gesture. It was also decided, with Indian help, to create at least a token national defence force.

Previously Bhutan's army had consisted of a few hundred men – scarcely more than a royal bodyguard. To man an army of even 10,000 men, which was the target set in 1962, meant a major upheaval in the life of the country. All able-bodied men between the ages of eighteen and forty-five became liable for conscription and supply, alone, became a serious problem. At the two main training centres, at Thimpu in the West and Tashigang in the East, no thorough supply system for feeding the troops had been worked out in advance. The result was that in Thimpu daily air-drops from India became necessary in order to keep the army in the necessities of life. Rice was in particularly short supply.

To meet this situation, Jigme made an appeal, particularly aimed at wealthy landowners, to sell stocks to the government as a patriotic duty. The first reaction of many Bhutanese, who had no experience of this sort of situation, was to deny that they had any surplus stocks. When Jigme discovered that one man had in fact bought a thousand sacks of rice intended for the army and was hoarding it in his warehouses, he felt it was time to make an example. The man was arrested, his house and property were confiscated and he was sentenced to six years' imprisonment. He turned out to be someone who had acted as an agent for the King, who had often transacted business for him and no doubt imagined himself to be under royal protection. He had already been convicted, when acting as a supply contractor for the Road Project, of diverting large sums. Lobsang admits that he thinks it would have been wiser of Jigme not to have made this particular demonstration of authority.

Inside the army itself, there had also grown up an anti-Dorji faction. Under the agreement with India for the expansion and modernisation of the army, selected young men were sent to military colleges in India to be trained as officers, and then to the new Bhutanese officers' training school at Ha, where many of the Dorji family's houses had been requisitioned to accommodate the cadets and their instructors. After crash courses of six months, these trainees were commissioned and posted to command units of the new national army.

It would have been an almost impossible task in the time available to re-train the old officer corps as leaders of a modern military force. To begin with, most of them would have had to learn how to read and write. Very few of them had any knowledge of English or Hindi, the languages used in the basic training of the new army. If there had been more time, it is possible that more tactful ways could have been devised of softening the blow to the pride and prestige of the old school of officers. As it was, it became increasingly clear to them that they were regarded as out of date and that they were going to be phased out and replaced by young officers with a little book-learning but no experience of actual command. They argued, understandably, that there had never been any trouble along Bhutan's frontiers while they commanded the army and asked what guarantee there was that the new army, under its young Indian-trained officers, would do any better.

When the Indian troops suffered their humiliating reverse at the hands of the Chinese in the North-East-Frontier Agency in 1962, the old Bhutanese officers scathingly reproached Jigme Dorji for putting Indian instructors in charge of the new army whose only example was apparently to run away in face of the enemy. The Indian officer who commanded the Indian Military Training Team, Brigadier Uppadhaya, himself confessed that he was ashamed of his uniform, although he had taken no part himself in the actual fighting.

Even if the King had not had to hand over to Jigme Dorji and leave for Europe, this problem of discontented senior army officers would certainly have existed. The plan, which had been agreed by the King, was that they should be retired, as far as possible, by 1964. As it was, it was Jigme rather than the King who incurred the unpopularity that inevitably went with these revolutionary changes. The malcontents tended to identify him with their grievances and to make common cause with others who, for quite different and often less honourable reasons, resented the authority which the King's absence had placed in Jigme's hands.

At the time of the Indian-Chinese fighting on Bhutan's Eastern frontier Lhendup Dorji, Jigme's youngest brother, was sent to take charge of the Bhutanese Eastern Command at Tashigang. On instructions he insisted that Indian troops who had straggled over the frontier should be sent back at once, as Bhutan naturally wished to avoid complications with China. The Indians no doubt resented this attitude and this was certainly another cause of Indian complaint against the whole Dorji family both at this time and later.

There was also another more personal source of friction – Yangki, the Tibetan woman who had been present at the archery match on the day of the King's heart attack. She was the wife of a groom in the King's stables called Chiru. At first her meetings with the King were conducted with discretion. Lobsang remembers driving her from her house to the palace at Thimpu in his truck in order not to excite comment. The Queen, for a long time, was unaware of the relationship, and Lobsang says that Jigme Dorji helped to explain away Yangki's continual presence in court circles by letting his sister think that she was his own girl-friend. Gradually, however, Yangki grew less careful and more ostentatious. The King had been lavish in setting her up in style and had also provided her with considerable sums of money. These she spent not only on herself and her immediate family circle. She entertained freely and made many influential friends among government officials and key army officers, not hesitating to distribute largesse and gifts when it advanced her purposes. Lobsang himself was often invited to her house to play cards or to dances when he was in Thimpu and was able to form a pretty accurate idea of the extent of her ambitions. These had grown when she bore the King their first child. She had already had one son by her husband Chiru. She became increasingly bold and began to make a practice of driving publicly in the royal jeeps, whose special markings and number-plates – Bhutan 7 or Bhutan 8 – made them instantly recognisable. Her ambition, no doubt, was to get herself acknowledged as the King's second official consort. The King's father had taken two wives, both of whom simultaneously enjoyed the title and privileges of royalty. Indeed the son of his second wife was at this time one of the King's principal officials.

After the departure of the King and Queen to Switzerland, towards the end of 1963, Yangki went to India on a shopping spree. She had had a brand new house built at the King's expense in Thimpu and went to choose furniture and fittings in her usual prodigal style. Clearly she was contemplating heavy personal and commercial purchases because, on the way out, the King's private secretary Shinkalam asked the army Commander-in-Chief to put two military vehicles at her disposal for their transport back to Thimpu. The Commander-in-Chief passed the request to the Quartermaster-General who, in turn, gave orders to make the two vehicles available at Phunscholing.

Unfortunately one of these lorries was overturned on the road by its driver, who was drunk, and discovered by Jigme, who was travelling down the road from Thimpu to Phunscholing. The Prime Minister was furious and gave orders to the civilian government's Bhutan State Transport organisation to take over the army's trucks. When he reached Calcutta, the Prime Minister summoned the Quartermaster-General and gave him a thorough dressing-down and a strict warning against allowing any army transport to be used for private purposes unconnected with army or state business. There had also been cases of the Quartermaster-General providing Yangki with money out of army funds at the request of the same Private Secretary who had made the original approach to the Commander-in-Chief about the loan of the trucks. All this gave the top army command another reason to resent Jigme.

In Lobsang's opinion the Commander-in-Chief never forgave this affront. Jigme's brother Lhendup had also been in Calcutta. He was even more indignant than the Prime Minister and had argued in favour of confiscating the trucks and transferring them permanently for the use of Bhutan State Transport. At this time development projects were often behind schedule because civil transport was commandeered by the army. This irresponsible use of valuable transport, often for private trade, offended both Jigme and Lhendup, particularly as the army was often needlessly negligent in its maintenance of valuable vehicles.

About a month after this incident Yangki's father came down to Phunscholing from Thimpu. Lobsang, who was also in Phunscholing on three months' leave from the Thimpu Dzong project, warned him against trying to commandeer any more army trucks. 'When the King comes back', retorted the old man menacingly, 'we shall see who's master.' There had been another occasion in 1963 when an army transport officer had tried to hold up some of Lobsang's own trucks going down from Thimpu to Phunscholing. Lobsang had made a complaint against this to army headquarters, but it worried him to discover that the army was beginning to throw its weight about as though it was the real power in the land.

There had been several small incidents which did not amount to much in themselves, but which, cumulatively, made Lobsang suspect that the army officers were scheming for some end of their own. The senior officers all of a sudden became very reluctant to accept any civilian appointments, however attractive. For example, Jigme Dorji had offered the post of *Nirchen Chompen*, or official in charge of rations, finance and supply, in Paro to an elderly colonel named Aku Tomi, who had begun his career as a band-master.

Ordinarily, he would have jumped at such an honour, but now he firmly declined. It began to look as if the army was beginning to consider itself an élite institution with a policy of its own. It had even put out a curious feeler in Lobsang's direction. The Commander-in-Chief, at the end of 1963, had sent a man named Chogyul to Lobsang's house to ask if he would be interested in joining the army and taking charge of tank training. Lobsang knew very well that there were no tanks in the Bhutanese army and no prospect of it acquiring any and, at the time, treated the matter as a joke. Now he began to wonder if this had not been an attempt to buy him. But if so, for what purpose? Decidedly, there was something fishy going on.

Lobsang's presence in Phunscholing was officially the result of a request for a spell away from Thimpu, where he had been overworking on the Dzong Reconstruction Scheme. The winters are very hard in Thimpu and Lobsang had not been well. But he had other reasons for wanting to get away from Thimpu. He had an uneasy feeling that things were going seriously wrong. In December, after the incident with Yangki's father, he had already warned Rimp Dorji in Phunscholing about his suspicion that a dangerous movement against the Prime Minister was building up around Yangki and among her circle. He told him frankly that Jigme, because he was responsible for so much, had also become the target of much discontent. Lobsang said he felt that the atmosphere had changed for the worse in the last few months. He did not feel able to speak personally to the Prime Minister in a way which might seem to imply criticism or disrespect and hoped that Jigme's own brother might be in a better position to pass on his warnings in the spirit in which they were meant. Rimp Dorji either found no opportunity to do so or may himself have felt it difficult to broach the subject for fear of worrying or angering Jigme. He did, however, implore Lobsang not to mention his fears to his other brother, Lhendup, saying he was so impetuous by nature that he might do something rash.

When next he met the Prime Minister in Phunscholing, Lobsang again raised the question of terminating his assignment in Thimpu. He had, after all, only been temporarily seconded from his real work on the Road Project and the workshop at Phunscholing. Jigme, who was placed in an awkward position, told him to ask the King, but by this time he had already left Thimpu for Europe. Finally the medical officer at Phunscholing gave Lobsang a certificate which said that his lungs needed supervision and advising that he should not do anything in the way of heavy work for the present. Lobsang says he feels that Jigme may have thought that he had some private business he wanted to attend to. With his usual consideration and understanding for Lobsang, he arranged with the Financial Secretary to extend Lobsang's three months' normal leave by a further three months' medical leave on full pay.

Lobsang, with the prospect of some enforced leisure in the pleasantly warm climate of Phunscholing, after all his strenuous work on the road and at Thimpu, seized the opportunity to get his domestic life organised on a more permanent basis. He asked Jigme if he might build a house for his family on the outskirts of Phunscholing and was told to choose himself a site. Having selected a pleasant spot on a hill overlooking the market, and with a commanding view of the river and the mountains, Lobsang went to work and put up a comfortable modern four-roomed house in two months. It was a congenial task, occupying him and taking his mind off the political storms which he now felt certain were brewing.

For the first time he was able to live with his wife and children in a real home of his own and enjoy a feeling of domestic security which had eluded him for so many years. His new house was conveniently situated within easy reach of the workshop and the Bhutan Engineering Service. He was also once again brought into regular contact with Jigme Dorji, whose duties still kept him constantly moving between India and Bhutan and so took him frequently through Phunscholing.

So it was that on the evening of 5th April, 1964, Lobsang was at home when Jigme arrived on his way up to Thimpu from India. Normally, if he had not been on leave, he would have gone, as a government official, to greet the Prime Minister on arrival at the Rest-House. As it was, at five o'clock, when Jigme reached the

Government Rest-House, Lobsang was in the Druk Hotel, a new enterprise started by Rimp Dorji in Phunscholing, and Bhutan's first hotel. Jigme spent the evening in the main lounge of the Rest-House, a bungalow building with a broad terrace in front and large modern glass windows which were an innovation in Bhutan, where the windows of the traditional houses have no panes but fasten with heavy wooden shutters. To pass the time until dinner, he started a game of rummy with his brother Rimp, his wife and Mary MacDonald, the Prime Minister's Anglo-Tibetan private secretary.

The room grew stuffy – Phunscholing is low-lying and by the beginning of April it can often be hot – and Jigme got up and opened a window. Then he returned to the table. It was a quarter past eight. There was a shot and Jigme collapsed in his chair.

The bullet, which had been fired through the open window from the darkness outside, passed through his right arm and lung and still had enough velocity to hit Rimp Dorji's wife, wounding her in the wrist. In the confusion which followed, the assassin, who in any case would have been invisible from inside the lighted room, escaped into the night.

23

WHO HIRED THE ASSASSIN?

Jigme Dorji was still alive and conscious but his condition was clearly desperate. If he could have been got to a properly equipped hospital Lobsang is convinced that his life could have been saved. The only doctor on the spot, a young and newly qualified Bengali, had little experience or equipment. Messengers were dispatched to Cooch-Behar and some of the tea-gardens across the Indian frontier to try to fetch oxygen cylinders. While Jigme was still able to speak, his thoughts were mainly for the political dangers into which his assassination, coming on top of the King's heart attack, might plunge his country. He asked that his murderer, if he was caught, should not be too severely treated, but he told his brother and the others present to try to find out why he had wanted to kill him.

On a more personal note, he explained that he did not want a lot of fuss and religious pomp at his funeral. Above all he urged his family to be loyal to their country and to treat the assassin, if he was apprehended, with clemency. He urged them only to try to find out the motive for the assassination since, although he was aware that he had enemies, he could not think of anyone who hated him to the point of wanting his death.

The first that Lobsang himself knew of the tragedy was around half past eight. The local Quarter-master, Major Dewan, a former Indian officer, came to his house, where he was already undressed for bed, and told him the news. He threw on some clothes and went out, to discover that the Quarter-master had brought thirty or forty soldiers with him as an escort. Lobsang mentions this as evidence of how strong Indian suspicions of everybody Chinese, including himself, were at this time. Even Dewan, not having seen him at the Rest-House, evidently thought he might be involved in the assassination plot and was taking no chances.

At the guest house Lobsang found Rimp Dorji and his wife. Rimp at once asked Lobsang for his opinion on the identity of the assassin. Who, he asked, could possibly have had a motive for wanting to get rid of his brother? Could it be discontented Nepali settlers in Southern Bhutan, who had organised some sort of a political movement for more privileged treatment? Nothing seemed to make sense. Lobsang took the distraught Rimp out on to the verandah and told him soberly where his own instinctive suspicions pointed. 'I told him I thought that the conspiracy must be Bhutanese in origin. I reminded him of my earlier fears and the warning I had asked him to pass on to Jigme.' Lobsang also said that he thought the assassin must have been the tool of the army officers who resented Jigme – possibly even of the Army Commander, Namgyal Bahadur, himself.

Rimp Dorji protested that he knew him as an honest and loyal man and could not believe he would carry his sense of grievance to the point of murder. It was, as a matter of fact, Jigme himself who in 1957 had recommended Namgyal Bahadur's appointment as Army Commander in order to counterbalance the King's promotion of four very young officers who had only just completed their training course in India, to senior command posts. Namgyal was a more experienced officer who had at one time served a training period with the Assam Rifles. Lobsang replied that it was the only plausible explanation he could think of. By the time Lobsang reached the bungalow, Jigme, although he lived for nearly three hours, was no longer able to speak.

Gradually, other members of the Dorji family began to gather at the deathbed. Jigme's youngest brother Lhendup had been at Samji, thirty miles away, where the Development Wing had its winter headquarters, in order to attend a reception for the new Indian Political Officer. Jigme's wife, Tess, had just returned to Bhutan from India. The eldest Dorji sister, Tashi, was at her mother's house at Namseyling, near Thimpu. Lhendup was the last of the family to reach the Rest-House. At the sight of his unconscious brother, he threw his revolver down on the table and wept.

Through their grief everyone was aware of the cold-blooded urgency of identifying and tracing the assassin, but until there was some clue to his nationality and motive, it was virtually impossible to guess in which direction he would try to make his escape. If he was acting for a foreign power, he would presumably head out of Bhutan into India. If, as Lobsang suspected, he had been given his orders by the army, it was more likely that he would return to Thimpu to report and seek the protection of whoever had sent him.

Lobsang left the two Dorji brothers conferring and went out into the kitchen to question the servants. The first real clue came from a kitchen boy who said he had noticed a tall stranger smoking a 'piri' (a kind of local cheroot) outside the kitchen quarters in the backyard. He had offered him one, but when asked what he looked like, the kitchen boy said it was dark outside and that he had not looked at him carefully. With precious time ticking away, Lobsang was not satisfied and told him he would be held for interrogation. The boy then volunteered that he thought he was a soldier from the army camp in Phunscholing. The duty officer in charge of the camp was fetched and asked if there was anyone in his camp not on the locally paid strength, but being paid by central army headquarters. The lieutenant in charge was at first unco-operative, but Lobsang had seen him earlier in the evening drinking at the Druk Hotel when he should have been on guard for the Prime Minister at the Rest-House. When Lhendup threatened to have him arrested for being away from duty, he admitted that there was a soldier of the name of Jambay who had no special duties and had left the camp to go to the Rest-House. He recollected that he had a German Mauser .38 revolver. When Lhendup Dorji was told this, he was able to add the information that a soldier of that name had served a prison sentence of a few months in Thimpu recently.

There was now enough to go on. Lobsung felt fairly sure that, if his suspicions were correct, Jambay would try to get back to Thimpu. In his haste, he had dropped a shoulder bag he was carrying and also lost one of his spare shoes outside the Rest-House. The night of 5th April was spent trying to follow the scent with tracker dogs flown from Calcutta by the Indian Government. Rimp Dorji, Lobsang and more than twenty others, mostly local Nepalese, passed a frustrating night, with the dogs trying to take them over rough forest country which was very difficult to negotiate in the dark. The party returned to Phunscholing around four o'clock in the morning and, after a discussion with Lhendup, it was decided that two separate search parties should work up the old footpath into the centre of Bhutan which all travellers had used before the motor road existed. Lobsang and a State Transport Officer named Lari Lama formed one party and the other was made up of soldiers from the Phunscholing garrison under a sergeant, Norbu. In a small hamlet named Tara where there was a frontier checkpost orders were left with the village headman that if he saw or heard of a man in shorts and a shirt he was to have him held.

On the second day of the search Jambay was run to ground. The alert for strangers had spread quickly through the countryside and a local postman who had seen Jambay guided the soldiers to a place near a little hamlet where he alleged he was hiding. The postman was carrying a shotgun, and, as they closed in on Jambay, fired by mistake. Lobsang's party, hearing the shot, ran up just as he was being apprehended by Norbu. He was secured and taken by truck back to Phunscholing. During the drive the prisoner, who was exhausted and frightened began to plead with Lobsang. 'Lobsang Sahib,' he entreated, 'I'm not an enemy of the Prime Minister. I was ordered from above.' He went on to explain that he had followed the Prime Minister to India in an unsuccessful attempt to find an opportunity to shoot him undetected. Jigme had gone to Samji on arrival in Bhutan, to welcome the New Indian political officer, Avtar Singh, and had left early to drive to the guest house at Phunscholing in his own car. On the way he had overtaken a new Mercedes mini-bus which had just gone into service. As he had not yet inspected this latest addition to the country's public transport, Jigme stopped it, made the driver take his own car, and took the wheel of the mini-bus, which he drove on to Phunscholing. Jambay was in fact a passenger in the bus, which he had taken in order to catch up with Jigme at the Rest-House where he knew he would spend the night.

No one could be certain that officers in the army camp at Phunscholing were not involved in the conspiracy, so it was decided that the prisoner should be kept somewhere where there was no danger of the army attempting to release him. He was put under guard in the safe-room of the SDO's office, which had a steel door, and orders were given that no unauthorised persons, whatever their nationality or rank, should be admitted. By this time Phunscholing was full of rumours. The first report published in the Indian Press, almost certainly with official approval, suggested that the assassin was probably a Chinese agent. At this date, less than eighteen months after China's attack on India, Peking had further offended the Indian Government by publishing maps in which large areas of Bhutan appeared as part of Tibet, and consequently of greater China, and New Delhi was convinced that China had long-term designs on Bhutan.

By the time the prisoner had been brought back to Phunscholing on the morning of April 7th, Jigme's body had already been removed and a funeral procession was on its way to lie in state at his mother's house at Namseyling, which stands above the road not far outside Thimpu. Already ceremonial scarves and flowers had been heaped by mourners at the Rest-House in Phunscholing and on the way up into the interior Bhutanese, Nepalese and Indians using the road spontaneously showered rhododendron petals on the cortege as it passed.

Tashi Dorji had gone, at her mother's suggestion, to see the King's mother at her house just above Thimpu. She was told that arrangements had been made for Jigme's body to lie in state at the army headquarters, where the whole Dorji family could pay their respects. Having already heard by radio from Phunscholing that the arrested suspect was an army man, Tashi objected to this arrangement and the Queen Mother then suggested as an alternative the school in Thimpu. Tashi said she would have to consult her mother, but on her way back to her mother's house she was temporarily stopped at an army check-post and told that this was on the orders of the Army Commander.

Lhendup Dorji, as Secretary-General of the Development Wing, stayed in Phunscholing, ready to receive the King on his arrival back from Switzerland. Lhendup told Lobsang that the position of the Dorjis looked very grave. Lobsang therefore took two truckloads of arms from the Phunscholing depot and motored up at speed to Namseyling to block the road leading to Jigme's mother's house in case the Army Chief made any attempt on the rest of the Dorji family. The arms were distributed to members of the household who formed an improvised guard round the house. By the time Lobsang arrived at Namseyling rumours of a plot to liquidate the entire Dorji family were widespread in Thimpu itself, as contemporary reports in the Indian Press from a correspondent on the spot bear out. Lobsang spent several nights on guard at the Dorji house and remembers that the intense cold, quite apart from the state of alert, made sleep impossible.

Meanwhile, in Phunscholing, the first official inquiries had already been completed. The King had cabled orders from Switzerland, as soon as news of Jigme's assassination reached him, addressed to Lhendup Dorji, to his step-brother Namgyal Wangchuk and to the Army Chief Namgyal Bahadur, to investigate the crime and arrest the assassins. The preliminary investigations in Phunscholing were conducted by the Commissioner for Southern Bhutan, Rinchen Drukpa. It was he who took Jambay's statement after he was brought to Phunscholing. This was recorded on a tape recorder and contained passages in which he stated that the Army Commander had ordered him to kill Jigme and alleged that these orders had had royal approval.

On 9th April the King reached Hasimara from Switzerland, a border town between India and Bhutan. He took a helicopter to Thimpu, but bad weather forced him to turn back to Phunscholing. The same evening the King summoned Rinchen and asked how he knew that Namgyal Bahadur was behind Jambay. Rinchen replied that Jambay had confessed to receiving the gun from Namgyal. The King also asked if his mother was suspected. On being told yes, the King appeared overcome by grief and said that even if it was true, his mother would have to be forgiven, as he was her only son, and could do nothing to hurt his mother. The King asked Rinchen whether it was thought that he himself was involved. When Rinchen had to admit that this was also so, the King wept and said that Jigme had been very good to him and so had his queen. If anyone had been in the plot, it could only be his mistress, who was greedy for more and more, in spite of the wealth that he had given her. He also expressed his concern to Rinchen that Jambay's wild accusations, if they became public knowledge, might cause people unjustly to suspect that he himself was in some way connected with the conspiracy, and that this could be harmful to the nation's unity. On the King's orders Jambay was sent under strong guard to the royal palace at Thimpu for further interrogation.

In Thimpu itself preparations had been made to welcome the King on his return to his country – the flags and bunting at the Army Headquarters, where his helicopter was expected to land, contrasting strangely with the mood of mourning and the mounting anxiety over the political implications of Jigme's assassination. At first the King had been expected to arrive on April 9th and the next day a guard of honour and reception committee, headed by the Army Commander, was mustered on the parade ground of the military training centre to receive him. After hours of waiting news came that bad weather had delayed the King and the parade was dispersed. In some sections of the crowd a fresh rumour spread of an army conspiracy to take the King into custody and force him to submit to its demands.

On the morning of April 11th the ceremony was repeated. At last two helicopters were sighted, but flying too high to make a landing on the parade ground. When they returned, only one alighted and it was not the King who disembarked but a former Indian Political Officer, Appa Pant. The other helicopter had already put down the King in his own palace compound, in the safe protection of his own royal bodyguard.

That afternoon the same two helicopters returned, one to pick up the Indian official from the Military Training Centre and the other to put down Lhendup Dorji in a field below his mother's house at Namseyling. On the palace roof white cloths had been laid out as a prearranged signal to Lhendup that the King was safe and in control of the palace. If they had not been there Lhendup was to presume that the King was being held under duress by the conspirators. At Namseyling the atmosphere on the morning of April 12th was electric. In the late morning a helicopter came to pick up Lhendup and take him to the Palace, leaving his family still uncertain whether he might not be flying into a trap. He was back in half an hour with the news that the King was safe but that a showdown with the Army Commander was still awaited. Tension and rumour continued throughout the day. Namseyling was now an armed camp in a state of siege. Military movements were in progress up and down the road, with reports that the Army Commander had had road blocks erected and was questioning all travellers about the strength and disposition of forces at Namseyling and at the Indian training mission's guest house.

On the morning of April 13th the King sent one of his most trusted officers, the Chief of General Staff, Colonel Tangby, to summon the Army Commander to the Palace. He arrived, accompanied by the former Quarter-Master General, Bachu Puche, and some escorting junior officers. The King had given orders to disarm all visitors, irrespective of rank, at the front gate of the Palace grounds. He himself met the Brigadier at the front door of the palace itself and informed him without further ado that he was under arrest. He had taken the precaution of putting Tangby behind the door with one of his own attendants. With the Brigadier safely inside the palace, Tangy went outside and arrested the two ADC's who had come with their chief. The ex-QMG was also arrested and confined in the palace. Tangby then went back to Army Headquarters and informed the officers that the King would be coming to address them. They were ordered to hold themselves ready, but told that it must be strictly understood that in view of the prevailing confusion, no arms were to be carried. Meanwhile the commander of the royal bodyguard at the palace had surrounded Army headquarters with his own troops and proceeded to arrest about forty individual officers.

The King never went to address the assembled officers. Instead, the same night, on April 13th, he had the Army Commander brought to him in the palace for a private confrontation. Colonel Tangby, concealed behind a door with a gun in his hand in case the Army Commander attempted violence, was the only witness of this interview. The King, according to Lobsang, dropping the tone of icy authority in which he had ordered Namgyal Bahadur's arrest, now proceeded to talk to him man to man. This was natural enough. The Commander was an uncle of the King by marriage, and the two men had always been on friendly and even intimate terms.

The gist of what the King now had to say was that the Army Commander must admit full responsibility for Jigme's assassination, thus corroborating the assassin's own confession. Besides the statement taken by Rinchen Drukpa at Phunscholing, the King had already interrogated Jambay privately in the palace at Thimpu in the presence of Tangby.

The King stressed how important it was, in view of the accusations contained in Jambay's confession, that there should be no public suggestion that members of the royal family were in any way involved in the assassination or its planning. He called upon Namgyal Bahadur to corroborate Jambay's statement that it was from Namgyal that he had received his orders and admit that he was solely responsible for them. If, in this way, a public scandal harmful to the state was avoided, the King even held out the hope that the Army Commander might look forward to royal clemency. He also spoke about the grievances and fears of the officers of the old school and gave Namgyal assurances that they would be properly treated and looked after. He went on to discuss the points that the Army Commander could legitimately make in his own defence at his coming trial.

First he could say that, because of the number of doctors Jigme had brought to see the King and the succession of drugs and medicine he had been given, he had feared that Jigme was putting the King's life at risk. Secondly, he could admit his resentment at Jigme's handling of army reforms and at the promotion of young Indian-trained officers at the expense of senior men of the old school. Thirdly, he could say that Jigme's jibes about these older officers being unable to read and write had particularly rankled and develop the theme of his sympathy for these trusted men who, after long years of loyal service, saw themselves threatened with redundancy just when the army was, for the first time in Bhutan's history, becoming a privileged and prosperous military caste and an influential institution.

All the men accused of the conspiracy were now under lock and key in the royal palace. Two days later the director of medical services for the Development Wing, a Dr Tobje, was in attendance on the King at the palace. There he was suddenly called by Tangby to the ex-Quartermaster General's cell, where he found the prisoner with a long knife embedded in his stomach. He was still conscious and was able to whisper to the doctor that the story would be that he had taken his own life, but that he had been disarmed and searched at the moment of his arrest and had in fact just been stabbed. The doctor hurriedly reported what he had found to the King who, according to Lobsang's account, took the line that the Quartermaster General had made his guilt clear by attempting suicide and that it would consequently be better for his own sake if he was allowed to die as he had intended.

Besides Jambay another accomplice named Sangye Dorji had been arrested. He had also been recruited by the Army Commander and given orders to assassinate Jigme, but had failed in his mission and squandered the money he had been given in drink.

The King lost no time in appointing a special commission to investigate the conspiracy. It was composed of the Chief Secretary Tinley Dorji, the Chief of General Staff, Colonel Tangby, the Deputy-Chief Secretary Paljor Sangay and the Commissioner of Southern Bhutan, Rinchen Drukpa. The proceedings of the inquiry and the trial were recorded by the King's private secretary Shinkalam.

Bhutan had no established legal practice which provided a precedent for dealing with the present situation, so the procedure had to be largely improvised for the occasion. Ordinarily justice was administered either summarily by the magistrates in the dzongs or by the King or his principal officials. With Bhutan so much in the public eye, it was important that the trial should be properly conducted. The Dorji family also had a special interest in seeing that justice should be done. Their brother's reputation as Bhutan's Chief Executive during the King's absence was, after all, in a sense involved.

The Queen, Kesang, naturally refused to give any credence to Jambay's allegation that the King had in any way connived at her brother's death. This made her all the more determined to find out the truth. In Paro, where she was now staying, was a young man named Dawar Tsering, a protégé of the Dorjis. He was recognised as possessing powers as a medium – not uncommon in Bhutan and other countries of South East Asia – and a séance was arranged. When the medium was asked whether Namgyal Bahadur, the Army Commander, had instigated the murder, he replied that others were behind him. This séance was held about a week after Jigme's death and before the setting up of the tribunal of inquiry and the trial.

Lhendup, the youngest Dorji brother, had been brought up in the tradition of unquestioning loyalty to King and country. He held the high office of Secretary-General, and must have felt he had an important role to play in helping to steer his country along the difficult path of transition on which Jigme had launched it and that, whatever his personal feelings, his over-riding duty was to Bhutan. After the assassination, the King asked Lhendup to carry on his brother's work for Bhutan. This expression of trust and the King's visible sorrow at Jigme's death made it as difficult for Lhendup as for the Queen to take Jambay's accusations of royal connivance in his brother's assassination seriously.

Tashi Dorji, the eldest sister, was above all concerned for her sister, the Queen. In spite of her skill as a diplomatist, Tashi is a strong and even passionate character to whom compromise on issues of family loyalty does not come easily. The rumours of a wholesale plot to liquidate the Dorjis made her genuinely afraid for the safety of the Queen and her children if a real power struggle developed in the country.

As the royal commission pursued its inquiries, the circumstances of Jigme's assassination seemed to become more and more complicated. When the Army Commander was confronted with the statement made by Jambay to Rinchen, he in turn declared that the attempt to kill Jigme had started some four months earlier. He had given Jambay a gun to carry out his mission and had made several plans, all of which had miscarried, to commit the crime so that Jigme's death would appear accidental. He then became increasingly afraid that the conspiracy would be discovered and ordered Jambay to return the gun he had given him. It was an old .38 Mauser and, when it was issued to Jambay, its magazine had contained nine bullets. When the new Bhutanese army was equipped by the Indian military mission with modern weapons, about forty of these Mausers, which had been in service in the old army, were called in. The Army Commander, in his statement to the commission of inquiry, said that all the Mausers except one, which the King had kept for his personal use and which he had given to one of his mistresses, were left in his safe-keeping. So that after Jambay had returned his pistol, together with its magazine, he had been astonished to learn that the murder weapon was also a Mauser, but that its magazine had contained eleven instead of nine bullets. Whether or not to protect himself, the Army Commander hinted strongly that, in the King's absence in Switzerland, someone in the King's entourage, who was presumably also aware of the plot and Jambay's part in it, must have had access to the other pistol and given it to Jambay. As, at the trial, no witnesses were called to give evidence on this point, the truth or falsity of the Army Commander's explanation was never publicly established. It is, however, Lobsang's conviction that this was a point of real substance and that, if it had been pursued, it might have revealed that several people in court circles were privy to the assassination conspiracy throughout.

When Rinchen reported this statement of the Army Commander to the King, he dismissed it as untrue.

Towards the end of April, everything was set for the trial. It was held in the dzong and the public was admitted. Lobsang sat through the proceedings and so did Tashi and Lhendup Dorji and the King's step-brother Namgyal Wangchuk. The King did not attend the court, but received detailed reports after each session from the members of the tribunal.

The upshot was that Brigadier Namgyal Bahadur made his confession, defending the assassination on the ground that he had ordered it in good faith as a patriotic duty.

The culmination of the trial was a summing up by the Chief Secretary, Tinley Dorji, who acted as President of the Tribunal. On the question of fact, the Army Commander's confession and those of the actual assassins left little for him to say. But in dealing with the prisoner's plea of justification, he told the Army Commander that, whereas all Bhutan's responsible officials had worked together for their country, he had betrayed it by removing Jigme Dorji, Bhutan's loyalest and most selfless servant. In the circumstances, the Court felt it had no choice but to impose the severest penalty. Accordingly he was sentenced to death by shooting.

Bhutan, as a Buddhist state and a former theocracy, had no death penalty. In the past, murderers who had to be got rid of were sometimes sewn into a yak's skin and dropped into a river – so that the fiction was maintained that they had drowned accidentally, thus exonerating any individual from the responsibility of having actually taken human life. The fact that all three accused in the assassination trial were serving soldiers and that the country was in a state of military emergency served as a pretext for the imposition of a death sentence for treason and the use of a firing squad.

How much the condemned man still hoped for the exercise of royal clemency at this stage of the proceedings is, like so many things about this web of confused motives and loyalties, difficult to conjecture. He was visibly moved by the President's stern summing up and was in tears by the time sentence was passed. For a man of his reputation and self respect, the imputation of betraying his country and the disgrace of public rebuke must have been as hard to bear as the sentence itself.

After the trial the King summoned the Army Commander to a final meeting in his room at the palace. It was a bitter confrontation. The King explained that public opinion was now so incensed at Jigme's assassination that the country's whole future was at risk. He said he feared that, if things got out of hand, a situation would arise in which established order would be threatened and everyone's life, including his own and that of his family, would be in danger. Consequently the whole situation had changed and the only way of restoring it, for the sake of Bhutan, was for the sentence to be carried out so that the public would be satisfied that justice had been done.

When the Army Commander tearfully reminded him of his earlier assurances, he could only console him by promising that he would see to it that his family was provided for – a pledge which was subsequently honoured. Brigadier Tangby, according to Lobsang, was again the hidden witness of this dramatic encounter.

The Army Commander was now taken from the Palace to a dungeon in the Thimpu Dzong, which was to serve as the condemned cell.

It was after this interview that two of Namgyal Bahadur's old officers, Colonel Penjo Ongdei and Colonel Lam Dorji, came to visit him while he was awaiting execution. These officers brought him food and drink and spent half the night with him trying to console him. He told them that, although they were much younger than he was, they had enjoyed a better education and were cleverer than himself. Had he had the same advantages, he said bitterly, he might not have found himself in his present plight. 'And', he concluded, 'my advice to you is never to allow yourselves to be made a scapegoat for other people. Let my example be a warning to you.'

Apart from the official proceedings of the Commission of Investigation and the trial itself, the Queen had taken steps of her own to clear up the doubts and contradictions surrounding her brother's death. She had been staying at the palace in Paro after Jigme's funeral, while the King was at his palace in Thimpu. The Queen took Dawar Tsering to Thimpu, where they installed themselves in the Palace guest house. Her intention was that Dawar should pay a secret call on the Army Commander in prison and ask him specifically if he was the sole instigator of the plot against her brother.

She was unaware that royal orders had been given that no one, irrespective of rank, was to be allowed access to the prisoners. These orders laid down that the guards should shoot any attempted intruders on sight. Dawar told Rinchen Drukpa of his mission and asked him to accompany him on his visit to the prisoner as a corroborating witness. Rinchen at once informed him of the King's orders and the risk he would be taking in trying to carry out the Queen's instructions. After much heart-searching they decided to pretend that they had seen the Army Commander and that he had confirmed that he, and he alone, had planned Jigme's murder.

Meanwhile Tangby, in charge of security at the Palace, had discovered the real purpose of the Queen's and Dawar's presence in Thimpu and had reported it to the King. It was then agreed that if Rinchen was questioned by the King, he would tell him the truth – that he and Dawar had never tried to visit the prisoner. To the Queen, however, they would stick to the story they had previously concocted. The King, when he learnt of their intention, rewarded them for their discretion by giving Dawar a fountain pen and awarding Rinchen the coveted Red Scarf – the same insignia of senior officialdom he had promised Lobsang if the Thimpu Dzong project was completed in three years.

The whole episode illustrates the complexity of the loyalties and fears which played their part behind the trial, both as they affected the King in his relations with his subjects and in his relations with the Queen and her family. Rinchen himself wrote a letter to his father about this time which leaves no doubt about his feelings. 'I know the truth,' he wrote, 'but the whole truth will never be publicly known.'

On 29th April, Brigadier Namgyal Bahadur, handcuffed and dressed in a scarlet and yellow striped *boku*, was taken to the Army Training Centre just outside Thimpu. He walked firmly to the execution post and, after only a few seconds, at the drop of a white handkerchief, was shot before a large and silent crowd. It was the first time that a death penalty had been carried out in Bhutan and, among the lamas and ordinary people, was regarded as offensive to Buddhist principles.

Jigme Dorji and the Master Builder on the site during the rebuilding of the Dzong at Thimpu. Below, the King and Queen of Bhutan at about the time of Lobsang's arrival in Bhutan; the little boy on the left is the present King

Above, the first road in Bhutan, which Lobsang helped to engineer, from the foot-hills on the Indian border up into central Bhutan

Below, the re-construction of the dzong at Thimpu – on the left, pre-fabricated beams and on the right, workers' lunch break in the courtyard

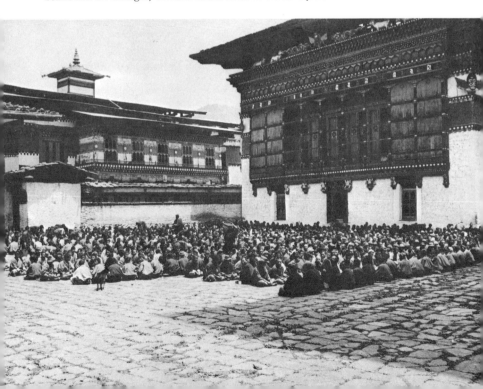

Lhendup Dorji, Jigme's brother; archery is the national sport of Bhutan. Below, the Commander-in-chief, Bahadur Namgyal, led from court after sentence of death

It was two weeks before the assassin Jambay and his accomplice, Sangay Dorji, were taken to the same parade ground and shot.

According to Lobsang, they actually had been taken to watch the execution of the Army Commander. They were then taken back to prison where they were again interrogated by members of the tribunal. Lobsang says that the strongest pressure was put on them, now that their commander was no longer alive, to refute their testimony, to swear solemnly that he, and he alone, had given them their orders to kill Jigme. With these final sworn statements on official record in the tribunal's findings, Jambay and Sangay Dorji were driven out and shot in their turn by an army firing squad.

24

INTO A DUNGEON AND
OUT INTO EXILE

It was now May 1964 and the King was under his doctor's orders to continue his convalescence and treatment in Switzerland as soon as the affairs of state allowed. The problems of delegating authority in his absence were now, if anything, even more complicated than before when he had first had to go to Europe to convalesce. Lhendup Dorji, whom he had appointed as acting Prime Minister, was understandably anxious to have his position made quite clear before the King left the country. He had seen the difficulties that Jigme had had to contend with when he was left as the King's deputy in sole charge of the country. He must have concluded that he would need all the official authority possible in order to hold the country together.

The Indian Government, in the transaction of some routine business connected with the aid programme, had inquired who was now Prime Minister of Bhutan, because it needed his signature for the receipt of certain moneys. Lhendup Dorji had drafted a reply with two senior permanent officials, saying that he was acting Prime Minister. This draft was submitted to the King, who approved it without comment. He also told Lhendup that he would be publicly confirmed as Prime Minister on June 6th and invitations were actually sent out for the ceremony at which he was to be appointed. Then, on June 5th, the King suddenly started for Switzerland, leaving Lhendup still with only the status of acting Prime Minister. Before leaving the country the King had circulated secret instructions to all the local governors and the magistrates at the various dzongs that nothing of any importance was to be done while he was away without his written orders. To avoid any misunderstandings he added that he, and he alone, was master in Bhutan.

When Lhendup Dorji discovered the existence of these orders, which virtually deprived him of any real authority, besides amounting to a calculated vote of no confidence in him, he was naturally very angry and discouraged. How could he carry out his duties as acting Prime Minister in the face of this gesture of the King? To make matters worse, when he had recently questioned a visiting Indian Political Officer about the removal of a radio transmitter, the officer had reported to New Delhi that Lhendup was anti Indian.

If the King hoped that the Army Commander's execution would put an end to the divisions which had come to the surface over Jigme's assassination, his hopes were quickly disappointed. He had, Lobsang feels, realised how disruptive his association with his Tibetan mistress had proved for Bhutan and expressed remorse for his treatment of the Queen. At all events Yangki was sent, in company with her brother-in-law, Chira, and Capt. Wangdi to Bumtang, in East Bhutan, far away from the court and the seat of power. Lobsang even remembers talk of a scheme, which was supposed to have had royal approval, to engineer an accident on the way which would have got rid of Yangki altogether. But even with Yangki banished to Bumtang, the country was still in a very unsettled mood.

The Queen retired to stay with her mother in Kalimpong, leaving the King's own mother to accompany him to Switzerland.

For the next four months Lhendup tried to keep the momentum of day to day government and the development plans going, but became increasingly aware that, because of the King's parting orders to the chief officials, people at all levels were sitting on the fence until the King returned to Bhutan. There was a widespread feeling that there was no point in getting too involved in any undertaking if, when the King returned, he might disapprove of it and blame those connected with it. In these circumstances Lhendup, as acting Prime Minister, asked Lobsang if he would act as his personal security officer. It seemed a sensible precaution and Lobsang, although he was reluctant to interrupt his own work, accepted. This meant that he spent longish spells in attendance on Lhendup, wherever he happened to be. From time time he was relieved in his security duties by one or other of two transport officers named Lari Lama and Gurung Lama. During these reliefs he usually returned to Phunscholing to see his family and attend to his own work along the road or at the workshop.

In October Lhendup paid a visit to the Queen and their mother, the Rani Chuni Dorji, in Kalimpong. The Rani Chuni, a sister of the King of Sikkim, was an old lady of considerable experience and character. This family reunion developed into a discussion of the situation in Bhutan in general and Lhendup's problems of government in particular. Some of his senior officials also came to Kalimpong. These included Tangby, who had been promoted brigadier and made Army Commander after Namgyal Bahadur's execution, Colonel Penjo Ongdei, Colonel Lam Dorji and the Commissioner for Southern Bhutan, Rinchen Drukpa. The simultaneous presence of so many important Bhutanese in Kalimpong was immediately reported to the King in Switzerland. Lobsang suspects that a Chinese businessman who knew the Dorjis and was in Kalimpong at the time may have told the Indian security branch about the gathering and that the Indians relayed it to the King, possibly with political embellishments. Lobsang denies that the Kalimpong meeting was in any way directed either against the monarchy or the regime but admits that it could have given that impression to anyone with a suspicious mind. One of the points that came under discussion was the possibility, now that the King appeared determined to eliminate Dorji influence, that a situation might arise where the King's mistress might try to persuade the King to transfer the succession from the Queen's son, Jigme, to her own child. In such an event Lhendup wished to be sure that he could count on the officials present to support the Crown Prince as the rightful heir to the throne.

As soon as the King heard of the meeting, he sent an angry cable to Tangby, asking him what he was doing away from his post and telling him he would deal with him when he got back from Switzerland. Shaken by the tone of the message, Tangby and the other officers left at once for Bhutan. Lhendup Dorji also went back, via Calcutta, where he picked up the Chinese businessman who had been in Kalimpong and a friend of his and took them back with him to Bhutan.

There now occurred an incident in Eastern Bhutan which was to transform what had become a situation of uncertainty and suspense into a full-scale crisis. Possibly bored with life in Bumtang, or possibly in the genuine belief that her own safety was threatened, Yangki left Bumtang by road and drove south to Hatisar on the Bhutanese side of the Indian border. The wireless operator in Bumtang informed Thimpu of her departure and the Chief Secretary issued orders to prevent her leaving the country. There are at least two conflicting versions of what happened next. According to one, Yangki was simply escorted back to Bumtang. According to the other she was arrested in circumstances more or less humiliating either to herself or to members of her party. Lobsang is sure the first version is the accurate one. But it was the second version that appears to have reached the King in Switzerland. His reaction, at any rate, was immediate and furious. He ordered the arrest of those responsible for intercepting Yangki, two of whom at least Lobsang knows subsequently served long prison sentences.

The King also sent a message to the Queen, asking her to join him in Switzerland. She actually started from Kalimpong but, when she got to Calcutta, Lhendup told her that he felt that he should go instead. The King's reaction to the Yangki incident, coming on top of his cable to Tangby after the Kalimpong meeting, had completely demoralised Lhendup's senior officials. Besides, he was now determined to find out from the King precisely where he himself stood in order to be able to decide whether he could continue in office or not. He flew at once to Switzerland but, on arrival, the King refused to receive him on the ground that he had left Bhutan without instructions and had no right to abandon his post at such a critical time.

Lhendup then went to London, where he issued to the Press a short but dignified statement of his position. In this he stated categorically that there was no question of organised opposition to the King in Bhutan and reaffirmed his own complete loyalty to the Crown. In order to explain his presence in London, he said that he was on leave and let it be understood that he might look into some development business during his stay in Europe. The statement ended with a declaration that he remained at the King's entire disposal at any time and in any capacity.

The King, apparently under the impression that Lhendup had returned directly to Bhutan and having heard nothing of his arrival, appears to have suspected that he might be busy preparing to seize power in Bhutan itself. Lobsang says that by this time the idea of a Dorji conspiracy to take control of the country had become an obsession with him.

Just how far this idea was deliberately encouraged, both before and after Jigme's death, by people who had access to the King and had their own reasons for wanting to see the Dorji family excluded from power, Lobsang finds it hard to assess. But he makes full allowance for the fact that, after his heart attack, the King was subject to intermittent bouts of severe depression during which he may have been unduly susceptible to rumours and malicious gossip. He also believes that, during the King's second stay in Switzerland, his immediate entourage included people who, to say the least, did nothing to allay his suspicions of a Dorji takeover back in Bhutan. This bogy of a takeover had already been in his mind when he explained to the Army Commander why he would have to die in order to save the monarchy and appease public opinion and the pro-Dorji faction.

In any event, the King now sent orders to Brigadier Tangby, with a copy to the Chief Secretary in Thimpu, to arrest Lhendup if he tried to enter Bhutan and, if he resisted arrest, to shoot him. Coming on top of the King's displeasure at the meeting in Kalimpong, these orders understandably threw Tangby and the other officers into a state of real alarm. Before Lhendup's departure they had already discussed the advisability of fleeing the country. Threatened with the wrath of an absolute monarch, their instinctive reaction was to put themselves out of his reach. Before he left, Lhendup had dissuaded them from leaving the country until he had tried to straighten matters out with the King in

Switzerland – not only in respect of his own position, but also of theirs.

But the officers were now thoroughly scared. Without consulting the Chief-Secretary, Tangby and Penjo left Thimpu by road for Phunscholing on the morning of November 21st, 1964. By four o'clock in the evening the Chief-Secretary, realising that they had fled, telephoned the Sub-Divisional Officer at Phunscholing, Latsering, and told him to arrest them both. When the Sub-Divisional Officer took the call, Tangby and Penjo were standing beside him and heard everything that was said. The unfortunate officer tried to temporise with the Chief-Secretary by saying that he was too junior and doubted whether he would be able to carry out the arrest. The Chief-Secretary insisted that he must obey orders and the S.D.O. assured him he would do his best. Eventually, after talking the whole thing over with Tangby, Latsering decided he would join him and leave the country.

On November 21st after working hours, Lobsang went from his workshop in Phunscholing to the Druk Hotel. He had had a message from Tangby to join him there for a drink, but when he reached the hotel he found everyone gone. The officers had already crossed the border and made good their escape to Nepal. There they asked for and were granted political asylum. The sense of insecurity had become so general that many minor officials in Southern Bhutan fled across the border at this time.

Lobsang had been broadly aware of this fast-moving and complicated sequence of events. He had heard more or less the whole story of the Kalimpong meeting when the officers had returned to Bhutan on the King's orders. On the day they passed through Phunscholing on their way home from Kalimpong he had dined with Tangby, Penjo and Rinchen in the house of a Chinese contractor and they had told him everything that had happened. They trusted him and valued his opinion because he was so openly identified with Jigme Dorji and the Dorji family and because he had never made any secret of his own suspicions about the origins of the conspiracy against Jigme. Rimp Dorji had once summed it up by saying 'Lobsang doesn't always say much, but he knows a great deal. He was the first person to realise that Jambay had done the murder and who was behind it.'

Things now moved very fast. On 24th November, the King arrived at the airport of Hasimara, just across the Indian frontier and was flown direct to his palace at Thimpu by helicopter. He had travelled from Switzerland via Calcutta, where the Indian authorities had told him of the officers' escape. There the Head of the Indian Ministry of External Affairs, T. K. Kaul, gave him the news of their flight. The King asked, 'Tangby too?' and when Kaul replied, 'Yes, Tangby too,' the King was so upset that he appeared on the verge of collapse. The King then inquired who was left of Lhendup's entourage and on learning that Lobsang was still in Phunscholing, issued orders for his immediate arrest. The arrest was carried out at Lobsang's own house in Phun-scholing by the Captain of the King's bodyguard, Captain Wangdei. This officer had followed Lhendup to Calcutta on his last visit before he went to Switzerland and had stayed on in Calcutta in order, Lobsang says, to spy on the Queen's move-ments for the King until his return. He travelled with the royal party as far as Hasimara and then proceeded to Phunscholing. There he had Lobsang's house surrounded by armed soldiers and asked Lobsang to hand over his arms. The only arms in the house had been given him by Lhendup Dorji during the last few troubled months while he was acting as his personal bodyguard.

Lobsang had been expecting arrest. Two evenings before, he had met Jigme's widow, Tess Dorji, and Dawar Tsering, who were returning from London, where they had been assisting Tashi Dorji on Colombo Plan work. Lobsang had told Tess Dorji that he thought the King would arrest him because he had acted as security officer to Lhendup, whose own arrest the King had ordered. Dawar Tsering, as a matter of fact, brought instruc-tions from Lhendup in London to the remaining officers on the southern frontier, who were mostly pro-Dorji, not to try to leave the country but to be loyal to the King. He did not however mention this to Lobsang or anyone else in Phunscholing. This order of Lhendup confirmed the declaration of his own personal loyalty that he had made in London.

Lobsang himself made no attempt to escape. For one thing, he had no wish to try conclusions again with the Indian Security Services now that he was out of favour with the King. He also felt that he had nothing to reproach himself with as far as the King was concerned. He had served him to the best of his ability and felt fairly confident that he would not kill him because of his work on the Thimpu Dzong which was completed in the time stipulated when the King had promised him the Red Scarf if it was finished within three years.

At the same time Lobsang had no illusions about the King's displeasure. He recalls an incident not long before the King's second departure for Switzerland which had made him realise how much the King resented his loyalty to the Dorjis after Jigme's assassination and the fact that he had accepted the duties of Lhendup's security officer. During one of the King's visits to Paro Lobsang had accompanied Lhendup in this capacity to the King's small palace. Lhendup had already gone in but, as Lobsang made to follow him, the major in charge of the King's guard, Tsering Ngeudu, drew him aside and told him he must give up his side-arms before going into the Palace. When Lhendup saw Lobsang, he asked him where his gun was and Lobsang raised the question with the major, who would be responsible if anything happened to Lhendup while he was in the Palace. Later, while Lobsang was standing by himself, the King arrived and Lobsang greeted him. The King's only reply was to mutter gruffly, 'You've lost your senses,' using a Bhutanese turn of phrase which conveyed grave disapproval. Lobsang was made to feel that the King particularly resented the fact that, after working so closely under him at Thimpu, he had now thrown in his lot so openly with the Dorjis.

After his arrest Lobsang was taken to the jail in Phunscholing. There he was joined by the two transport officers Gurung Lama and Lari Lama, the second of whom was a cousin of Dawar Tsering. Lobsang had not told his wife of his expectation of arrest, and she was at the school where she taught when he was taken away. All the rooms in his house were afterwards put under seal, leaving his wife and children only one room to live in.

The three prisoners were driven by jeep to Thimpu. Lari Lama was taken on to Paro, where the King had now gone. Lobsang was taken to the Thimpu Dzong, handcuffed and put in leg-irons and placed in the dungeon. By a strange irony, he was one of the first prisoners in the dzong since he had helped to rebuild it. The new dzong, by Bhutanese standards, had every modern convenience, including windows with glass panes, but the central tower, beneath which the dungeon lay, had been left as it was before, no doubt because of the Lamas' objections to the demolition and because the great square tower itself contained all the chapels and historic treasures of the monastery. He was housed in the same cell where Namgyal Bahadur had spent the night before his execution. On November 25th, the day after he was taken into custody, the Indian newspapers carried a report which said that two Chinese spies had been arrested by the Government of Bhutan who went by the names of Lobsang Thondup and Lari Lama.

Lobsang's new prison was a classical dungeon. It had no windows, no bed and no blankets. He had to lie on the floor and, even if he had been in a state of mind to sleep, would have been kept awake by the rats which scampered over him with fearless curiosity in the dark. 'Huge rats,' he says with disgust, 'as big as cats.' His handcuffs had been so tightly fastened that he immediately suffered severe pains through constriction of circulation in his hands. They were not loosened for twenty-four hours. To this day the skin of his left hand remains cold and dry and, if he is not in good health, becomes scaly. Even this discomfort was not as bad as the cold. Lobsang was dressed in what he had been arrested in at Phunscholing, whose low-lying climate is warm, even in November. Now, at Thimpu, at an altitude of nearly 8,000 feet, the nights were freezing and the stone underground chamber of the dungeon was at all times below the temperature of the rest of the building. Lobsang is convinced that he would not have survived if a former official of the Thimpu Dzong had not sent him one quilted blanket. 'It saved me and, apart from preventing me freezing to death, it helped me cover myself from those damned rats, which would sometimes nibble at my hair when I was half asleep before I could shake them off.'

On the third day of his confinement at Thimpu, he received an unexpected caller. This was an Indian Political Adviser to the Government of Bhutan, named Mari Rustomjee. He knew Bhutan well and had previously held a political appointment in Gangtok, the capital of Sikkim, which until 1963 also served, as it had in the days of British India, as New Delhi's diplomatic link with Bhutan. Rustomjee had known Jigme Dorji well and accompanied him on a tour of Eastern Bhutan. After the King's heart attack he had been recalled to Bhutan from an administrative appointment in Assam at Jigme's request.

From Lobsang's point of view, it was a pointless interview. 'He began by saying that the King had sent him to ask if I had any difficulties for living. Considering the conditions of my dungeon, the question seemed a mockery.' Rustomjee then asked why the officers had run away and Lobsang replied that if he really did not know that he was hardly qualified to act as political adviser. Lobsang asked in turn why the King should have had him arrested. Clearly their conversation was getting nowhere and it began to irritate Lobsang. Rustomjee then said that the King had told him that Lhendup Dorji had had a plan for taking over the country and asked what this plan had been. Lobsang then frankly lost his temper and told his visitor that he thought Jigme Dorji had picked the wrong sort of political adviser. He asked him not to come to see him again. 'Forgive me,' he added, 'but I have to take a strong line, and not the line they are trying to make me take in order to save my own skin. I won't do that.'

His next visitor was the Deputy Chief Secretary, Sangay Penjo, a cousin to the King who was later to become Bhutan's Chief Delegate at the United Nations. Lobsang is pretty certain that he also came to see him on the King's instructions. 'He asked substantially the same questions, but he knew much more about the situation in Bhutan than Rustomjee and was very careful and circumspect in what he said.'

Two much less guarded inquisitors were the King's private secretary and the Chompen Lama, who was in charge of Palace supply. They took a tough line, insisting that Lhendup Dorji had had a plan to seize power and that Lobsang himself was one of its authors. This plan, they said, had included blowing up the road and cutting all telephone wires in order to isolate Bhutan while the Crown Prince was smuggled out of the country. They also implied that the plot included the murder of the King himself. They warned Lobsang that all this had been disclosed by other prisoners under arrest. Lobsang was later told that Rustomjee informed the Queen that not a single one of the prisoners had remained loyal to the Dorji family under interrogation. Lari Lama, according to Rustomjee's reported version, had said that Lobsang and the signals officer Chawna had plotted with Lhendup to murder the King and abduct the Crown Prince. Lobsang and Chawna were to dynamite the road and paralyse the telephone system while they smuggled the Crown Prince out of Bhutan. Lobsang suspects that Dawar Tsering told Lari Lama, who was his cousin, to invent this story to protect himself while he was in jail in Paro.

Lobsang was repeatedly asked by the people the King sent to question him why he had become bodyguard to Lhendup. His stock reply was to remind them that the King himself had appointed Lhendup acting Prime Minister and that he had simply obeyed Lhendup's orders. Far from compromising the Dorjis under interrogation, Lobsang insists that he always threw the questions back at his interrogators by asking them, 'What's wrong with the King to dream up these absurd ideas?'

Some four and a half months after his arrest the sergeant-major in charge of the soldiers at the dzong who acted as prison guards came to the dungeon during the night and took him to a cell on the ground floor. This was now occupied by Lari Lama who had been transferred from Paro. Gurung Lama, who had been in another cell at Thimpu all the time, had also been brought there. They were given a drink and the sergeant-major, like all the soldiers as a general rule in their dealings with the prisoners, was informal and friendly. He told Lobsang that he had heard that the old master-builder Apa Usui had recently taken the King aside in the dzong and shown him vehicles and tractors lying rusting in a state of bad disrepair. He had said to him reproachfully, 'When Lobsang was in charge, this sort of thing never happened,' and the King replied, 'You think I should let him out?' 'I do think so,' said Usui respectfully but emphatically, but the King had ended the discussion, not unkindly, 'But, you see, times have changed.'

Lobsang's reflections on his months in the Thimpu dungeon are mixed. The solitude, he admits, was 'very difficult.' The discomfort, with his handcuffs and ankle-fetters, was often appalling, but, he concedes philosophically, if he had been fitted with a wooden neck-wheel, as long term prisoners in Bhutan often were, sleeping would have been an even more difficult exercise. Food was better than a dungeon dweller might have expected. The Bhutanese are hearty eaters and Lobsang's diet, though not very fancy, was copious and sustaining, with plenty of filling rice. Sometimes the same friend who had supplied his quilt managed to send him yak's meat and other delicacies. 'It's a funny thing. I never got ill. I kept moving, to keep my circulation going. I think that's what did it.' The soldiers who guarded him, too, were friendly and ready to talk in quite a human way, so different from his unsmiling tormentors in Lhasa. One night they smuggled his wife Rinzi Om and their two daughters in to visit him. 'She had no permission. They just let her in out of kindness.'

On March 24th, 1965, the day after his meeting with the two other prisoners, with no forewarning, soldiers from outside the dzong came and took the three of them from Thimpu. Their hands were handcuffed behind their backs and they were jolted down the road to Phunscholing in an Indian one and a half ton Dodge truck. The bumps and lurches made this an excruciating journey and Lobsang was also racked by uncomfortable speculation about what it had been decided to do with him. His guess was that the King had agreed to hand him over to the Indian authorities and so be rid of an awkward witness who knew too much. After they had been a couple of days lodged in Phunscholing jail, the Queen must have got news that the prisoners had been transferred there and that the King was proposing to send them to India. She sent a jeep from Kalimpong to Phunscholing and one of her servants came to the local quartermaster's garage to deliver five packets of vitamin tablets for each of the prisoners. Later Lobsang was told that she had also sent a message to the King, saying, 'If you hand over these people, who will believe that you are King of a sovereign country?'

The King's intention to do precisely that is confirmed by a cable which Lobsang says he addressed to the Indian Political Officer in Sikkim saying he would put Lobsang, Lari Lama and Gurung Lama over the border and by a cable sent by the Political Officer from Delhi to the Sub-divisional Officer at Phunscholing asking him not to release the prisoners till he himself arrived in Phunscholing. Suddenly on March 29th, a Sunday morning, an order came to the SDO's office to release the three prisoners immediately. It was still very early, and the chances were that the Indian police and security men waiting at Jaigaon, on the other side of the frontier, would be having their Sunday off.

There followed a scene of frantic activity. The guards were very slow in removing the prisoners' leg-irons. Lobsang, mad with impatience, got them to fetch a hack-saw, with which he sawed expertly through his fetters. He managed to send a message to his wife and began improvising a plan with his two fellow prisoners. As soon as they were free of their shackles, they were driven at full speed across the border, and Lobsang asked the driver to leave them as quickly as possible so that his vehicle, with its distinctive Bhutan number plate, would not attract attention to them. He also asked him to return to his wife a parcel of clothes she had managed to send to him.

Gurung Lama was a Nepalese, but had Indian citizenship. If he were picked up by the Indian authorities, there was no reason why he should be in serious trouble. So it was decided that he would go on foot through the tea-gardens, by-passing Jaigaon and any Indian security reception party, and rejoin the main road which runs from the Bhutanese frontier to Hasimara. Lati Lama's sister was a school teacher in Samji, just in Bhutan thirty miles from Phunscholing. Her husband worked on the Bhutan East-West highway project and so had easy access to plenty of motor vehicles. The plan was that Gurung was to contact him and tell him to meet Lati Lama and Lobsang at a point where the railway and a road crossed and show flashing lights as a signal. Actually Lari Lama's sister had already heard that the prisoners had been sent to Phunscholing and had told her husband, who said he would go to see them there. By pure chance, he met Gurung Lama walking along the road and agreed to wait for the other two at the point they had chosen.

Meanwhile Lobsang and Lari Lama had made for the river and swam downstream about one and a half miles to throw any pursuers off the scent. They then took to the forest, rested and continued downstream parallel to the river to where it met a railway line, following the railway six or seven miles to the agreed junction with the road. There, after what had seemed an interminable wait for Lari's brother-in-law sitting in his car, they could see headlights being flashed on and off in the darkness and heard the sound of a horn. Terrified that the car would leave without them, they tried to run. After four months in prison their legs were horribly stiff and they were physically and mentally exhausted by their sudden burst of activity. They shouted, 'Who's there?' and stumbled on. Fortunately the Assistant Transport Officer knew all the roads in the area by heart. He drove them as fast as he could to the border of Nepal at a point some eighteen miles from the town of Siliguri. There he engaged the soldiers at the frontier check-post in conversation while Lobsang and Lari Lama once more took to the water and crossed the river which forms the frontier into the Kingdom of Nepal at that point.

With money provided by Rinzi Om, Lobsang and Lari Lama flew next day to Kathmandu. Tashi Dorji and the fugitive officers were already there. They had submitted evidence to the King of Nepal of their reasons for leaving their country which had decided him to grant them all political asylum.

POSTSCRIPT

Since March 1965, with a few brief interruptions, Lobsang has lived in Nepal, where he was joined by his wife soon after his arrival. He and Rinzi Om now have a family of four – two girls and two boys.

He has kept himself occupied in a number of small enterprises, some with other exiles from Bhutan, others on his own account. He has enjoyed his longest unbroken spell of domestic life, but these years in Nepal have been a period of marking time and frustration, aggravated by a nagging sense of injustice over his imprisonment and banishment from Bhutan. This, and his enforced leisure, helped to decide him to embark on this book. In Nepal he has had ample opportunity to compare notes and verify the events he describes in the concluding chapters with the other members of the group who sought refuge from Bhutan. Like them, he has always hoped that things in Bhutan would resolve themselves in a way which would make it possible for them to return.

In 1972, while Lobsang was in London working on this book, King Jigme Dorji Wangchuk died and was succeeded by his seventeen-year-old son. Lobsang hopes and believes that, under its new King, who is both a Wangchuk and a Dorji, the misunderstandings and rivalries which divided Bhutan will disappear and the country will again be united.

In telling his story, he has no wish to impair that unity or revive old enmities. But, having gone to prison rather than subscribe to the official version of the assassination of Jigme Dorji and the events which followed, he believes that, in justice to himself and to others, the truth as he saw it should be placed on record, quite apart from the fact that, without his years in Bhutan, his own biography would be incomplete.